JUSTICE AND F
IN THE C

C000186493

A multi-disciplinary approach to 'ordinary' cities

Edited by Simin Davoudi and Derek Bell

First published in Great Britain in 2016 by

Policy Press
University of Bristol
1-9 Old Park Hill
Bristol
BS2 8BB
UK
t: +44 (0)117 954 5940
pp-info@bristol.ac.uk
www.policypress.co.uk

North America office:
Policy Press
c/o The University of Chicago Press
1427 East 60th Street
Chicago, IL 60637, USA
t: +1 773 702 7700
f: +1 773-702-9756
sales@press.uchicago.edu
www.press.uchicago.edu

© Policy Press 2016

British Library Cataloguing in Publication Data
A catalogue record for this book is available from the British Library

Library of Congress Cataloging-in-Publication Data
A catalog record for this book has been requested

ISBN 978-1-4473-1839-2 paperback
ISBN 978-1-4473-1838-5 hardcover
ISBN 978-1-4473-2337-2 ePub
ISBN 978-1-4473-2338-9 Mobi

The right of Simin Davoudi and Derek Bell to be identified as editors of this work has been asserted by them in accordance with the Copyright, Designs and Patents Act 1988.

All rights reserved: no part of this publication may be reproduced, stored in a retrieval system, or transmitted in any form or by any means, electronic, mechanical, photocopying, recording, or otherwise without the prior permission of Policy Press.

The statements and opinions contained within this publication are solely those of the contributors and editors and not of the University of Bristol or Policy Press. The University of Bristol and Policy Press disclaim responsibility for any injury to persons or property resulting from any material published in this publication.

Policy Press works to counter discrimination on grounds of gender, race, disability, age and sexuality.

Cover design by Andrew Corbett
Front cover image: Getty
Printed and bound in Great Britain by CMP, Poole
Policy Press uses environmentally responsible print partners

Contents

List of tables and figures

Notes on contributors

Derek Bell
Currently Professor in Environmental Political Theory at Newcastle University, he was born in Newcastle upon Tyne. He studied philosophy, politics and economics at Balliol College, Oxford, before returning to Newcastle to complete a PhD at Newcastle University. He has worked in the School of Geography, Politics and Sociology at Newcastle University since 2001. His main research interests lie at the intersection of environmental politics and analytical political philosophy. He has published widely on environmental justice, liberal environmentalism, environmental citizenship, democracy and the environment. His most recent work has been on local and global climate justice.

Elizabeth Brooks
Following two years as a research associate at Newcastle University, working on environmental governance in the School of Architecture, Planning and Landscape, she moved to take up a post-doctoral research fellowship jointly between Glasgow University and the Crichton Carbon Centre in southern Scotland, where she is currently working on a resource to support the development of the environmental sector across the region. Her research interests include land reform, coastal resilience and the transition to a low carbon society.

Helen Coulson
PhD candidate in the School of Architecture, Planning and Landscape at Newcastle University, Helen has a background in geography and urban planning. Her current research draws upon urban political ecology and feminist care ethics to explore community food growing spaces in Edinburgh, Scotland.

Simin Davoudi
Professor of Environmental Policy and Planning, and Associate Director of the Institute for Sustainability at Newcastle University, her research is at the interface of society and ecology and focuses on questions of spatiality, governance, politics and justice. She is past president of the Association of the European Schools of Planning, Fellow of the Academy of Social Sciences and the Royal Society of Arts and held visiting professorships at European, American and

Australian universities. She has led the UK Office of Deputy Prime Minister's Planning Research Network; served as expert advisor for UK government departments and EU Directorates General; been a member of the 2014 sub-panel of the UK Research Excellence Framework, several research councils' assessment panels and universities' advisory boards in the UK and Europe. Some of her latest books are *Reconsidering localism* (2015, Routledge), *Conceptions of space and place in strategic spatial planning* (2009, Routledge) and *Planning for climate change* (2009, Earthscan). Simin is co-editor of the *Journal of Environmental Planning and Management*.

Jan Deckers

Jan is a Senior Lecturer in Bioethics at Newcastle University's School of Medical Education. The majority of his research is on the ethical issues associated with reproduction, genetics, stem cell research, environmental issues such as climate change and the consumption of animal products. Publications include: (2013) 'In defence of the vegan project', *Journal of Bioethical Inquiry*, 10(2): 187-95; (2011) 'Could some people be wronged by contracting swine flu? A case discussion on the links between the farm animal sector and human disease', *Journal of Medical Ethics*, 37(6): 354-56, and (2011) 'Justice, negative GHIs, and the consumption of farmed animal products', *Journal of Global Ethics*, 7(2): 205-16.

Bob Giddings

Chair of Architecture and Urban Design in the Department of Architecture and the Built Environment at Northumbria University, Newcastle upon Tyne, his research in urban design is based on a post-city structuring approach to cities. A focus for this work has been the design and use of public squares in European city centres, which ranges from geometric configurations, pedestrian activity and microclimate, to the privatisation of public space and alternative informal uses of the public realm. An important factor is the perception of the city centre by different user groups, and the way in which citizens across the demographic divide can be accommodated without conflict.

Rose Gilroy

Professor of Ageing Policy and Planning in the School of Architecture, Planning and Landscape at Newcastle University, Rose's research explores the impact of the ageing population, particularly in relation to planning and housing. Rose explores how place supports everyday life in later life. As a planner, she is interested in the transactional relationship between people and their environment that embraces how people individually and collectively may influence their environments. Rose Gilroy's research has included research in urban China, rural Japan and India. Locally, she is a member of Newcastle Age Friendly City, working to make Newcastle a better place in which to grow old.

Faith Goodfellow

Faith has a BEng in Environmental Engineering and Resource Management from the University of Nottingham, Master of Research in the Built Environment from the University of Leeds and an Engineering Doctorate in Environmental Technology from the University of Surrey. Her doctoral thesis was titled *Environmental management of chemical incidents: Improving the public health response*. Faith has worked as an environmental advisor for BP plc and environmental public health scientist for the former Health Protection Agency (now Public Health England). She now works on a freelance basis and her interests are in the fields of environment, social justice and philosophy.

Michael Jeffries

Mike is University Teaching Fellow in the Department of Geography at Northumbria University, Newcastle upon Tyne. His research into the reinvention and appropriation of Tyneside's urban spaces by skaters, BMXers and free runners grew out of his interest in the maligned 1960s 'Brasilia of the North' architecture of Newcastle, which had serendipitously created an ideal urban sports-scape. The work also dovetailed with Mike's use of visual methods: photography, video, doodled maps and comic books, all of which helped involve the skaters and free runners with a participatory approach allowing them to represent their worlds at events and exhibitions beyond the academy.

Ashok Kumar

Ashok is Professor and Head of Regional Planning at the School of Planning and Architecture, New Delhi. In his teaching post he plays a critical role in managing the School's postgraduate department. He has been teaching courses on planning theory to undergraduate and postgraduate planning students for over 20 years. His research work focuses on urban justice and fairness and he has many years of experience working in the area of spatial justice and capabilities with specific focus on low income settlements including slums in Indian cities. He draws heavily on the work of Michel Foucault and the concept of 'capabilities' from Amartya Sen and Martha Nussbaum.

Karen Laing

Senior Research Associate at Newcastle University, her work has centred around the impact of legal, policy and practice initiatives on children, young people and families, and she specialises in research with vulnerable and disadvantaged families about sensitive issues that concern them. She works from a social policy perspective, while crossing interdisciplinary boundaries in family law, criminology, social work and education. She was co-author of a report on fairness in education for the Newcastle Fairness Commission in 2012.

Elisa Lopez-Capel

Research Associate in Urban Soil Sciences in the School of Agriculture, Food and Rural Development at Newcastle University, her research is primarily on soil engineering and environmental sciences, investigating mitigation technologies to engineer soils for organic and inorganic carbon sequestration. Her current research focuses on sustainable use of land resources in urban environments, such as regeneration of derelict land into greenspaces. In her role as Higher Education STEM (Science, Technology, Engineering and Mathematics) Science, Agriculture and Engineering faculty ambassador, Elisa runs a wide range of outreach workshops and events for young people at schools and community groups in the region.

Laura Mazzoli Smith

Laura is Research Associate in the School of Education, Communication and Language Sciences at Newcastle University and Honorary Research Fellow in the Faculty of Education, University of Cumbria. Previously she was Senior Research Fellow at the National Academy for Gifted and Talented Youth, University of Warwick. Her main area of research is sociology of education with specific interests in social inclusion, gifted education and the use of narrative methods in educational research. She has published a range of articles and reports, and a co-authored book with Professor Jim Campbell, entitled *Families, education and giftedness: Case studies in the construction of high achievement* (2012, Sense Publishers).

Jane Midgley

Jane is a Senior Lecturer in the School of Architecture, Planning and Landscape at Newcastle University. Before this, Jane was a research fellow at the UK's leading think tank, the Institute for Public Policy Research, where she established and led its food policy research. Jane has an interdisciplinary social science background and her research focuses on poverty, exclusion and insecurity. Her work currently explores care through the lens of food, particularly the food provisioning practices of vulnerable individuals within British society.

Roberto Palacin

Senior Research Associate at Newcastle University, leading the Seamless and Inclusive Transport Research Theme as well as the Railway Systems Research Group, Roberto has a background in engineering and design with a focus on transport. His research interest is focused on system level efficiency of transport networks, connectivity and mobility, particularly exploring human–systems interaction aspects both from an engineering/technology perspective as well as a social/end user angle.

Sean Peacock

Sean is a recent graduate of the MPlan degree programme at the School of Architecture, Planning and Landscape, Newcastle University. Sean's current research interests include mobility and social justice, community engagement, and the participation of young people in the planning process. In his time at university he assisted several members of staff in their projects as a research assistant and is aspiring to continue study at PhD level. He is currently working in local government as a Planning Policy Officer, assisting in the preparation of an emerging Local Plan.

Lee Pugalis

Lee is Professor of Urban Studies at the Institute for Public Policy and Government, University of Technology, Sydney, Australia. He has worked for local, regional and national government, and gained undergraduate, postgraduate and doctoral qualifications from Newcastle University. Lee is a World Social Science Fellow and an editor of the journals *Regional Studies, Regional Science* and *Local Economy*, which reflect his research interests in urban regeneration, local and regional development and entrepreneurial governance. His most recent book is *Enterprising places: Leadership and governance networks* (2014, Emerald).

Suzanne Speak

Suzanne is Senior Lecturer in International Spatial Planning in the School of Architecture, Planning and Landscape at Newcastle University. Her original research focused on the housing issues for vulnerable young parents in the North East of England. However, for the last 15 years, her research has shifted to the developing and emerging countries of Asia, Middle East, Africa and Latin America, where she has developed a deep understanding of housing and homelessness in a range of social and cultural contexts. In particular, she has viewed housing and urban policy through a feminist framework.

Neil Stanley

Neil is a Lecturer in the School of Law at the University of Leeds. After qualifying and practising as a solicitor for several years, Neil moved to the University of Leeds, where he lectures in pollution control law and planning law. Neil's research focuses upon risk, risk perception and environmental decision making. Neil is the co-author of *Wolf and Stanley on environmental law* (2014, Routledge).

Teresa Strachan

Professional Practice Tutor at the School of Architecture Planning and Landscape, Newcastle University, she has a background in planning practice in both the public and private sector, with further experience gained in the third sector before joining the School in 2007. Teresa's work is centred on the academic support for town planning students in their placement employment. Her area of research is increasingly focused on developing skills for effective engagement with the community and especially with young people.

Jon Swords

Jon is Senior Lecturer in Economic Geography at Northumbria University, Newcastle upon Tyne. His interests focus on critical forms of development at the local and regional scale. The methodologies Jon adopts range from the traditional to the participatory, with a particular focus on visuals and how visual methods provide a way to break down barriers that traditional methods erect. Jon also uses visualisation to feed back research findings by representing participants' insights through academic lenses.

Liz Todd

Liz is Professor of Educational Inclusion at Newcastle University. She led the enquiry into fairness and education in Newcastle Council's Fairness Commission. Her main research areas are the social and educational inclusion of all children and young people in schools, and the use of collaborative non-normative ways of promoting change in relationships through video interaction guidance and narrative practices. She was awarded Investing in Children's membership (quality mark) as a result of the quality young people's involvement in research projects. Her monograph with Dyson and Cummings, *Beyond the school gates*

(2011, Routledge), was prize winning and highly commended by the Society of Educational Studies.

Geoff Vigar

Geoff Vigar is Professor of Urban Planning in the School of Architecture, Planning and Landscape, Newcastle University. A key element of his research focuses on the politics of mobility, infrastructure supply and demand, and their translation into transport policy. A particular focus rests on how environmental and social justice discourses compete for attention in policy debates.

David Webb

David is a Lecturer in Town Planning in the School of Architecture, Planning and Landscape at Newcastle University. His interests stem from a belief in usable knowledge and a feeling that the potential for knowledge transfer via formal political or professional routes is overstated. Consequently, David's research focuses partly on critical analyses of urban government, including interests in urban policy and heritage and in the fate of the alternative or progressive content within such schemes. A second research interest lies in the instructive potential and formal reception of subaltern, or weakly connected, spaces through which concerns for the future of the built environment are pursued.

Pamela Woolner

Lecturer in Education, Research Centre for Learning and Teaching, Newcastle University, Pam has a growing reputation in understanding learning environments, with research interests in underlying issues as well as the design and use of educational space. Her work combines a rigorous approach to the evidential basis for claims about the impact of surroundings with an understanding of the needs and concerns of the users. Publications include an influential review, *The impact of school environments*, numerous articles, a book about school space and an edited interdisciplinary book, *School design together*, exploring collaborative approaches to school design and use.

Acknowledgements

On 27 May 2011, we held a workshop to launch the *Justice and Governance* theme of the then Newcastle Institute for Research on Sustainability (NIReS) and develop a network of academics whose research interests were related to the theme. In the coming years, we organised several other workshops and seminars to explore multiple approaches to the concepts of justice and fairness in our particular fields. With generous financial support from NIReS and Newcastle University's Sustainability Challenge Committee, we secured a visiting professorship position for Professor David Schlosberg who made invaluable contributions to our work on justice including a public lecture and presentations at two workshops in November 2011: one on *Global Justice and Climate Change* and the other on *Fairness at a Time of Financial Austerity*.

The idea of an edited book to which members of the network could contribute was inspired by the work of the Newcastle Fairness Commission which was established by Newcastle City Council in 2011 and chaired by Professor Chris Brink, the Vice Chancellor of Newcastle University. The Commission was invited to develop a set of justice principles which could inform the Council's decisions at the time of financial austerity. The book idea was then finalised in a brainstorming session in 18 January 2012. Subsequently, potential contributors presented and discussed their ideas and commented on draft chapters in four other workshops (14 December 2012, 24 April 2013, 31 October 2013 and 8-9 September 2014). We are grateful for the financial support provided by NIReS and its successor, the Institute for Sustainability (IfS). We are also grateful for the useful comments from the participants of the above-mentioned workshops as well as from those who took part in other related events including a roundtable discussion on *Environmental Justice and the City*, in which Professor William Rees (a visiting professor at Newcastle University) and Philip Hunter from Newcastle City Council took part (22 March 2012), and a symposium on *Justice and the City* (15-16 November 2012) funded by the Global Urban Research Unit (GURU), Newcastle University.

Our main gratitude goes to Dr Faith Goodfellow. Without her editorial assistance and support it would have been impossible for us to undertake this long-term book project. Throughout the process, Faith helped us generously with organising workshops, keeping track of the progress, liaising with authors, ensuring that various draft versions of chapters were submitted on time and according to guidelines, formatting and copy editing the final drafts, putting together the prelims and making the manuscript submission-ready. Given her own academic expertise in environmental issues and her interest in philosophy, Faith also provided us, the editors, with insightful comments and observations for addressing the intellectual and practical challenges that edited volumes such as this often face.

The authors would also like to thank the following individuals and organisations: the Institute for Local Governance for funding and Newcastle City Council for commissioning and supporting the study that underpins Chapter 2, and Najla Mansour, research student at Newcastle University, for her assistance with Figures 2.1 to 2.4; staff and students at Farne Primary School in Newcastle, Jesmond Gardens Primary School in Hartlepool, Washington School in Washington, schools involved with the Open Futures programme and all other schools and colleges for their contribution to ideas underpinning Chapter 3; the Newcastle University's Institute for Sustainability (grant no. BH140193) for financial support of the work undertaken for Chapter 4; Adam Jenson and Sebastian Messer for help with the research and the skateboarders, BMXers and free runners of Tyneside for participating in the research underpinning Chapter 7; the financial support from the Engineering and Physical Sciences Research Council's Sustainable Urban Environments Thematic Grant EP/I002154/1 and the School of Architecture Planning and Landscape's Engagement Committee for the research base of Chapter 8; Andrew Wanley and the young people from Benfield School at Walker and from Byker for their time and participation; the financial support of the Joseph Rowntree Foundation for the 2009 study on the Elder Count and the people who willingly gave their time to talk to the authors of Chapter 11; Linnea Laestadius for her contribution to Chapter 13; and all reviewers of the chapters and the book for their constructive and helpful comments. The opinions expressed in the relevant studies and the chapters are entirely those of the authors and do not necessarily reflect the views of the editors or funding organisations.

Foreword

The editors very generously say that this book was inspired by the work of the Newcastle Fairness Commission. Reading that took me back in time to early 2011, when the aftershocks of the global financial crisis were still being felt daily, and the first shocks of the austerity policies of the Coalition government were felt at local authority level. It was then that Newcastle City Council invited me to chair a Commission to consider how it could make fair decisions in planning and resource allocation in the face of a shrinking budget and a mood of concern about the delivery of public services.

The Fairness Commission, as it emerged, was a broad-ranging group of people from various areas of civil society: charities, faith groups, activists, academics, teachers, and so on. It was not a pressure group, it was not a group of experts, and in a sense it was not a group at all – just a collection of individuals who shared a concern about the future of the city and a willingness to try and make a contribution.

Early on, we decided to try and get to the heart of the practicalities by isolating some principles of fairness. This was an endeavour before which professional philosophers might quail, but fortunately we completed the task before anyone could point out that it was impossible. I drafted an initial set of ideas, and then we refined and adapted these over the course of various discussions. Eventually we did something even more ambitious: we summarised the entire report in the title: 'Fair Share, Fair Play, Fair Go, Fair Say'.

'Fair share' is about resource allocation. When your budget is shrinking, and you have competing priorities, how do you come to a position where people feel they have received a fair share of whatever there is, matched to their needs? 'Fair play' is about due process and even-handedness. It is the realisation that no matter how you allocate resources, people won't feel they have been fairly treated unless they trust the way in which it was done. 'Fair go' is about equality of opportunity. Anybody should be enabled to have a go at anything – education in particular – no matter what their starting position, and a chance to fulfil their aspirations. And finally, 'fair say' is about participation. We have to make sure that everybody's voice is heard – even those who would not normally speak up.

It is very gratifying, a few years later, to be able to trace in this book, written and edited by academic experts, many of these same ideas made manifest in a number of practical contexts. These contexts, as you will see, range from environmental justice to skateboarding, from transport to food, from the young to the old. Across all these contexts, I believe it is fair to say that the views expressed about resources, process, opportunity and participation never contradict and often support the principles that a loose conglomeration of ordinary people had come up with a couple of years ago. And so, overall, I think the Fairness Commission did not do too badly. Perhaps this is an example of what I believe is now called the wisdom of crowds: that ordinary people, properly mobilised, can come up with ideas and predictions at least as good as those of the experts.

But of course we need the experts. We need them for conceptualisation, for contextualisation, for making comparisons, raising alternatives, clarifying assumptions, drawing conclusions, and pointing out consequences. All of these can be found in this book. In particular, the book renders the valuable service of putting fairness in the context of cities. Newcastle, our city, is what the authors and editors call an 'ordinary city', which I think we should take as a compliment, in the same sense as I have used 'ordinary people' as a complimentary term above. Fairness, surely, should not be something extraordinary. The whole idea is that fairness should be something ordinary, even when circumstances are extraordinary.

I am sure this book will contribute to the ideal of fairness as something embedded in the city, and I am pleased to recommend it to you.

Chris Brink
Newcastle upon Tyne
March 2016

ONE

Understanding justice and fairness in and of the city

Derek Bell and Simin Davoudi

Introduction

More than half of the world's population live in cities. Many of those people live in grinding poverty while some enjoy unimaginable wealth. The juxtaposition of extreme wealth and poverty in a single city might be surprising but for the fact that such radical inequalities are a common feature of almost all cities. Moreover, economic inequality is just one among many types of radical inequalities including, for example, life expectancy, health, education, mobility, access to services and social capital, and treatment by authorities. Many of us believe that some – perhaps, many – of these inequalities are *unfair* or *unjust*. However, justice and fairness are not simple or uncontested concepts. Neither is the 'city'. So, there is theoretical – analytical and normative – work to be done to move, first, from the empirical claim that there are inequalities to the moral claim that there are injustices, and second, from the conception of the city as a physical space and a container of (in)justices, to its understanding as a social and political space that is actively reproducing (in)justices. In this book, we bring together researchers from various disciplines and theoretical perspectives to 'look for' (in)justices *in* and *of* the city.

This chapter provides some theoretical background, explains our focus on one particular city and outlines the structure of the book. In the first section, we introduce the ideas of justice and fairness. We begin with liberal formulations of justice and briefly review key debates among liberals and between liberals and their critics. In the second section, we turn our attention to justice and fairness *in* and *of* the city by drawing on theories of spatial justice. Our aim is to situate debates about justice in and of the city in the broader context of debates about conceptualisation of justice. We conclude this section by arguing for a multi-disciplinary and pluralistic approach to thinking about justice, a relational approach to the city and a dialectic understanding of spatial justice. We suggest that this is an important first step toward bridging the gaps between different disciplinary perspectives on social and spatial justice and fairness. In the third section, we explain why this book focuses on a single city, Newcastle upon Tyne, and provide a short introduction to *our city*. Finally, we briefly set out the structure and content of the book.

Justice and fairness: liberal formulations and critical alternatives

For centuries, from the time of Aristotle and Plato, people have been interested in justice in its both formal and legal sense as well as its informal and moral sense. Political philosophers have been at the forefront of the debate about justice with John Rawls' *A theory of justice* (Rawls, 1972) dominating the contemporary debate for over 40 years. Rawls defended a liberal theory of justice, which prioritised individual liberties, including civil and political liberties, but also demanded 'fair equality of opportunity' and an egalitarian distribution of income and wealth (Rawls, 1972; Rawls, 2001). His version of 'political liberalism' is a 'left' leaning liberalism because it emphasises equality as well as freedom (Rawls, 2001). Both liberals and critics of liberalism have developed their theories of justice in response to Rawls' account of 'justice as fairness' (Rawls, 2001). In this section, we outline three key debates within liberalism before introducing a number of critical perspectives that aim to offer a more fundamental challenge to mainstream Rawlsian or 'political' liberalism.

The three key debates within liberalism over the last 40 years have been about the 'currency', 'principles' and 'scope' of justice. The most important late 20th-century liberal theories of justice, including Rawls' theory, were mainly concerned about the fair distribution of resources, especially income and wealth but sometimes also natural resources (Rawls, 1972; Dworkin, 2002). For them, the 'currency' of justice – or the good that should be fairly distributed – was resources. However, many leading justice theorists, such as Sen (1980), Arneson (1989) and Cohen (1993) argue that focusing on resources was not enough because what really matters is what people are able to do rather than how much money they have. Instead, they suggest alternative 'currencies' of justice, such as 'capabilities' and 'equality of opportunity for welfare' (Sen, 1980; Arneson, 1989). The capabilities approach, which focuses on the range of things that people are genuinely able to do, has become the main alternative to resourcism in the philosophical literature.

The second liberal debate has been about fair principles of distribution. How should resources or capabilities be distributed? Rawls famously advocated the 'difference principle', which requires that inequalities of income and wealth should only be permitted when they are to the advantage of the least well off (Rawls, 1972). The basic institutions of a society, including the tax and welfare systems, should be organised so that they maximise the income and wealth of the least well off. Some critics have argued that Rawls' commitment to maximising the minimum income in a society (maximin) is not sufficiently egalitarian because any deviation from equality is unjust. In contrast, others have argued for less demanding principles of justice that allow for greater inequalities so long as everyone has a sufficient level of resources or capabilities (sufficientarianism). This debate continues between those interested in imagining an ideally just society, but we have also seen more discussion of less demanding principles for non-ideal circumstances.

The third debate has been about the scope of justice. Rawls conceptualised justice at the scale of the nation state. On his account, we owe duties of justice to our fellow citizens but not to citizens of other states. Rawls' cosmopolitan critics have argued that the scope of justice extends beyond our fellow citizens to include everyone in the world (Beitz, 1979; Caney, 2005). For them, we should be interested in a fair *global* distribution of resources or capabilities. Again, this remains an ongoing debate among political philosophers with an increasing number of theorists trying to navigate a middle way between statists and cosmopolitans (Valentini, 2011). These three debates among political liberals highlight the contested nature of justice even within one (narrowly defined) philosophical tradition. We find more fundamental disagreements about how we should understand justice when we move beyond political liberalism. Political liberalism is not short of critics. We will introduce six critical perspectives: libertarianism, Marxism, democratic proceduralism, multiculturalism, environmentalism and spatial justice. This is not intended to be an exhaustive list of types of critics. Instead, we focus on critical perspectives that we believe raise important challenges for political liberalism and those that will be relevant for our later discussion of justice in and of the city.

Libertarians (Nozick, 1974) reject the political liberal's claim that the state should aim to ensure that resources are distributed fairly. For them, the distribution of resources is fair − irrespective of whether there are radical inequalities between the rich and the poor − if it is the outcome of a fair process. A fair process is one in which capital, labour and goods are exchanged in free markets and private property rights are protected from theft and fraud. So, the state's role is limited to ensuring that markets are free and that private property rights are protected.

Marxism stands at the opposite end of the right–left spectrum to neoliberalism (libertarianism) but it is similarly dismissive of the political liberal's conception of justice. For Marx, distributive justice was a diversion from the main problems of capitalist society. Marxists argue that justice is an ideological concept that serves the interests of the ruling class (Buchanan, 1982). They argue that political liberalism offers the false hope of a more egalitarian distribution of the goods of consumption and (deliberately or naively) fails to understand the political economy of capitalism and its underlying causes of mal-distribution. The distribution of the goods of consumption cannot be considered in isolation from the distribution of ownership of the means of production. If the capitalist class controls the means of production, it has the political and economic power to ensure that reductions in inequalities are, at best, marginal and only realised when they serve the interests of capital. So, for Marxists, 'justice' that serves the interests of the working class requires revolution and the end of capitalism.

Democratic proceduralism, like libertarianism, rejects the political liberal's focus on substantive principles of distributive justice (Estlund, 2008). Instead, it is primarily concerned about the procedures for making political decisions, including decisions that affect the distribution of income and wealth. Justice requires nothing more or less than fair procedures for making decisions. There are no independent principles of substantive justice by which we can critically judge the outcome of a fair democratic process. Most contemporary democratic proceduralists are deliberative democrats. For them, a fair procedure is an inclusive, deliberative process. Ideally, it is the 'force of the better argument' rather than unequal political or economic power that should determine our collective decisions about how our society should be organised.

Unlike the first three critical perspectives, multiculturalism shares the political liberal's commitment to substantive principles of justice. However, its advocates argue that there is more to justice than the fair distribution of resources (or capabilities). For them, recognition – or respect for group differences – is at least as important as redistribution (Young, 1990; Fraser and Honneth, 2003). It is a necessary condition of a just society that we recognise others as equals whether or not they share our culture, ethnicity, gender, sexuality, social background or values. A just society must be without discrimination, including institutional discrimination, and free from prejudice. Equal recognition is both an independently important dimension of social justice and a prerequisite for fair distribution. The leading advocates of equal recognition share the Marxist's concern that political liberalism offers a false hope of a more egalitarian society. However, they offer a different diagnosis of the political liberal's mistake. For them, the problem is that political liberalism has a naïve conception of social processes and, in particular, fails to recognise that distributive inequality is an inevitable outcome of unequal recognition and a lack of parity of participation in society.

Environmentalism, like multiculturalism, is concerned that political liberalism misses important dimensions of justice. Environmentalists argue that the scope of justice should be extended to include, at least, future generations and, perhaps, non-humans. They also argue for a broader conception of the currency of justice beyond income and wealth to include the distribution of environmental benefits (such as clean air, access to greenspaces, and the right to use the carbon absorption capacity of the earth's atmosphere) and environmental burdens (such as toxic waste and contaminated sites). More radically, some environmentalists argue that political liberalism's focus on distributive justice reflects and supports a conception of the human-environment relation that is inconsistent with our best scientific accounts of the environment (Bell, forthcoming). It is also rooted in anthropocentric and utilitarian views of the world, which 'places humans at the centre of the Universe and considers nature to be at their service' (Davoudi, 2012: 54). Political liberalism tends to conceive of the environment as part of the economy, infinitely divisible, passive or controllable, always able to provide circumstances of moderate scarcity and as property (Bell, forthcoming). In contrast, an ecologically informed conception of justice should conceive of the economy as embedded in the environment and the environment as systemic, dynamic and often beyond our control (Daly, 1995). An ecologically-informed theory of justice will not be concerned with the distribution of property rights but rather with justifying our use of (parts of) the environment in light of the competing claims of other subjects of justice now and in the future (Wissenburg, 1998). It will place environmental values – and our responsibilities towards nature for nature's sake – firmly in the framework of social justice (Davoudi and Brooks, 2014).

Finally, spatial justice theorists also argue that political liberalism's account of justice, or indeed any account of justice that ignores its spatial dimensions, is incomplete and fails to acknowledge the significance of space in social relations (Lefebvre, 1974; Soja, 2010). There are two sides to the debate about spatial justice. The first one focuses on the 'spatiality of injustice'. On this approach, space is conceived in absolute or Euclidean terms. Injustice is done in particular spaces, such as the territory of a state or a city. Moreover, Euclidean space is a fixed resource and the unequal access to it is a matter of injustice. So, for example, radically unequal ownership of land (with exclusive access rights) and the exclusion of young people from some areas of cities after dark are matters of spatial justice in this sense. The second side to the debate about spatial justice focuses on the 'injustice of spatiality'. On this approach, space is conceived in relational or Leibnizian terms as socially and culturally produced. The social construction of spatial relations among persons and between persons and physical objects (such as houses and workplaces) and natural environment (such as greenspaces) plays a major part in creation and entrenchment of injustices. Spatial justice theorists have drawn attention to the specific injustices of, for example, ghettoisation and other forms of locational discrimination, which disadvantage poorer communities by, for example, directing them to inferior services, such as lower quality health care and education (Marcuse, 2009). Moreover, injustice is created, sustained and exacerbated through the spatial processes of capitalist development and urbanisation (Harvey, 2009). The spatial organisation of capitalist societies entrenches the injustices that Marxists identify as central features of capitalism by ensuring that the capitalist class preserve their advantages over the working class.

Justice *in* and *of* the city

It is helpful when we are thinking about justice *and* the city to distinguish justice *in* the city from justice *of* the city. Discussions of justice *in* the city adopt the Euclidean conception of space: cities are neutral containers or spaces in which justice and injustice occur. In contrast, discussions of the justice *of* the city focus on the role of the city in creating and maintaining (in)justice, drawing on the spatial dialectic of injustice recognised in work on the injustice of spatiality (Dikeç, 2001). In this section, we discuss both justice *in* the city and justice *of* the city. We elaborate on these in turn.

Justice in the city

Debates about justice *in* the city tend to focus on the question of scale but are interpreted differently. For some, scale raises the problem of boundaries: where does the urban end and rural begin? It also highlights the difficulties of capturing the flows: what should be the geographical unit of analysis and how inclusive ought that to be? Acknowledging this limitation, David Harvey (1973) noted that, for example, justness of a distribution at the aggregate regional level may bear little relation to its disaggregated city level. For others, scale raises questions that are similar to scope and mentioned earlier. Critics argue that contemporary political philosophers, with very few exceptions, have not considered what justice requires at the scale of the city (Fainstein, 2010) by which they mean not scale in terms of a pre-given geographical boundary but, like scope, in terms of administrative and jurisdictional authority. The focus is on the powers, responsibilities and duties of city governance for pursuing justice. While political theorists' debates about the scope of justice have focused mainly on the nation state (statism) versus global governance (cosmopolitanism), scholars from other disciplines, especially geography and planning, have paid more attention to justice at the city governance level. A common justification of why the city scale matters is that we live in an increasingly urbanised world; that by 2050 more than two thirds of the world's inhabitants (or six billion people) will live in cities where extreme wealth often stands against abject poverty. Together, the sheer number of people living in cities and the radical inequalities in cities suggest a powerful prima facie argument for the importance of thinking about justice at the scale of the city.

The case against thinking about justice at the city scale (understood not as geographical but as a governance scale) rests on two arguments. First, cosmopolitans and statists would both argue that the scope of justice extends beyond the city. The duties of justice that we owe to fellow inhabitants of a city are simply the duties of justice that we owe to fellow nationals (for the statist) or to everyone in the world (for the cosmopolitan). There are no special duties of justice among fellow city dwellers. Second, it has been argued that there is no point in thinking about justice at the city scale because city institutions are powerless to tackle injustice within the city. For example, Peterson (1981) argues that cities cannot promote justice because any attempt to introduce redistributive policies will lead to capital flight, unemployment and a reduction in the tax base. More generally, city institutions are subservient to the combined power of national (or regional) government and international capital.

However, neither argument undermines the prima facie case for thinking about justice at the city scale. The second argument exaggerates the weakness of city-level institutions. Although the power of city-level institutions is limited and 'cities cannot be viewed in isolation; they are within networks of governmental institutions and capital flows', 'there are particular policy areas in which municipalities have considerable discretion and thus the power to distribute benefits and cause harm, … [including] urban redevelopment, racial and ethnic relations, open space planning, and service delivery' (Fainstein, 2010: 21). Moreover, the differences between cities, even cities in the same country, suggest that city institutions may influence outcomes. So, it seems an exaggeration to say that cities have no power to reduce (or increase) injustice.

This response to the argument from powerlessness also suggests a qualified response to the argument made by cosmopolitans and statists. We can avoid taking a position on the question of whether, as a matter of ideal theory, city dwellers have special duties of justice to each other that they do not have to those living outside the city. In our existing, non-ideal, circumstances, city-level institutions have responsibility for some policy areas affecting city dwellers and some power to affect the relative positions of and relations among city dwellers. In such circumstances, city-level institutions should, at least, seek to promote justice among city dwellers. So, justice in the city matters here and now. This does not rule out the possibility that city-level institutions should also consider whether their policies are consistent with the requirements of statist or cosmopolitan conceptions of justice. It also leaves open the possibility that a more ideally just society would not devolve responsibility or power to city-level institutions.

Based on this conviction, Fainstein has developed a liberal multiculturalist conception of the just city, arguing that a just city is one that realises three values: 'equity, diversity and democracy' (Fainstein, 2010: 5). Here, 'equity' refers to the political liberal's concern about the fair distribution of the material and non-material resources as well as capabilities (2010: 54-6). However, Fainstein proposes a more modest principle of fair distribution that requires only that the distribution of benefits 'derived from public policy … [should] not favor those who are already better off at the beginning' (2010: 36). She explicitly rejects the goal of equality as 'too complex, demanding, and unrealistic to be an objective in the context of capitalist cities' (2010: 36). The idea of 'diversity' refers to multiculturalism's concern about recognition, endorsing Young's ideal of 'social differentiation without exclusion', which affirms the value of group difference, rejects assimilation and demands 'respect for group differences without oppression' (Young, 1990: 238, 47, cited in Fainstein, 2010: 43). Her account of the third value, 'democracy', is developed in direct opposition to democratic proceduralism, which she argues has become the 'normative standard for planning' (2010: 24). She rejects the democratic proceduralist's 'assumption that a just process necessarily produces a just result' (2010: 24) and argues that democratic proceduralism 'ignores the reality of structural inequality and hierarchies of power' (2010: 30). So, democracy is not likely to deliver either equity (fair distribution) or diversity (equal recognition) in an already unequal city. Using this three-dimensional conception of justice she provides some fine-grained analysis of the relative merits of the policy choices made by different cities and concludes that overall, some cities (notably Amsterdam) have done better at promoting justice than others (such as New York).

Justice of the city

The debate about justice of the city rests on a relational, rather than absolute, view of space. The absolute view is rooted in Euclidean three-dimensional geometry while the relational view originates from Leibniz's philosophy, suggesting that 'spatial properties are relational, and the position of any object is to be given in terms of its relation to any other objects' (Scruton 1996: 362). 'Space is relational in the sense that it does not exist independent of objects and events but is constructed from the relations between them' (Davoudi and Strange, 2009: 13). Acknowledging that cities are socially and culturally produced became particularly prominent in the 1960s and 1970s when the highly influential works of geographers and sociologists, such as Henri Lefebvre's *The production of space* [1974 (1991)], David Harvey's *Social justice and the city* [1973 (2009)] and Manuel Castells' *The urban question* (1977), began to apply Marxist analyses to space and a structural reading of the city. This is despite the fact Marx remained remarkably uninterested in the question of space even though his close collaborator, Friedrich Engels, made intriguing observations on the spatial distribution of classes in mid-19th-century Manchester (Davoudi and Strange, 2009). As regards the spatial justice debate, two seminal publications have come to dominate the field: Lefebvre's *Le droit a la ville* or *The right to the city*[1] and Harvey's *Social justice and the city*. We briefly sketch their key contribution and position within the broader justice theories.

Lefebvre's notion of 'the right to the city' is a right of both individuals and groups to be included and present in the processes that produce their city. As Isin (2000: 14) suggests, 'the right to the city [involves] the right to claim presence in the city, to wrest the use of the city from privileged new masters and democratize its spaces'. However, the right to the city requires more than democratic proceduralism for three reasons. First, democratic proceduralism in a capitalist society leaves the production of the city in the hands of the capitalist class. The city is produced for its exchange value rather than its use value. Second, democratic proceduralism, like political liberalism, separates the 'political' and the 'personal'. However, the city is not produced by the 'political' actions of (local) government but rather by all of the actions, including the everyday actions, of its citizens and inhabitants (within and beyond the city boundaries) who influence the lives of city dwellers. So, the political is pervasive and democratising the city's spaces requires far more than participation for everyone in local government. Third, democratic proceduralism suggests that justice is purely procedural. However, for Lefebvre, the pervasiveness of the political implies that city dwellers only enjoy the right to the city when they are genuinely included in the daily production of their city and that is only possible when they have the resources (or capabilities) necessary to access the city's spaces and the processes that shape them on equal terms with their fellow city dwellers.

Furthermore, the right to the city is not 'a simple visiting right or a return to the traditional city', but '*the right to urban life*, in a transformed and renewed form' (Lefebvre, 1993:435 original emphasis). Dikeç (2001) argues that Lefebvre's insistence on this expanded right is in some ways a response to Immanuel Kant's idea of the rights of strangers. Kant stated that the 'stranger' 'cannot claim a *right of residence* but rather a *right of visit*' (quoted in Dikeç, 2001: 1789). Citizenship originates from the rights to the city as the site of politics. Thus, the right to the city is not just about the citizen's participation in urban social life, but also in urban political life. It is about both having access to all aspects of urban life and being able to make and remake our cities and ourselves.

Lefevbre also considers the right to the city as the right to be different. He suggests that 'the right to the city, complemented by the right to difference and the right to information, should modify, concretise and make more practical the rights of the citizen as an urban dweller (*citadin*) and user of multiple services' (Lefevbre, 1996: 34). So, although Lefebvre and his followers do not specify principles of substantive justice in the same way as political liberals or multiculturalists (Attoh, 2011), his insistence on the right to be different resonates with multiculturalism. What they share is the rejection of abstract, ideal notions of justice that are devoid of time and space.

Harvey's *Social justice and the city* [2009 (1973)] suggests that we cannot understand injustice in the city without thinking about *both* the social and the spatial processes and relations that create the city. So, political liberalism, which fails to pay any attention to spatial relations, cannot provide us with the necessary theoretical resources to understand injustice in the city. In Section One of his book, Harvey tries to develop an alternative 'liberal' account of justice that takes into account the effects of spatial relations on the distribution of 'real income' in an 'urban system' (2009: 50). He adopts a resourcist conception of the currency of justice and draws on Rawls' account of the principles of justice but pays particular attention to 'the "hidden mechanisms" of income redistribution in a complex city system' (2009: 52). In particular, he focuses on spatial mechanisms, such as 'the redistributive effects of the changing location of jobs and housing' (2009: 60) and argues that these mechanisms tend to 'increase inequalities [in the distribution of real income] rather than reduce them' (2009: 52). Therefore, a liberal theory of justice for an urban system must control or 'make use of' these hidden spatial mechanisms to reduce inequality or promote a more egalitarian distribution of real income (2009: 53).

Harvey's own assessment of his attempt to apply a 'geographical imagination' to political liberalism is that it is ultimately unsuccessful because political liberalism not only fails to understand how spatial relations produce injustice in the city but also fails to understand the relationship between cities and a capitalist economy (2009: 23). On Harvey's account, the city is the dominant 'built form' and 'urbanism' is the dominant 'social form' when capitalism is the dominant 'mode of production' and 'market exchange' is the dominant 'mode of economic integration' (2009: 203, 210). The growth of cities is a direct consequence of the dominance of capitalism and market exchange. Capitalism and market exchange together create 'permanent concentrations of surplus value' in the hands of a capitalist class (2009: 227). The logic of capitalism demands that the capitalist class has to continually reinvest the surplus value that it appropriates to generate more surplus value. Developing and expanding cities – by building homes, offices, shopping malls, and the surrounding urban infrastructure – has become one of the most important ways of continually reinvesting surplus value (2009: 322). So, cities are created by the capitalist class to generate more surplus value for the capitalist class. As Harvey puts it, cities 'are founded upon the exploitation of the many by the few' (2009: 314). The political liberals fail to recognise that exploitation is built into cities from the very beginning and, moreover, the continuing growth of cities depends on continuing opportunities for exploitation.

On Harvey's account, 'a genuinely humanizing urbanism' requires the revolutionary overthrow of capitalism and 'democratic control over the production and utilisation of the [social] surplus' (2009: 314, 328). This is echoed by other Marxist accounts such as Merrifield and Swyngedouw's *Urbanisation of Injustice* (1997: 13) which asserts that, 'every emancipatory and empowering politics inevitably involves a spatial strategy: a struggle not just in but for space'.

In this section, we began by explaining why we believe that it is important to discuss justice *in* and *of* the city. We briefly introduced key contributions to this debate, which has until recently been dominated by Marxist theorists but has recently been complemented with poststructuralist approaches as well as liberal and multiculturalist conceptions of justice. The key point emerging from the literature is the acknowledgment of the spatial dialectics of injustice (Dikeç, 2001); that cities are not simple containers of justice and injustice but their active producers and reproducers; that we cannot understand justice without situating it in space (and time). The works of spatial justice theorists that we reviewed reject democratic proceduralism and neoliberalism and do not emphasise environmentalism. This is, of course, a very selective introduction but our reading of the literature leads us to three tentative conclusions. First, discussions of spatial justice have drawn on several theoretical traditions that think about justice in quite different ways. Second, there is considerable scope for further fruitful debate and critical engagement between different theoretical perspectives on justice, including some that are relatively underdeveloped in discussions of justice and the city, such as political liberalism and environmentalism. Third, one way of deepening our understanding of different theoretical perspectives on justice and the city – and what is at stake in the debates between conceptions – may be to examine (in)justice in and of a particular city from a range of different disciplinary and theoretical perspectives. If we reflect on what social, environmental and spatial 'injustices' we see – and what 'injustices' we don't see – from each perspective, we may begin to see theoretical debates in a new light.

An ordinary city: Newcastle upon Tyne

The literature on cities has been dominated by discussion of 'world cities' or 'global cities', such as New York, London, and Tokyo, which play a key role in the global political economy (Sassen, 1991; Knox, 1995). However, critics have challenged the global cities approach in urban studies. For example, Jennifer Robinson emphasises that the global cities approach, first, leaves many cities 'off the map' and under researched (Robinson, 2006: 94), and second, tends to focus attention on a 'limited range of economic activities with a certain global reach', while ignoring many other aspects of the economic, social and political organisation of cities (Robinson, 2006: 98). Furthermore, she suggests that the 'Global City as a concept becomes a regulating fiction' for all cities. So, cities must either aspire to the status of 'global city' or accept (and work towards) their proper place further down the 'hierarchy of world cities' (Robinson, 2006: 111).

Robinson (2006: 108), following Amin and Graham (1997), suggests that we should see all cities as 'ordinary'. This conceptual move should help us to overcome the problems associated with the global cities approach. First, if all cities are 'ordinary', we have no reason to research only a small subset of cities. Instead, all cities are 'on the map' for researchers. Second, we can recognise that ordinary cities are 'diverse, complex and internally differentiated' and they 'assemble many different kinds of social, economic and political processes' (Robinson, 2006: 109). Our view of the ordinary city encompasses much more of city life than we see through the lens of the global city approach. Third, if all cities are 'ordinary', we can also recognise that each city is 'diverse and distinctive with the possibility to imagine (within the constraints of contestations and uneven power relations) their own futures and their own distinctive form of cityness' (Robinson, 2006: 113). The ordinary city approach recognises both the individuality of cities and the potential that each city – its people and institutions – has to shape its own future.

In this book, we are interested in thinking about justice and fairness in relation to ordinary cities with a primary focus on the city of Newcastle upon Tyne (hereafter Newcastle) in the north east of England (in the United Kingdom). We concentrate on one city for two reasons. First, the ordinary city approach encourages us to think about the distinctive features of each city, including the distinctive injustices and their particular causes and potential remedies. Second, as we suggested earlier, we believe that studying one city from a range of theoretical and disciplinary perspectives may help us to deepen our understanding of injustice and think more clearly about what is at stake in debates between competing conceptions of justice in and of the city. Our particular choice of Newcastle is multifaceted. Most of us live and work in the city and have experiential knowledge of the city. Some of us have studied the city, its evolution, its urban problems and its policy solutions over many years. In addition to these pragmatic reasons, we also believe that Newcastle provides a fertile ground for exploring claims of (in)justices.

Newcastle City Council was one of a small number of local authorities in the UK that organised an independent fairness commission to consider how it might make fair decisions in planning and resource allocation during a time of austerity. The Newcastle Fairness Commission, chaired by Professor Chris Brink, Vice Chancellor of Newcastle University, reported in 2012 (Newcastle City Council and Newcastle University, 2012). The Commission's report was a thought-provoking attempt to tackle some very difficult questions of fairness and justice. It provided the direct stimulus for us to organise a series of workshops with colleagues, which has now developed into a multi-disciplinary discussion of justice and fairness in ordinary cities.

Newcastle is situated on the north bank of the River Tyne and 8.5 miles from the North Sea (see Figure 1.1). The municipal authority administering the city, Newcastle City Council, covers an area of 44 square miles and a population of over 280,000 people. The location of the city has a history of settlement dating back to Roman times but 'New Castle' was founded toward the end of the 11th century when a new castle was built on the ruins of Monkchester after the Norman conquest of England. Newcastle is most famous for its history of coal mining and shipbuilding in the 19th and 20th centuries. Its traditional industries declined during the latter part of the 20th century and the city became more reliant on public sector employment and services.

Newcastle is now the seventh largest conurbation in England but tends to fare poorly on many indicators compared to the national average. For example, the unemployment rate (10%), the fuel poverty rate (13.4%) and the rate of child poverty in Newcastle (31%) are all well above the national average (Bridge North East, 2014; Department of Energy and Climate Change, 2014). The city consistently appears in the bottom quartile of local authorities in England on a range of health indicators (Public Health England, 2012; Office of National Statistics, 2014) and the average life expectancy in Newcastle for both men and women is approximately two years less than the national average. While these show disparities at the national level, our concern is primarily with the city itself. Newcastle, like many other ordinary cities, is suffering from inequalities (see Figure 1.2). Over a quarter of its population live in the 10% most deprived areas in England, while over a third live in the top half of affluent areas (NCC, 2011a). There is a striking gap in disability-free life expectancy between the least deprived (such as South Gosforth) and the most deprived wards (such

Figure 1.1 Location of Newcastle upon Tyne in the United Kingdom

Source: UK National Archives, Open Government Licence.

as Byker) standing at 19.3 years for men and 16.4 years for women (NCC, 2011b: 3). As we will see in the chapters that follow, these inequalities are exacerbated by a range of other social, environmental, educational, food, health and procedural injustices.

Figure 1.2 Carstairs index of socioeconomic deprivation, 2001

Least Deprived Quintile of Wards
in Newcastle Upon Tyne

Most Deprived Quintile of Wards
in Newcastle Upon Tyne

Castle

Woolsington

Fawdon   Grange

Blakelaw

Westerhope   Kenton   South Gosforth   Dene

Denton   Jesmond   Heaton

Newburn   Fenham   Wingrove   Moorside   Walkergate

Lemington   Sandyford   Monkchester

Scotswood   Elswick   Byker   Walker

Benwell   West City

Source: Davoudi and Brooks (Chapter 2).

The outline of the book

This book consists of four sections: Section One: local environmental justice; Section Two: spatial justice and the right to the city; Section Three: participation, procedural fairness and local decision making; and Section Four: social justice and life course. Each section is organised around a key theme in thinking about justice *in* and *of* the city. Section One focuses on local environmental justice and includes four chapters, each engaging with the question of justice from different perspectives. As we noted earlier, theories of environmental justice have not been at the centre of major theoretical discussions of justice and the city. However, we believe that reflecting explicitly on environmental justice *in* the city and how the environment *of* the city (re)produces (in) justice can help us to understand better the diverse challenges (and opportunities) for reducing the injustice of ordinary cities. The four chapters in Section One cover various aspects of local environment including urban greenspace, mobility, food and the potential role of schools as local environmental assets. The range of topics reflects the breadth of the contemporary environmental justice literature, which has expanded well beyond the classic discussions of pollution to recognise the pervasiveness of environmental issues in everyday life (Schlosberg, 2013).

Section Two is about spatial justice and the right to the city. Its three chapters apply the spatial justice theories outlined above to various practices, ranging from displacement in Global North and South to the appropriation and use of space by young people in general, and skateboarders in particular. As we have seen, the discussion of spatial justice has dominated the work of major theorists working on justice and the city. Moreover, Lefebvre's notion of the 'right to the city' has become a focal point for academics thinking about, and activists seeking to challenge, the injustices of ordinary cities. The chapters in Section Two apply these theoretical ideas to new case studies to show how space in the city is (re)constructed and contested in the everyday lives of city-dwellers at the political, social, economic – and often spatial – margins of the city.

Section Three is about participation, procedural fairness and local decision making. The major theorists of justice and the city reject democratic proceduralism but they recognise the value – as well as the challenges and shortcomings – of procedural fairness and democratic participation in city politics. This section explores some of these challenges and shortcomings in two chapters, one focusing on people's perception of fair participation and the other on the significance of the past in making fairness real.

Section Four deals with social justice and life course and discusses how people's understanding of what matters to them most and what is fair or unfair changes throughout their life. This is another theme that has received little explicit attention from the leading theorists of justice and the city. However, thinking about justice through the life course – and the very different issues faced by different age groups – should help to deepen our understanding of how injustice is (re)produced over time through the different stages of individuals' lives and (re)produced across generations through the marginalisation of communities in cities. The three chapters in this section focus on old age and the significance of relationships; children and the significance of educational opportunities; and the working age and the significance of pay differentials.

The chapters collected together in this book are not intended to provide a comprehensive and exhaustive analysis of justice *in* and *of* the city. They are however indicative of the multiple ways in which people experience justice and injustice in ordinary cities. We will further elaborate on the substantive work of the contributors to this book in our section introductions and in the concluding chapter. In doing so, our aim is to reflect on both the injustices that we see (and don't see) in and of the city and how they can be located in some of the theoretical debates about justice.

Note

[1] This was published in French in 1968 and took nearly 30 years to be translated to English.

References

Amin, A. (2006) 'The good city', *Urban Studies*, 43(5/6): 1009-23.

Amin, A. and Graham, S. (1997) 'The ordinary city', *Transactions of the Institute of British Geographers*, 22(4): 411-29.

Arneson, R. (1989) 'Equality and equal opportunity for welfare', *Philosophical Studies*, 56: 77-93.

Attoh, K. (2011) 'What kind of right is the right to the city?', *Progress in Human Geography*, 35(5): 669-85.

Beitz, C. (1979) *Political theory and international relations*, Princeton, NJ: Princeton University Press.

Bell, D. (forthcoming) 'Justice on one planet', in S. Gardiner and A. Thompson (eds) *The Oxford handbook of environmental ethics*, Oxford: Oxford University Press.

Bridge North East (2013) 'Local authority profiles', in *Bridge North East State of the Region Report 2013*. [online] Available at: http://www. bridgenortheast.com/documents/_view/533aa3167cbb88893a0000a6 [accessed January 2016].

Buchanan, A. (1982) *Marx and justice: The radical critique of liberalism*, Cambridge: Cambridge University Press.

Caney, S. (2005) *Justice beyond borders: A global political theory*, Oxford: Oxford University Press.

Castells, M. (1977) *The urban question: A Marxist approach,* London: Edward Arnold.

Cohen, G. (1993) 'Equality of what? On welfare, goods, and capabilities' in M. Nussbaum and A. Sen (eds) *The quality of life*, Oxford: Oxford University Press, pp 9-30.

Daly, H. (1995) 'Consumption and welfare: two views of value added', *Review of Social Economy*, 53: 451-73.

Davoudi, S. (2012) 'Climate risk and security: new meanings of 'the environment' in the English planning system', *European Planning Studies,* 20(1): 49-69.

Davoudi, S. and Brooks, E. (2014) 'When does unequal become unfair? Judging claims of environmental injustice', *Environment and Planning A,* 46: 2686-702.

Davoudi, S. and Strange, I. (2009) 'Space and place in the twentieth century planning: an analytical framework and an historical review', in S. Davoudi and I. Strange (eds) *Conceptions of space and place in strategic spatial planning*, London: Routledge, pp 7-42.

Department of Energy and Climate Change (2014) *Fuel poverty sub regional data under LIHC indicator*'. [online] Available at: https://www.gov.uk/government/uploads/system/uploads/attachment_data/file/318998/2012_Sub-regional_LIHC_Final.xlsx [accessed January 2016].

Dikeç, M. (2001) 'Justice and the spatial imagination', *Environment and Planning A,* 33: 1785-805.

Dworkin, R. (2002) *Sovereign virtue: the theory and practice of equality*, Cambridge, MA: Harvard University Press.

Estlund, D. (2008) *Democratic authority: A philosophical framework*, Princeton, NJ: Princeton University Press.

Fainstein, S. (2010) *The just city*, Ithaca, NY: Cornell University Press.

Fraser, N. and Honneth, A. (2003) *Redistribution or recognition: a political-philosophical exchange*, London: Verso.

Harvey, D. (2005) *A brief history of neoliberalism,* Oxford: Oxford University Press.

Harvey, D. [1973 (2009)] *Social justice and the city*, Athens, GA: University of Georgia Press.

Isin, E.F. (2000) 'Introduction: democracy, citizenship, and the city' in E.F. Isin (ed) *Democracy, citizenship and the global city*, Cambridge, MA: Blackwell, pp 1-22.

Iveson, K (2011) 'Social or spatial justice? Marcuse and Soja on the right to the city', *City*, 15(2): 250-9.

Knox, P. (1995) 'World cities in a world-system' in P. Knox and P. Taylor (eds) *World cities in a world-system*, London: Routledge, pp 3-20.

Lefebvre, H. (1996) *Writings on cities*, trans. E. Kofman and E. Lebas, Cambridge, MA: Blackwell.

Lefebvre, H. [1974 (1991)] *The production of space,* Oxford: Blackwell.

Marcuse, P. (2009) 'Spatial justice: derivative but causal of social injustice', *Spatial Justice*, 1: 1-6.

Merrifield A. and Swyngedouw E. (1997) 'Social justice and the urban experience: an introduction', in A Merrifield and E Swyngedouw (eds) *The urbanization of injustice*, New York: New York University Press, pp 1-17.

Newcastle City Council (2011a) *Equalities statistics*. [online] Available at: http://www.newcastle.gov.uk [Accessed January 2016].

Newcastle City Council (2011b) *A fair budget for a fairer city. Newcastle future needs assessment: what we know about the people of Newcastle.* [online] Available at: http://www.newcastle.gov.uk [accessed January 2016].

Newcastle City Council and Newcastle University (2012) *Fair share, fair play, fair go, fair say. Report of the Newcastle Fairness Commission.* [online] Available at: http://www.ncl.ac.uk/media/wwwnclacuk/socialrenewal/files/fairnessreport.pdf

Nozick, R. (1974) *Anarchy, state and utopia*, New York: Basic Books.

Office of National Statistics (2014) *Life expectancy at birth and at the age of 65 by local areas in the United Kingdom.* [online] Available at: http://www.ons.gov.uk/ons/rel/subnational-health4/life-expec-at-birth-age-65/2006-08-to-2010-12/rft-table-1.xls [accessed January 2016].

Peterson, P. (1981) *City limits*, Chicago: University of Chicago Press.

Public Health England (2012) *Longer lives.*. [online] Available at: http://longerlives.phe.org.uk/ [accessed January 2016].

Rawls, J. (1972) *A theory of justice*, Oxford: Oxford University Press.

Rawls, J. (2001) *Justice as fairness: A restatement*, Cambridge, MA: Harvard University Press.

Robinson, J. (2006) *Ordinary cities: Between modernity and development*, Abingdon: Routledge.

Sassen, S. (1991) *The global city: New York, London, Tokyo*, Princeton, NJ: Princeton University Press.

Schlosberg, D. (2013) Theorising environmental justice, the expanding sphere of a discourse, *Environmental Politics* 22(1): 37-55

Scruton, R. (1996) *Modern philosophy: An introduction and survey*, London: Mandarin.

Sen, A. (1980) 'Equality of what?' *The Tanner Lecture on Human Values* delivered at Stanford University, 22 May 1979. Available at: http://tannerlectures.utah.edu/_documents/a-to-z/s/sen80.pdf

Soja, E. (2010) *Seeking spatial justice*, Minneapolis, MN: University of Minnesota Press.

Valentini, L. (2011) *Justice in a globalised world*, Oxford: Oxford University Press.

Wissenburg, M. (1998) *Green liberalism: The free and green society*, London: UCL Press.

Young, I.M. (1990) *Justice and the politics of difference*, Princeton, NJ: Princeton University Press.

SECTION ONE

Local environmental justice

Simin Davoudi and Derek Bell

> There is an immense need patiently to disseminate information, to dwell repeatedly on the concrete cases of injustice and on the concrete cases of ecological unsustainability. (Naess, 1999: 28)

People care deeply about their local environment because its quality affects their quality of life, wellbeing and contribution to environmental sustainability. Local environmental justice is a critical component of social justice. Like other forms of social inequality, environmental inequalities worsen health and wellbeing, hamper economic development and diminish social cohesion. Environmental justice matters because access to environmental benefits and protection from environmental harms constitutes basic human rights (UNEP, 2001). The history and origin of environmental justice go back to environmental justice movements (EJM) and their links with civil rights movements of the 1950s and 1960s in the United States. This was a time when the poor and predominantly non-white communities suffered most from pollution especially from toxic waste disposals. Today, the political reach of environmental justice has moved beyond race to include deprivation, age, gender and other vulnerabilities. The question of 'who gets what' has been extended to include other questions such as 'who counts', 'whose voice is listened to' and 'what counts as a legitimate claim'. Similarly, its substantive scope has moved beyond toxic waste and hazards to incorporate a wide range of both environmental 'bads' (burdens) and environmental 'goods' (benefits). The breadth of issues covered in discussions of environmental justice reflects the pervasiveness of the environment in everyday life.

The four chapters that make up this section of the book address a number of local environmental concerns including, urban greenspace, local schools, transport and food. The authors draw on their knowledge and experience of Newcastle to provide examples of various ways in which people experience justice and fairness in the city. The section starts with Chapter 2, which focuses on urban greenspace and its benefits to local environmental quality and local communities. Drawing on their earlier work, Simin Davoudi and Elizabeth Brooks present a multidimensional framework for understanding justice that goes beyond a concern with the geographical distribution to concerns about recognition, responsibility and capability. Based on this framework, they develop a number of key principles that can be applied to judge claims of injustice in relation to urban greenspace in Newcastle city. The chapter demonstrates how the uneven distribution of greenspace in the city can be interpreted as unfair when it is examined in interaction with other vulnerabilities and inequalities. They put a particular emphasis on the role played by what they call, qualities of and qualities in greenspace in people's access to and use of this urban environmental asset.

In Chapter 3, Pamela Woolner focuses on the school in the city, attempting to shift the debate away from a sole focus on poor physical quality of schools in deprived areas, to highlighting their potential contribution to improve the quality of the local environment. She argues that, the conventional justice debate about schools focuses on the former and is concerned with its negative impact on learning, teaching and, ultimately, student outcomes. However, Chapter 3 puts the emphasis on the positive role the school in the city can play to address environmental, and perhaps social, injustices. Woolner shows how efforts rooted in improving the school space can create a centre for sustainable living and an environmental resource for the wider community. She demonstrates how this broadened understanding of the role of the school in the city parallels the reconceptions of environmental justice that go beyond simple distributive justice to consider the importance of participation and recognition.

Chapter 4 by Roberto Palacin, Geoff Vigar and Sean Peacock focuses on transport poverty and urban mobility. As the authors argue, social exclusion in transport is double edged in the sense that mobility and accessibility are unevenly given in society and this is reinforced by policy and investment that favours certain modes and speed for a few over accessibility for all. They show how the choices of the 'hyper-mobiles' impact disproportionately on the disadvantaged and less mobile sections of society who are also more likely to be subject to the harmful consequences of transportation such as air pollution, road crash, noise and so on. They pay particular attention to two key dimensions of transport poverty, car ownership and public transport service and show how deprived households in Newcastle are disproportionately affected by lack of access to both. More importantly, they argue that poverty can also be experienced by those who are forced to own a car, in spite of their ability to afford one, because no other transport options are available or affordable.

In Chapter 5, Jane Midgley and Helen Coulson discuss the growing concerns about food justice, and show how different aspects of social and environmental justice interrelate with food. They focus particularly on how food justice has emerged as an organising concept for contemporary society and how its development and adoption have been informed by particular political debates. A notable example is the influence of the environmental justice movement on the food justice discourse by drawing attention to the fact that certain communities experience disproportionate lack of access to healthy foods. Midgley and Coulson explore the various practices and institutional arrangements surrounding the urban food systems that can be captured by the notion of food justice, using Newcastle as an example. They argue that without radical reform of the institutional arrangements and practices in urban food systems the pervading structural inequalities and injustices will remain.

The contributions to this section of the book demonstrate the importance of work on environmental justice for understanding justice *in* and *of* the city. Together, the four chapters show some of the very different ways that environmental injustices – in access to greenspace, the effects of air and noise pollution in schools, mobility and the effects of the hyper-mobile, and access to healthy food – contribute to the injustice *of* the city. They highlight the effects of environmental bads on the everyday lives and the life chances of city dwellers already enduring social and economic disadvantages. However, they also illustrate how the reproduction of injustice might be challenged through both planned interventions, such as improving access to greenspace, and community activism, such as local initiatives to tackle food poverty or schools repurposing their outdoor space to create new opportunities for children and the wider community.

This section of the book shows that, like social justice, defining and assessing environmental justice is not straightforward; that questions of justice and fairness are not technical or statistical questions but rather ethical and political questions. The chapters, especially Chapters 2 and 3, illustrate how different theoretical perspectives highlight different injustices. Therefore, identifying and addressing injustice requires theoretically-informed practical judgments about specific cases at specific times and places. So, as Davoudi and Brooks argue in Chapter 2, there is a need to combine quantitative analyses of spatial distributions of environmental benefits and burdens with fine-grain qualitative narratives of how people experience injustices in their everyday life, and what aspects of local environmental qualities matter most to them.

References

Naess, A. (1999) 'An outline of the problem ahead', in N. Low (ed) *Global ethics and environment*, London: Routledge.

UNEP (2001) 'Living in a pollution free world a basic human right'. *UNEP News Release* 01/49. [online] Available at: http://www.unep.org/Documents.Multilingual/Default.asp?documentid=197&articleid=2819 [Accessed January 2016].

TWO

Urban greenspace and environmental justice claims

Simin Davoudi and Elizabeth Brooks

Introduction

> The budget for new road building, if used differently, could provide 1,000 new parks at an initial capital cost of £10 million each – two parks in each local authority in England. (CABE study, quoted in Marmot, 2010: 25)

Urban greenspace provides a vivid illustration of the debate over how multiple factors can coincide to turn the distributional unevenness of environmental benefits into a case for claims of injustice. What underpins this debate is a pluralistic understanding of justice that goes beyond distribution to include recognition, participation, capability and responsibility. The focus is not only on who gets what, but also on who counts, who gets heard, what matters, and who does what. Based on this inclusive framework, Davoudi and Brooks (forthcoming) have suggested a set of guiding principles that can be used for judging justice claims about environmental burdens. These, adjusted for environmental benefits, are shown in Table 2.1.

The aim of this chapter is to show how these principles can be applied to the fairness of access to urban greenspace in the city of Newcastle upon Tyne (hereafter Newcastle). More specifically, we aim to explore whether the uneven distribution of greenspace in Newcastle can be interpreted as unfair for this particular case and time. The chapter is structured under four headings. After this introduction, we discuss the significance of urban greenspace as an environmental benefit for human health and wellbeing. We then draw on the justice dimensions and the guiding questions in Table 2.1 to discuss how the uneven distribution of greenspace may lead to claims of environmental injustice. The chapter's conclusions are drawn together in a final section.

Table 2.1 Guiding questions for judging environmental justice claims

Justice dimension	Examples of questions in relation to environmental benefits
Distribution	Does a deprived community suffer disproportionately from a deficient (a lack of or limited) environmental benefit? Is it particularly vulnerable to the impacts of deficiency in the environmental benefit? Is it provided with compensatory measures?
Recognition	Does the deficiency in the environmental benefit result in, or add to, misrecognition for a deprived community or stigmatisation of a deprived area? Is the area perceived as an unsuitable location for other environmental benefits, or as a more suitable location for environmental burdens and does it therefore suffer from their cumulative impact?
Participation	Is a deprived community excluded from decisions about locating, or strategies to remediate the poor quality of, an environmental benefit?
Responsibility	Is the deprived community the least contributor to the cause of the deficiency in the environmental benefit? Is the deficiency made up for by any compensatory benefit? Can the community contribute to remediation measures?
Capabilities	Does a deficiency in an environmental benefit limit the freedom of a deprived community to pursue its valued goals?

Greenspace as an environmental 'good'

There is a growing body of literature that underwrites the multiple benefits of urban greenspace. As part of 'ecosystem services', greenspaces function as carbon sinks, cooling the temperature, reducing surface water runoff and providing green corridors for wildlife (Heynen, 2006). Greenspace in urban areas reduces the effect of air pollution through biogenic regulation (Freer-Smith et al, 1997), with tree canopies being particularly effective in capturing particles due to their greater surface roughness (Manning and Feder, 1980).

In addition to these environmental benefits, research has shown that urban greenspace is important for people's physical and mental health throughout their lives (White et al, 2013; UCL IHE, 2014). For example, epidemiological studies have found strong links between health and greenspace in large cities (de Vries et al, 2003), particularly in relation to longevity in the elderly and more generally (Takano et al, 2002; Mitchell and Popham, 2008) and healthy childhood development (Sadler et al, 2010). There is evidence of association between greenspace and a reduced risk of anxiety and depression (Maas et al, 2008). It is suggested that contact with nature can promote better mood (van den Berg et al, 2003), improve attention (Ottosson and Grahn, 2005), provide restorative benefits (Taylor et al, 2002), and enhance self-discipline (Taylor and Kuo, 2009), self-awareness and self-esteem (Maller et al, 2002). There are also social benefits: it is shown that natural settings provide inclusive places to meet that can improve social interaction and cohesion (Bird, 2007). It is also argued that properly managed urban greenspace enhances neighbourhood image and adds to property values (Scottish Natural Heritage, 2014: 2). However, the materialisation of many of these benefits depends on a number of factors such as the availability (size and distance to where people live), accessibility (physical and sociocultural) and quality (actual and perceived) of urban greenspace. While later sections will explore these factors in greater detail, we will first begin by presenting the case study area of Newcastle and its greenspace endowment.

Greenspace in Newcastle city

Newcastle is a birthplace of the Industrial Revolution, which brought wealth for some but created destitution for others and left a legacy of environmental problems. While reducing inequalities has remained a challenge, major progress has been made in reducing the environmental burdens in the city and enhancing its environmental benefits. A notable example of the latter is greenspace, which the city, despite its industrial past, is well provided with. This was a major factor in Newcastle being twice voted (in 2009 and 2010) as 'the greenest city' in Britain by Forum for the Future (Forum for the Future, 2010). Some 55% of the city (around 68 km² from a total of 123 km²) consists of greenspace, of which about one quarter (17 km²) is publicly accessible. A further 5% (6 km²) of the city's area is water, mainly in the form of the River Tyne, which borders the southern edge of the city and the Ouseburn, which is the Tyne's main tributary in the city.

The average built up area in European cities ranges from 20-80% (EEA, 2010: 14), so Newcastle with its 40% built up area is positioned in the middle (EEA, 2010: 26). However, Newcastle has a particularly dense built environment with only 7.5% of homes being detached[1] compared to an England average of 22.5%; while over 30% of homes are flats/apartments compared to an England average of 19.3% (NCC, 2011a), indicating the importance of greenspace in the city. In terms of per capita provision, Newcastle has a high level of publicly accessible greenspace standing at 8.4 ha per 1,000 people; however, as will be discussed in the following section, and shown in Figure 2.1, its distribution is not even. Notably, over 20% (4 km²) of the public greenspace is in the form of one large, protected pasture called the Town Moor (UK NEA, 2011) at the centre of the city.

Figure 2.1 Greenspace in Newcastle upon Tyne

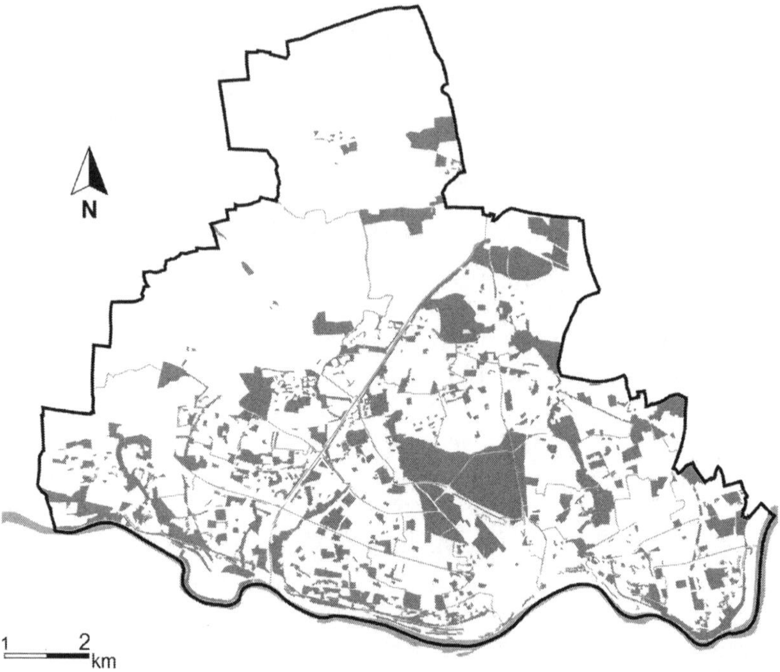

Source: the authors, based on data provided by Newcastle City Council.

Newcastle's greenspace: fair or unfair?

In order to address the above question, we draw on the guiding principles outlined in Table 2.1, beginning with the distribution of greenspace in the city. We then examine potential claims of justice in relation to recognition, participation, capabilities and responsibility.

Distribution

Distributional concerns have been at the centre of environmental justice struggles as early as the 1950s when the environmental justice movement (EJM) came to prominence in America and became tightly connected to the civil rights movement. However, for some time, the focus remained largely on environmental harms, especially the disproportionate exposure of non-white communities to toxic wastes and hazardous industries (Taylor, 2000). Today, both the substantive scope and political reach of EJM have expanded. In terms of the former, concerns about the distribution of environmental 'goods' (such as greenspace) have been added to concerns about environmental 'bads' (such as air pollution). As regards the latter, concerns about race, ethnicity and deprivation have been complemented with other vulnerabilities such as age, gender, health and disability (Lucas et al, 2004).

Existing research on the distribution of greenspace in the United States has already shown a strong link between its availability and higher socioeconomic groups (Heynen et al, 2006). In England, a Commission for Architecture and the Built Environment (CABE) study demonstrated that the most affluent 20% of wards in England have five times the amount of greenspace as have the most deprived 10% (CABE, 2010); while the Marmot review found that the more deprived the ward, the more likely it was to suffer from a number of environmental negatives, including a lack of greenspace (Marmot, 2010).

Implicit in these studies is a focus on availability (size and distance) of urban greenspace, because it is shown that some of the benefits from greenspaces depend on their distance from where people live. 'On average, people living closer to a park typically derive more benefits from its presence than those living further away' (UK NEA, 2011: 390), because, for example, their impacts on noise abatement and pollution reduction tend to be greater the closer people live to them and the proportion of people using greenspaces for recreational purposes decreases with distance from them. Close proximity to greenspace also encourages people to make short trips on foot or by bicycle (Bird, 2004), both of which are beneficial to health and environment. Some studies have found a connection between proximity to certain types of greenspace and children's levels of physical activity (Lachowycz et al, 2012) with implications for their health as well as their familiarity with and confidence in natural surroundings. All this suggests that distance matters. But defining what is an appropriate distance, and to what size of greenspace, differs according to different standards. One of the commonly used standards in the UK is produced by Natural England, which has also formed part of the government guidance (Urban Green Spaces Taskforce, 2002). Known as the Accessible Natural Greenspace Standards (ANGSt), these recommend that everyone, wherever they live, should have an accessible natural greenspace of:

- at least 2 ha in size, no more than 300 m (5 minutes walk) from home;
- at least one accessible 20 ha site within 2 km of home;
- one accessible 100 ha site within 5 km of home;
- one accessible 500 ha site within 10 km of home; plus

- a minimum of 1 ha of statutory Local Nature Reserves per 1,000 population. (Natural England, 2010: 10)

It should be noted that while the term 'accessibility' is often used in greenspace literature, including the ANGSt, to refer to the distance between home/work and greenspaces, we use the term differently to refer to physical and social barriers and promoters, and examine them under the recognition aspect of justice (as 'qualities of' and 'qualities in' greenspace). We use the term 'availability' to refer to size and distance and examine it in this section (the distributive aspects of justice). We will then make some observations about other dimensions of justice namely participation, capabilities and responsibility with regard to greenspace in Newcastle.

We earlier established the uneven distribution of publically available greenspace in Newcastle, showing overprovision in the centre (the Town Moor). The map in Figure 2.1 also indicates underprovision in some of the outlying 'village and rural' wards to the north west of the city, with the southernmost wards appearing to have multiple small spaces. The discrepancies between the various wards emerge from analysis, with Wingrove, Newburn and Castle particularly well provided, while the southern part of Heaton ward (since 2004, South Heaton ward) and Westerhope have particularly small proportions of the city's provision. Furthermore, the city council notes that some greenspaces are isolated and poorly linked to the wider network of spaces, especially those to the east and west of the city (NCC, 2012: 24). In order to examine the distributional justice, we have compared patterns of availability of greenspaces with patterns of deprivation (defined by the Index of Multiple Deprivation and presented in Figure 2.2) in the city, based on the following analytical specifications.

First, we have simplified the city's geography for ease of reference because wards and their names have changed over the period for which data was available at the time of analysis. The main juxtapositions are drawn between the 'deprived riverside wards/areas' (the locations of former heavy industries) and the mainly 'affluent wards/areas' (the location of more middle-class housing) from the city centre northwards. Another relatively affluent area is the suburban, semi-rural north west of the city. Beyond these generalisations lies a more nuanced mosaic of poverty and affluence, such as areas of strong deprivation in the city centre (see Figure 2.2). However, whichever way we present the city's geography, we are confronted with the 'uncomfortable truth' that, 'inequalities within and between different parts of the city severely reduce the life chances of people from cradle to grave' (NCC, 2011b: 4).

Figure 2.2 Carstairs index of socioeconomic deprivation, 2001

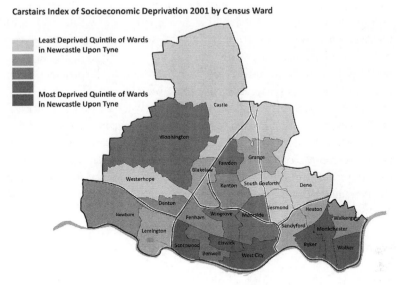

Carstairs Index of Socioeconomic Deprivation 2001 by Census Ward

Source: the authors

Second, we have drawn on Newcastle City Council's (2012) definition of urban greenspace, which includes eight categories. These are also recommended by the Urban Green Spaces Taskforce (UGST) (2002) and used by other local authorities to audit existing open spaces and assess the need for new ones in their areas. We will discuss the accessibility implications of such a broad definition of greenspace in the subsection on 'Recognition'.

Third, we have drawn on an analysis by Caparros-Midwood (2011), which focuses on fine-grained Census Output Area level[2] in the urban core rather than the entire city (as used in Figure 2.1). This is because the large peripheral parts of the city are mainly suburban or rural in character, with low-density housing and countryside access (Newcastle/Gateshead, 2011: 19), which arguably compensate for deficiencies in greenspace. The Caparros-Midwood analysis also takes into account the size (minimum 2 ha) and distance (applying various thresholds) according to the standards (ANGSt) recommended by Natural England (2010). Furthermore, distance is calculated by taking into account the road and path networks, rather than simply using a point-to-point straight line.

The results of the greenspace availability analysis are shown in Figure 2.3. These indicate that outlying wards (such as Elswick, West City and Sandyford)[3] have a lower provision of ample-sized greenspace. Overall,

69.7% of output areas in the city's urban core are within 1 km (15 minutes' walk) of a greenspace of 2 ha or more and 22.2% are within 500 m. However the standard of a 2 ha greenspace within 300 m of the home is only met by 10.5% of the city's output areas. Some of the deprived riverside wards, bordering the river Tyne and facing densely built up areas of Gateshead across the water, are underprovided with larger (2+ ha) greenspace. As well as these broadly geographical factors, the analyses show an overall relationship between higher deprivation in Newcastle and a greater distance from greenspace. Within the Newcastle urban core, the output areas with levels of deprivation in the bottom 50% for the city have larger mean distances to greenspace than the more affluent 50%, with a difference of about 157 m between the average for the most deprived and most affluent quarters (Caparros-Midwood, 2011).

Recognition

Both Marxist and feminist scholars have criticized the exclusive focus of distributive justice on the allocation of material goods. The former argue that such a focus leads to the neglect of the social structures and institutional contexts that shape distributional patterns (Simpson,

Figure 2.3 Greenspace of 2 ha and over in urban core of Newcastle upon Tyne

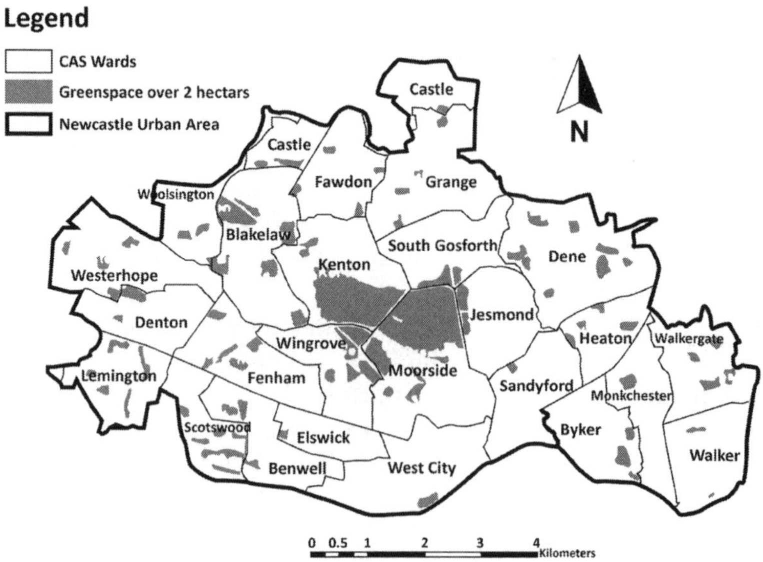

Source: Caparros-Midwood, 2011. Reproduced with the author's permission.

1980), such as historical patterns of land ownership, the operation of property markets, or the regulatory impacts of the planning systems, all of which can help or hinder the creation of a more equitable urban greenspace. Feminists suggest that distributive justice is difference-blind and unable to address cultural oppression; that it neglects the cultural politics of difference by overemphasising the social politics of equality (Young, 1990). A key argument is that some social or cultural groups tend to be systematically devalued and their voice excluded from public discourse. 'Identity politics' has sought to highlight the rights of such groups to equal consideration. However, rather than regarding recognition as an alternative to redistributive politics, scholars, notably Nancy Fraser, have argued for a 'bivalent' conception of justice that includes 'both distribution and recognition without reducing either one of them to the other' (Fraser, 1996: 30). While redistribution secures the objective condition of justice, recognition safeguards its intersubjective condition (Fraser, 2003). Justice requires the recognition of people's different identities and vulnerabilities because these affect people's physical and sociocultural access to available greenspace. We have conceptualised those factors that affect physical accessibility as the qualities *of* greenspace and those that affect sociocultural accessibility as qualities *in* greenspace, while acknowledging the intimate connections between the two. We will go on to discuss the cumulative effects of limited greenspace.

Qualities of greenspace refers to a variety of factors, ranging from the general upkeep to the availability of services such as seats, lighting, toilets, ramps and signposts. Accessibility might be reduced by both actual and perceived quality. A study in Scotland found that where there was the greatest need for open space, its low quality meant it did not make a positive contribution to quality of life (James, 2004). The general upkeep of parks seems to particularly affect their level of use by vulnerable groups. Drawing on a literature review, Williams and Green (2001) suggest that older, disabled, ethnic minority and female residents are less likely to use parks than other groups because of the parks' poor quality, poor access, a lack of toilet and other facilities, and safety.

Research in the UK (Duffy, 2000) has shown that parks run by local authorities in deprived areas had lower standards of maintenance than parks run by wealthier local authorities, suggesting that greenspace quality is at least partly an issue of resources. While Newcastle City Council is not a particularly affluent local authority, it has, nonetheless, made substantial investment in its greenspaces over the last decade, with 11 parks in the city being awarded the 'Green Flag' for quality, including parks in two of the deprived riverside wards (Newcastle/ Gateshead and ENTEC, 2011). Nevertheless, the quality varies across the city, as shown by a local audit conducted in 2004 seeking users' views. The result points out the variability of greenspace conditions between and within greenspace categories. Public parks and cemeteries still open for burials typically achieved the highest quality ratings. Amenity greenspace, outdoor sports facilities and natural and semi-natural greenspace received the lowest scores (NCC, 2004). More relevant to the discussions on justice claims, a 2011 residents' survey undertaken[4] by the council showed that, on the whole, people living in more affluent areas were significantly more satisfied about the quality and maintenance of parks and open spaces than those living in more deprived wards, although there were some exceptions.

As indicated earlier, most of the research points to the relationship between proximity to greenspace and its use. Proximity to greenspace is likely to encourage 'active' forms of travel. A report from the Chartered Society of Designers, for example, notes that 68% of journeys to greenspace are made on foot while 4% are made by bicycle (CSD, 2011). Regarding the remaining 28% of journeys to greenspace, those in deprived wards who lack locally available greenspace may be at a further disadvantage because of low levels of car ownership in those wards (see Davoudi and Brooks, 2014) and limited availability of regular local bus routes linking them to greenspace. In Newcastle, the focus is on providing routes that link city suburbs to the city centre, rather than to city amenities (Davoudi and Brooks, 2012: 115).

Qualities in greenspace refer to their appeal to different social and cultural groups. Research in the US has shown that certain qualities can repel or attract different age, gender and ethno-racial groups of users and hence affect access. For example, Byrne and Wolch (2009) show how different ways of perceiving the same greenspace by different groups of users affect their use; a park may be perceived as either intolerant and unwelcoming, or a safe and welcoming place for ethnic minorities (Byrne and Wolch, 2009: 752). With regard to safety, Roman and Chalfin (2008) suggest that fear of violence is likely to discourage women in particular from using outdoor space. Furthermore, the combination of gender, race and class can have a strong negative impact on people's ability to take advantage of greenspaces.

Taking qualities in greenspace seriously requires a more nuanced understanding of what constitutes greenspace. The definition of greenspace used by Newcastle City Council and adopted in Figures 2.1 and 2.3 includes a wide range of areas, which besides the various types of natural space, parks and gardens, includes outdoor sports facilities, cemeteries and churchyards. The latter is an example of insensitivity to social and cultural diversity that creates different meanings of a place for different people. In this case, cemeteries and churchyards may be perceived as inaccessible to people of non-Christian background. The former category includes golf courses and school playing fields, which some people may not consider tranquil and welcoming, and as a result may find them inaccessible. When considering the breakdown of greenspace in Newcastle by category (as shown in Figure 2.4), it becomes clear the accessibility of generally available greenspace may be more limited than the impression given in Figures 2.1 and 2.3.

Cumulative effects

Another guiding question with regard to recognition is whether the lack of environmental benefits in some areas is compounded with environmental burdens. Some studies show that environmental disbenefits are cumulative and are concentrated in areas of high social deprivation (for example Marmot, 2010). Our research has shown that in Newcastle, the deprived riverside wards suffer from higher levels of air pollution (see Davoudi and Brooks, 2014). The absence or under provision of greenspace takes away their mitigating potentials, increases the likelihood of poor air quality, aggravating existing health problems in those areas, and hence adds additional weight to claims of injustice.

Furthermore, a lack of access to greenspace may be compounded by other deficits in the provision of local environmental benefits. This includes, for example, a dearth of private gardens, which is a characteristic of Newcastle's high proportion of flatted accommodation as mentioned earlier. Deprived areas also tend to suffer from poor indoor conditions (such as cold, damp and unsanitary living spaces). In Newcastle, such unsatisfactory living conditions were concentrated in the deprived riverside wards (Davoudi and Brooks, 2012: 65). This is compounded by unsatisfactory local environmental quality standards in the neighbourhood (such as litter, graffiti, fly-posting and fly-tipping), also tending to be higher in the former industrial Tyneside wards (Davoudi and Brooks, 2012: 56). Together, these can contribute to an impression of a neglected, unsafe neighbourhood. In some wards, lack of greenspace is compounded by a lack of access to natural spaces, woodlands and bluespace (water). The latter is clearly more ample in the deprived riverside wards than other areas in the city. However, their quality varies between the affluent central wards, such as those transected by the Ouseburn, and the city's riverside wards, one of which

Figure 2.4 Greenspace in Newcastle upon Tyne by category, 2011. Extract from Green Infrastructure Study – Evidence Base, prepared for Gateshead Council and Newcastle City Council by Entec (January 2011).

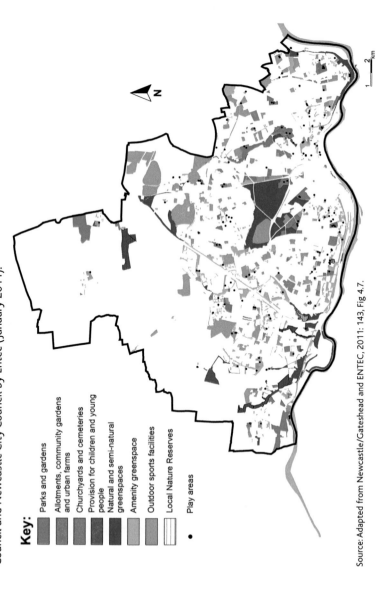

Key:

Parks and gardens

Allotments, community gardens and urban farms

Churchyards and cemeteries

Provision for children and young people

Natural and semi-natural greenspaces

Amenity greenspace

Outdoor sports facilities

Local Nature Reserves

• Play areas

Source: Adapted from Newcastle/Gateshead and ENTEC, 2011: 143, Fig 4.7.

even hosts an unremediated site of contamination, which contributes a steady stream of industrial pollution to the river Tyne (Davoudi and Brooks, 2012: 50).

Participation

Participation is a better known component of justice and forms part of 'procedural justice'. According to Fraser (1996) what combines redistribution with recognition is 'parity of participation' in society and fair *representation* in decision making. The manner in which justice is decided and carried out is important to its material effects in terms of distribution. The locations of urban greenspaces are often determined by systems of landownership and land use planning decisions. Many urban greenspaces have originated from traditional common grazing lands and amenities that were provided for and by the wealthy landowners for use by urban residents. These were gradually made public as a result of popular pressure and endowments by philanthropists (Lasdun, 1992). In Newcastle, the Town Moor's history goes back to the 12th century and is now regulated by its own Act of Parliament[5] and managed through a partnership between the Freemen of the City and Newcastle City Council. Its importance for the city relates not just to its size, but also to the rental income that it generates from grazing. The historical origins of urban greenspaces such as Town Moor partly explain the often non-uniform distribution of greenspace in cities and the difficulties of altering this pattern.

However, cities are subject to new developments whereby land is turned from green to built-up areas and vice versa. The change of use provides opportunities for inclusive participation in the decisions affecting the location and nature of the newly created greenspaces, if environmental information is transparent and accessible to all. However, such opportunities may be less available to Newcastle's deprived due to their unequal engagement with sources of environmental information, which are increasingly communicated through the internet. A 2006 study showed that 60% of homes in the city's affluent areas had internet access compared to 37% in deprived areas (Crang et al, 2006). Although internet usage has by now risen to over 80% in the North East region as a whole (ONS, 2013), the gap between affluent and disadvantaged areas in Newcastle is unlikely to have narrowed much. This is because access is only one aspect of the digital divide: skills, attitudes and types of engagement with internet use are also significant (Helsper, 2012; Clayton and McDonald, 2013). For example, a pattern of pervasive ICT usage was found in an affluent neighbourhood of Newcastle, compared with sporadic use in a deprived neighbourhood (Crang et al, 2006).

Capabilities

Capabilities refer to the capacity of people to function in the lives they choose for themselves. The capability approach to justice was developed by Martha Nussbaum (2011) and Amartya Sen (2009), who challenged John Rawls' 'primary goods' metric[6] as being insensitive to human diversity and the differential values of particular goods to particular people and communities. They argued that the metric neglects the structural, institutional and cultural factors that affect the *conversion* of these goods into capabilities,[7] functioning[8] (being and doing), and wellbeing-driven freedom. Instead, Sen (2009: 233) suggests a 'serious departure from concentrating on the *means* of living to the *actual opportunities* of living'. Defining what to include in a capability metric has been subject to dispute, but Sen prefers 'group discussion' as a way of selecting, trading off and prioritising capabilities (Crocker, 2008). We concur with the latter because it reflects the situated nature of justice and respects cultural differences. Environmental burdens and benefits have a profound impact on people's capabilities. Limited availability and accessibility of urban greenspace can inhibit people who have reason to value it from converting other goods (such as income) to their wellbeing. For example, the perception of an unsafe area affects people's freedom of circulation, and in inhibiting their access to greenspace, can harm their quality of life.

An illustrative example from Newcastle is indicated by the pale brown areas in Figure 2.4, which as the key explains, represent 'outdoor sports facilities' – a category which includes both natural and artificial surfaces. These represent 17.24% of the city's overall provision of greenspace (2.94 km^2), making them the third largest category of greenspace in the city, preceded by amenity and natural greenspace (UGST, 2002; NCC, 2012: 21). Yet, as with the distribution of the latter, we can observe that sports facilities are quite unevenly located in the city with some of the larger sports areas clustering in the centre and east of the city, as shown in Figure 2.4. This implies limitations on the capabilities of those in the deprived wards who may wish to develop sporting proficiency, particularly as a high proportion will not have access to a private car (as noted in an earlier section).

Responsibility

Responsibility embraces a broad set of questions about the original causes of the environmental deficiency and who should take action to remediate that deficiency. This may go back to how an uneven distribution or poor quality environmental benefit came into existence, and how much the people who live with that environmental deficiency have contributed to it, or are able to take part in remedying it.

These questions are important because if people are subjected to environmental burdens or deprived of environmental benefits in which they had no choice, their sense of injustice is exacerbated. This, however, does not mean that rights and responsibilities necessarily go hand in hand: people may hold rights where they hold no corresponding responsibilities, because often people's choices are conditioned by structural and institutional constraints as well as physical and mental vulnerabilities, social norms and cultural values. For example, researchers have proposed the pressure imposed on 'cognitive bandwidth' by poverty may limit people's capacity to make good decisions (Mani et al, 2013). It is also difficult to separate individual from collective responsibility (Pierik and Robeyns, 2007: 148-9). Nevertheless, responsibility that arises from freedom and capabilities is an important part of environmental justice because 'it raises ethical questions about responsibility towards not only fellow humans but also non-human nature' (Davoudi and Brooks, 2014: 2690). Incorporating this dimension into the environmental justice debate helps challenge the dominant human-centric view which 'places humans as at the centre of the Universe and considers nature to be at their service' (Davoudi, 2012: 54). As Davoudi and Brooks (forthcoming) argue, 'A focus on responsibility places the discourses of environmental ethics firmly in the framework of social justice in much the same way as a focus on sustainability places 'the discourse of justice firmly within the framework of sustainability' (Agyeman and Evans, 2004: 156). Justice for people becomes entwined with justice to nature. It is therefore important that everyone has the opportunity to volunteer to contribute to the creation, maintenance or management of their local greenspace. The benefits of this go beyond recreation and health and include 'wider and longer-term social, economic and environmental benefits' (UGST, 2002: 11) because greenspace encourages more social inclusion.

The particular nature of greenspace means that it is difficult to retro-add to urban contexts. However, the conversion of brownfield land to greenspace, particularly in former industrial sites has become a key feature of many urban regeneration schemes. In Newcastle, a former riverside leadworks was converted to parkland in Walker ward. However, because of the extremely high level of lead contamination in the soil, it has been developed as a fenced off dense woodland area that borders the Hadrian's Wall Path in Walker Riverside Park, arguably adding little to the local amenities and potentially lessening the sense of security on that path. It appears that the deprived community of Walker had little input into the conversion of this site (Davoudi and Brooks, 2012). In contrast, in another project called 'Greening Wingrove' local residents were brought together to work on strategies for making better use of trees and plants as well as tackling refuse and reducing energy bills. The project also encouraged residents to monitor local services and put forward new ideas to improve their local environment (NCC, 2011c: 15).

Lack of opportunity to contribute to the quality, use and upkeep of greenspace underlines a further disadvantage for those who do not live near it. Acknowledging the benefit of co-responsibility, the Groundwork NGO has played a significant role in supporting deprived communities to take control of their local parks and open spaces at the national level (Fordham et al, 2002). In Newcastle, Groundwork has also supported Newcastle City Council and Community Groups in renovations and improvements to over 40 parks, open spaces and school grounds; 15 of these projects included Green Gyms, with outdoor exercise equipment for all (NCC, 2012: 27). Clearly, the social and environmental benefits of involvement in such projects will not be available to those communities lacking publicly accessible greenspace.

Concluding remarks

Environmental justice is at the heart of social justice because like social inequalities, environmental inequalities diminish people's health and wellbeing and society's prosperity and cohesion. However, defining the 'justice' in environmental justice has not been straightforward and remains an open question. In our previous paper (Davoudi and Brooks, 2014) we have built on the existing scholarship in this area to provide a pluralistic understanding of environmental justice that goes beyond the concerns for distributive justice to incorporate recognition, participation, capability and responsibility. While responsibility has received less attention, it is paramount for the consideration of justice for both instrumental and moral reasons. In terms of the former (nature for human's sake), claims of injustice are strengthened when the deficiency in environmental benefits for some people is due to the action of others, as is the case when publicly accessible greenspace is built upon for private profit with no clear benefit to local communities (as has recently been threatened, for example, at several sites in the city of Liverpool – see Our Ground, 2014). In terms of the latter (nature for nature's sake), not being able to exercise responsibility for the environment, such as creating and maintaining greenspaces, is an injustice not only to nature but also to the people who value such contributions.

Our application of the pluralistic understanding of justice to greenspace in Newcastle has revealed that the impact of its deficiency (lack or poor quality) is likely to be felt more in socially deprived communities where:

- because of their health and housing conditions, people have greater need for the benefits of such a resource nearby;
- people may be more likely to experience high levels of environmental pollution;
- people may be less able to make their voices heard;
- people may suffer from place stigmatisation;
- people's capabilities may be impinged.

As mentioned earlier, the proposed guiding questions shown in Table 2.1 should not be taken as all-encompassing or universally applicable to all situations but as a starting point to develop a fuller account of how multiple social, spatial and environmental factors can overlap to turn a distributional unevenness into an injustice – how unequal may become unfair.

Finally, it is important to reiterate what we have stressed in our previous work and highlight the conceptual limitations (in terms of the inability to explain the why and the how of injustices) and the methodological limitations (in terms of the inability to account for multiple flows and scales) of this approach. However, these limitations do not entail the abandonment of attempts to unearth cases of injustice, even though perfectly just institutions are not in place. Furthermore, we reiterate that quantitative socio-spatial analyses of environmental justice claims need to be combined with fine tuned qualitative narratives of how people experience injustice. A situated view of environmental justice is needed that enables affected people to prioritise the burdens, benefits and principles (such as those summarised in Table 2.1) that matter most to them. We are aware of the idealistic tone of such an inclusive approach to justice, but as John Rawls (1999) has suggested, in a non-ideal world, imagining a 'realistic utopia' is a good start for the pursuit of alternatives beyond the present-day political reality.

Notes

[1] These are homes that are surrounded by open land on all four sides.

[2] The lowest level of analysis for census data, comprising about 125 households.

[3] As defined before 2004.

[4] 16,688 questionnaires were sent out to a random sample of households of which 5,222 (31.3%) responses were received (NCC, 2011a).

[5] Originally by 1774 Town Moor Act, and now by the 1988 Newcastle upon Tyne Town Moor Act. See http://www.freemenofnewcastle.com/themoorhistory.html

[6] That includes general purpose goods, such as income and wealth, opportunities and liberties, and the social bases of self-respect (Rawls, 1971).

[7] For Sen, capabilities as freedoms refer to the *presence* of options or alternatives, in the sense of opportunities that do not exist only formally or legally but are substantively available to people and communities.

[8] Such as being employed, expressing oneself, breathing clean air, engaging with nature.

References

Agyeman, J. and Evans, B. (2004) '"Just sustainability": the emerging discourse of environmental justice in Britain?', *The Geographical Journal*, 170: 155-64.

Bird, W. (2004) *Natural fit: Can greenspace and biodiversity increase levels of physical activity?*, Bedford: Royal Society for the Protection of Birds.

Bird, W. (2007) *Natural thinking: A report for the Royal Society for the Protection of Birds.* [pdf] Available at: http://www.rspb.org.uk/Images/naturalthinking_tcm9-161856.pdf [accessed January 2016].

Byrne, J. and Wolch, J. (2009) 'Nature, race and parks: past research and future directions for geographic research', *Progress in Human Geography*, 33: 743-65.

CABE (2010) *Community green: using local spaces to tackle inequality and improve health*, London: CABE.

Caparros-Midwood, D. (2011) 'A GIS investigation of the relationship between urban greenspace and the socio-demographic of a city', unpublished BSc thesis, Newcastle upon Tyne: University of Newcastle.

Clayton, J. and McDonald, S. (2013) 'The limits of technology: social class, occupation and digital inclusion in the city of Sunderland, England', *Information, Communication and Society*, 16:945-66.

Comber, A., Brunsdon, C. and Green, E. (2008) 'Using a GIS-based network analysis to determine urban greenspace accessibility for different ethnic and religious groups', *Landscape and Urban Planning*, 86: 103-14.

Crang, M., Graham, S. and Crosbie, T. (2006) 'Variable geometries of connection: urban digital divides and the uses of information technology', *Urban Studies,* 43: 2551-70.

Crocker, D. (2008) *Ethics of global development: agency, capability and deliberative democracy*, Cambridge: Cambridge University Press.

CSD (2011) *Understanding the contribution parks and green spaces can make to improving people's lives.* [pdf] Available at: http://www.csd.org. uk/uploadedfiles/files/value_of_green_space_report.pdf [accessed January 2016]

Davoudi, S. (2012) 'Climate risk and security: new meanings of "the environment" in the English planning system', *European Planning Studies,* 20(1): 49-69.

Davoudi, S. and Brooks, E. (2012) *Environmental justice and the city: full report.* [pdf] Available at: http://www.ncl.ac.uk/guru/documents/ Environmentaljusticeandthecity.pdf [accessed January 2015].

Davoudi, S. and Brooks E. (2014) 'When does unequal become unfair? Judging environmental justice claims', *Environment and Planning A,* 46(11): 2686-702.

De Vries, S., Verheij, R.A. and Groenewegen, P.P. (2003) 'Natural environments – healthy environments? An exploratory analysis of the relationship between greenspace and health', *Environment and Planning A,* 35: 1717-31.

Duffy, B. (2000) 'Satisfaction and expectations: attitudes to public services in deprived areas', *CASE paper 45*, London: Centre for Analysis of Social Exclusion.

EEA (2010) *The European environment. state and outlook, 2010: urban environment.* [online] Available at: http://www.eea.europa.eu/soer/ europe/urban-environment [accessed January 2016].

Fordham, G., Gore, T., Knight-Fordham, R. and Lawless, P. (2002) *The Groundwork Movement: its role in neighbourhood renewal.* York: Joseph Rowntree Foundation/York Publishing Services.

Forum for the Future (2010) *Sustainable cities index.* [online] Available at: http://www.forumforthefuture.org/project/sustainable-cities- index/overview [accessed January 2016].

Fraser, N. (1996) *Social justice in the age of identity politics: redistribution, recognition, and participation*, Stanford, CA: Stanford University.

Fraser, N. (2003) 'Social justice in the age of identity politics: redistribution, recognition, and participation', in N. Fraser and A. Honneth (eds) *Redistribution or recognition? A political–philosophical exchange*, New York, NY: Verso, pp 7-109.

Freer-Smith, P.H., Holloway, S. and Goodman, A. (1997) 'The uptake of particulates by an urban woodland: site description and particulate composition', *Environmental Pollution*, 95(1), 27–35.

Helsper, E. (2012) 'A corresponding fields model for the links between social and digital exclusion', *Communication Theory*, 22: 403–26.

Heynen, N. (2006) 'Green urban political ecologies: toward a better understanding of inner-city environmental change', *Environment and Planning A*, 38: 499–516.

Heynen, N., Perkins, H.A., Roy, P. (2006) 'The political ecology of uneven urban greenspace: the impact of political economy on race and ethnicity in producing environmental inequality in Milwaukee', *Urban Affairs Review*, 42: 3–25.

James N (2004) *Making the links: greenspace and quality of life.* Scottish Natural Heritage Commissioned Report 60. [online] Available at: http://www.snh.gov.uk/publications-data-and-research/publications/search-the-catalogue/publication-detail/?id=480 [accessed January 2016].

Lachowycz, K., Jones, A., Page, A., Wheeler, B. and Cooper, A. (2012) 'What can global positioning systems tell us about the contribution of different types of urban greenspace to children's physical activity?', *Health and Place*, 19: 586–94.

Lasdun, S. (1992) *The English park: Royal, private and public*, New York, NY: The Vendrome Press.

Lucas, K., Walker, G., Eames, M., Hay, F. and Poustie, M. (2004) *Environment and social justice review: Rapid research and evidence review*, revised version, December 2004, London: Policy Studies Institute.

Maas, J., Verheij, R.A., Spreeuwenberg, P. and Groenewegen, P.P. (2008) 'Physical activity as a possible mechanism between greenspace and health: a multi-level analysis', *BMC Public Health*, 8: 206.

Maller, C., Townsend, M., Brown, P. and St Leger, L. (2002) *Healthy parks, healthy people: the health benefits of contact with nature in a park context: a review of current literature.* Melbourne, Australia: Faculty of Health and Behavioural Sciences, Melbourne University.

Mani, A., Mullainathan, S., Shafir, E. and Zhao, J. (2013) 'Poverty impedes cognitive function', *Science*, 341 (6149): 976–80.

Manning, W.A. and Feder, W.J. (1980) *Pollution monitoring series: bio-monitoring air pollution with plants.* London: Applied Science Publishers.

Marmot, M. (2010) *The Marmot Review: fair society, healthy lives.* London: UCL.

McPherson, E.G. (1994) 'Using urban forests for energy efficiency and carbon storage', *Journal of Forestry*, 92(10): 36–41.

Mitchell, R. and Popham, F. (2008) 'Effect of exposure to natural environment on health inequalities: an observational population study', *The Lancet*, 372 (9650), 1655- 60.

Natural England (2010) *Nature nearby: accessible natural greenspace guidance.* [online] Available at: http://publications.naturalengland. org.uk/publication/40004?category=47004 [Accessed January 2016].

Newcastle City Council (2004) *Greenspaces, your spaces: Newcastle's greenspace strategy*, Newcastle: Newcastle City Council.

Newcastle City Council (2011a) *Background evidence paper for housing delivery plan 2011/12.* [online] Available at: http://www.newcastle. gov.uk/housing/housing-strategy [Accessed January 2016].

Newcastle City Council (2011b) *Improving Newcastle's neighbourhoods: Working together to deliver decent neighbourhood standards across the city*, Newcastle: Newcastle City Council.

Newcastle City Council (2011c) *A fair budget for a fairer city. Let's talk Newcastle. Helping us understand people's priorities for their city and their council*, December 2011. [pdf] Available at: http://www.newcastle. gov.uk/sites/drupalncc.newcastle.gov.uk/files/wwwfileroot/your-council/budget_and_annual_report/lets_talk_newcastle_-_full_ report_-_dec_11.pdf [accessed January 2016].

Newcastle City Council (2012) *Green capital bid to the European Commission.* [online] Available at: http://www.thebiggreenpledge. org.uk/european-green-capital [accessed January 2016].

Newcastle/Gateshead (2011) *One core strategy 2030: Draft*, September 2011, Newcastle: Newcastle City Council.

Newcastle/Gateshead and ENTEC (2011) *Green infrastructure study: Evidence base.* [online] Available at: http://www.gateshead.gov. uk/Building%20and%20Development/PlanningpolicyandLDF/ LocalPlan/EvidenceLibrary/Planning-for-the-Future-Primary-Evidence/GreenInfrastructureStudy.aspx [accessed January 2016].

Nussbaum, M. (2011) *Creating capabilities: The human development approach*, Cambridge, MA: Bellknap Press.

ODPM (2002) *Living places: Cleaner, safer, greener*, London: ODPM.

ONS (2013) *Statistical bulletin: Internet access quarterly update, Q2, 2013*, Office for National Statistics. [pdf] Available at: http://www.ons.gov. uk/ons/dcp171778_323333.pdf [accessed January 2016].

Ottosson, J. and Grahn, P. (2005) 'A comparison of leisure time spent in a garden with leisure time spent indoors: on measures of restoration in residents in geriatric care', *Landscape Research*, 30 (1): 23-55.

Our Ground (2014) *Liverpool's local plan.* [online] Available at: http:// www.ourground.net/ [accessed January 2016].

Pierik, R. and Robeyns, I. (2007) 'Resources versus capabilities: social endowments in egalitarian theory', *Political Studies*, 55(1): 133-152.

Rawls, J. (1971) *A theory of justice*, Cambridge, MA: Harvard University Press.

Rawls, J. (1999) *The law of peoples,* Cambridge, MA: Harvard University Press.

Roman, C. and Chalfin, A. (2008) 'Fear of walking outdoors: a multilevel environmental analysis', *American Journal of Preventative Medicine*, 34(4): 306-12.

Sadler, J.P., Bates, A.J. and Hale, J. (2010) 'Bringing cities alive: the importance of urban greenspaces for people and biodiversity', in K.I. Gaston (ed) *Urban Ecology*, Cambridge: Cambridge University Press, pp 230-60.

Scottish Natural Heritage (2014) *Urban green infrastructure benefits factsheets*, June 2014. [pdf] Available at: http://www.snh.gov.uk/docs/A1328615.pdf [accessed January 2016].

Sen, A. (2009) *The idea of justice*, Harmandsworth, Middx: Penguin.

Simpson, E. (1980) 'The subject of justice', *Ethics* 90: 490-501.

Takano, T., Nakamura, K. and Watanabe, M. (2002) 'Urban residential environments and senior citizens' longevity in megacity areas: the importance of walkable greenspaces', *Journal of Epidemiology and Community Health*, 56: 913-18.

Taylor, D. (2000) 'The rise of the environmental justice paradigm: injustice framing and the social construction of environmental discourses', *American Behavioral Scientist*, 43(4): 508-80.

Taylor, A.F., and Kuo, F.E. (2009) 'Children with attention deficits concentrate better after walk in the park', *Journal of Attention Disorders*, 12(5): 402-9.

Taylor, A.F., Kuo, F.E., and Sullivan, W.C. (2002) 'Views of nature and self-discipline: evidence from inner city children', *Journal of Environmental Psychology*, 22, 49-63.

UCL Institute of Health Evidence (2014) *Local action on health inequalities: Improving access to greenspaces*, London: Public Health England.

Urban Green Spaces Taskforce (2002a) *Open spaces, better places*, London: DTLR.

Urban Green Spaces Taskforce (2002b) *Green spaces, better Places*, London: DTLR.

UK National Ecosystem Assessment (2011) *The UK national ecosystem assessment: technical report*, Cambridge: UNEP-WCMC.

Van den Berg, A.E., Koole, S.L., and Van der Wulp, N.Y. (2003) 'Environmental preference and restoration: (how) are they related?', *Journal of Environmental Psychology*, 23(2): 135-46.

White, M., Alcock, I., Wheeler, B. and Depledge, M. (2013) 'Would you be happier living in a greener urban area? A fixed effects analysis of panel data', *Psychological Science*, 24(6): 920-8.

Williams, K. and Green, S. (2001) 'Literature review of public space and local environments for the cross-cutting review', Oxford: Oxford Brookes University/DTLR.

Young, I. (1990) *Justice and the politics of difference,* Princeton, NJ: Princeton University Press.

THREE

The school in the city

Pamela Woolner

Introduction

Are city schools primarily a site for social injustice compounded by environmental ills, where the best we can do is ameliorate the problems in an attempt to close the gap between the achievement of rich and poor? Or could the school in the city spearhead community-based justice?

This chapter opens by considering the potential problems faced by the school in the city, particularly where schools are located in economically disadvantaged urban areas and serving poorer communities. Initially the focus is on the difficulties of the physical school environment, investigating the impact these issues can be expected to have on learning, teaching and, ultimately, on student outcomes. Although limiting the negative impact of these problems, most obviously by distributing these ills of city living more equitably, would seem a reasonable aim, the chapter then explores how we might move beyond this conception of the city school as a problem. The author presents and discusses the potential for the school in the city to be part of the solution to environmental, and perhaps social, injustice: efforts rooted in improving the school space begin to create a centre for sustainable living and an environmental resource for the wider community. As will be demonstrated, it is notable how this broadened understanding of the role of the school in the city parallels reconceptions of environmental justice that go beyond simple distributive justice to consider the importance of participation and recognition (for example Schlosberg, 2004; Davoudi and Brooks, 2012).

Challenges and consequences

There are many aspects of the physical school space that may make it awkward or unsuitable for educational use, which include teaching and learning but also social activities. A coherent body of mainly correlational evidence attests to a relationship between the quality of the school environment and student outcomes, where those in poorer environments tend to have poorer attitudes and behaviour as well as lower attainment (Durán-Narucki, 2008; Kumar et al, 2008). The diversity of the school community, range of outcomes that might be desired and the complexity of the relationships between setting, use and actors, however, tends to scupper any attempt at simple prescriptions or reliable causal relationships (Woolner et al, 2007; Uline et al, 2009). Yet it is possible to discern elements of school space where evidence has accumulated of direct and indirect effects, generally negative, on student learning and educational achievement. In what follows, the evidence related to the environmental aspects of noise, poor air quality and restricted space will be considered in order to develop an understanding of how they might impact within a city school. It is important to note that all three challenges to be discussed are likely to be inequitably distributed, with schools in poorer urban areas more likely to be troubled by them. Furthermore, the educational system and the school itself may be accelerating, amplifying or exaggerating economic and environmental disadvantage. This relates to the tendency of schooling to produce and reproduce injustice (see Chapter 12 in this volume), but also to the physical location of the school in an environmentally disadvantaged neighbourhood where the same environmental ills will be experienced at home and at school. The familiar tendency for environmental and economic disadvantage to compound each other, referred to by writers on social and environmental justice (for example Davoudi and Brooks, 2012), may thus be particularly amplified so that the school in the city fatally embeds injustice within a community.

Air quality

Poor air quality is likely to impact indirectly on educational outcomes through causing health problems that reduce attendance and so opportunity to learn (Rosen and Richardson, 1999), but there is also some evidence of contaminated or stale air having a direct impact on learning. Pollutants and contaminants in external air entering the school, which were previously common in the UK (for example lead), have in recent years been much reduced, of course, but there is still air of poor quality in urban areas and this tends to be inequitably distributed, affecting the poor more than the wealthy. The situation within Newcastle is explored by Davoudi and Brooks (forthcoming) and this is indeed the pattern. Children living in these unfairly affected areas of the city and attending their neighbourhood school will be breathing this same poor air at home and at school with possible consequences for their health. In addition, details of the school environment may heighten problems due to polluted air and, particularly, stale air. Specifically, researchers have warned that 'fleecy' furnishings or open storage may increase dust, which contains irritants and allergens (Smedje and Norback, 2001). This problem will be worsened if ventilation is inadequate and worryingly many studies have shown that classroom spaces tend to have low levels of ventilation, producing unacceptably high levels of carbon dioxide as well as of any contaminants. Recent research suggests that such high levels of carbon dioxide may have direct effects on learning through reducing students' attention and accuracy (Bakó-Biró et al, 2012). Although it is unclear how ventilation levels are distributed across schools, it seems probable that within city schools concerns about external air pollution or road noise are more likely to limit window opening, reducing ventilation rates.

Noise

A number of studies of environmental noise, due to proximity to airports, railway lines and major roads, have demonstrated that living with chronic noise appears to cause stress and ill health (Stansfeld and Matheson, 2003) as well as having a negative effect on learning (Haines et al, 2001). These noise problems are often present in urban areas but will be unevenly distributed across the city with poorer areas often found near noise sources, particularly busy roads. Research has indeed shown that Newcastle conforms to this pattern of inequitable proximity to major roads (Davoudi and Brooks, forthcoming). In addition to the studies of problems associated with living in noisy places, there is a body of research evidence linking noise in schools to specific learning problems. An early US study in an urban school found lower reading levels for children taught in classrooms on the noisy side of the building next to an elevated section of light urban railway (Bronzaft and McCarthy, 1975). Consistent evidence of detrimental effects on speech, language and reading (Evans and Maxwell, 1997) is backed up by controlled laboratory experiments that show noise adversely affecting elements of learning such as memory (for example, Salame and Wittersheim, 1978). As has been noted by researchers in this area, problems of external noise near the neighbourhood school will often be replicated in the nearby housing, so reinforcing the unfair distribution and, potentially, the negative impact on wellbeing and intellectual development (Shield and Dockrell, 2003: 102).

It must be noted, however, that more recent research measuring noise levels in UK schools (for example Shield and Dockrell, 2004) suggests that problematic noise levels tend to result from internal noise, either within the specific classroom or from adjoining school spaces. As the author has discussed elsewhere, requirements for reduction of internal noise in schools need to be treated with some caution, given that some noise may be productive and educationally important (Woolner and Hall, 2010). It is also worth remembering the consequences of poor air quality discussed earlier if schools are tempted to install carpets and softer furnishings to reduce noise or reverberation. Designing closed learning spaces and keeping internal doors shut to limit noise leakage may also have negative implications for ventilation, which staff in city schools may be reluctant to ameliorate by opening external windows, as discussed previously.

It is notable that these intrinsically linked problems of poor air quality and noise are frequently due, in a city setting, to transportation with inequities underpinned by the tendency of poorer people to be 'both "less travelled" and "travelled upon"' (SDC, 2011b: 5; 47; see also Chapter 4). This link to transport will be revisited later in connection with the school's potential to contribute positively to environmental sustainability in the locality.

It is also important to observe that alongside the direct detrimental effects on learning and health shown by research, the noise and air quality problems of our city school are likely to feed into more complex networks of effects. Less positive attitudes from students, reduced satisfaction of staff and a sense of constraints on teaching and learning practices feed into the complex processes through which physical problems drive and so compound usage, choices of activity and social relationships in school. Possible tangible results include problems like low staff retention rates or reduced student numbers. Within the current UK climate of heavy inspections and demands for particular academic outcomes, problems can accumulate and result in a 'less effective' school that may slide into a spiral of decline.

Limited space

Turning to the third challenge of the city school, it is worth noting that the evidence base for this aspect of the school environment is not as conclusive as for the challenges of air quality and noise. However, as we shall see, this may be an effect of circumstance and the history of research interests rather than a reflection of the evidence potentially available.

During the 1970s, evaluations of school design referred to the necessity of adequate space, and research found that overcrowding was often a problem (Bennett et al, 1980). A National Union of Teacher's (NUT) report into open plan schools, published when school numbers were particularly high, made this point about space quite forcefully. A teacher responding to their survey stated, 'There can be no movement or activity on any scale where there is no room to move' (NUT (England), 1974: 29). In addition to these direct problems with lack of space, a more crowded classroom or school is also likely to be noisier and more difficult to ventilate, problems, which, as described previously, can in themselves interfere with learning.

A small, but carefully conducted, piece of research in the 1980s attempted to compare the attitudes of learners in two spacious primary classrooms with those in two cramped classrooms, where the space per pupil was considerably less (Clift et al, 1984). Statistically significant differences were found between students in the cramped and spacious classrooms for questionnaire responses relating to relationships and attitudes within the classroom and class group, which we might expect to affect their learning. However, despite the need for further investigation, decreasing school populations during the 1980s and 90s meant that this issue seemed a less pressing concern and the possible impact of restricted learning space has received little attention.

In contrast, in both the UK and the US, there has been substantial research into the impact on learning of the closely related issue of class size, in terms of the number of students. In fact, research in this area generally conflates the two issues since classes reduced in size may be taught in existing classrooms and so experience both reduced class size and reduced classroom density. Yet when this issue is examined directly, it does seem to be important. A piece of US research specifically investigated the relationships of a number of variables with both area per child in the classroom and class size (Maxwell, 2003). This study did not find significant effects of class or school size on the outcome measures of learning but instead discovered statistically significant associations with classroom spatial density.

Although the relationship between restricted school space and the economic status of its neighbourhood is not straightforward, it is clear that many city schools are located on relatively small urban sites and do struggle with limited space (see Figure 3.1).

Due to the interactions with noise and air quality, limited space could particularly compound disadvantages accumulating in poor areas of the city. Also, as with the other environmental issues considered here, there is the likelihood that any problems with the school space

Figure 3.1 Restricted space inside and out, with mainly hard outdoor space, may constrain education

Source: the author

will parallel problems with local housing. Thus, children attending city schools with very limited space may too often be going home to overcrowded city housing, and there is some, mainly US, research evidence that shows that overcrowding in the home separately impacts on learning (Maxwell, 2003: 569). As in the home, the restrictions on space in the city school will tend to occur as both limited internal and external area. Previous eras of school design commonly found in city areas did not include particularly generous classrooms, but a tight urban site may also severely restrict the space available for outdoor activities, ranging from socialising, through sport and physical education, to opportunities for outdoor learning. This seems important, given the focus here on environmental justice (see also Chapter 2 for discussion of access to greenspace), and is an issue that will be returned to as part of a consideration of how even limited and awkward outdoor space might be developed to facilitate gardening, nature study and some less obvious learning opportunities.

The city school as part of the solution not part of the problem

So far this chapter has explored the elements that are likely to make the city school less conducive to learning as well as suggesting how these aspects, inequitably distributed as they are, are likely to interact with each other and with other features of social and environmental injustice. The logic is that the school in the city is potentially a problem for city inhabitants, and clearly steps could be taken to minimise these negative impacts through paying attention to deficiencies in the physical school setting. Such an understanding is clearly founded on a liberal account of environmental justice concerned with the distribution of environmental burdens and their impact on educational attainment. This leaves untouched, however, the bigger social injustices of which education is a part. It also, the author would suggest, underestimates the potential power of the school in the city to be part of the solution to the challenges of urban living, as opposed to merely less of a problem for city children. As the remainder of this chapter will demonstrate, through references to research, existing initiatives and government guidance relating to education, the city school has the potential to be a vital environmental resource for the whole community.

This framing of the school as part of the solution, not just a problem, comes mainly from understandings developed within education (for example, Facer, 2011; Clarke, 2012; Sutherland et al, 2014). However, as will be returned to, this distinction can be further illuminated by understandings of justice that foreground recognition and participation as opposed to those that see justice as more purely and narrowly distributive. The author's argument is that the 'part of the solution' actions involve, and may even necessitate, these aspects of environmental justice that are beyond distribution. Specifically, the author will explore how these proposed solutions relate to three of the six alternative conceptions of justice proposed in the introduction to this volume. As will become clear, some of these initiatives suggest the *environmentalist* perspective: changes made to environment and behaviour to benefit pupils now and in the future, centred therefore on concern for justice to future generations. Yet the more radical side of these activities appear to be founded on *democratic proceduralism* together with the recognition of *multiculturalism*, which in combination might aspire to become the 'thorough recognition and mutual engagement' desired by Schlosberg (2004: 536).

To explore these ideas, the author will consider some examples in practice. As Schlosberg (2004: 520) argues in the context of global environmental and economic justice, it is necessary to investigate practices because, in the social world, these constitute central parts of the abstract ideas we are hoping to define. In an educational context, practice is key to the experience of education: what actually happens as opposed to what is supposed or intended to occur.

Guidance, suggestions and examples for schools

The Sustainable Development Commission (SDC), established by the Labour government of 1997–2010, was clear that education needed to be a key part of the approach to improving the UK's environmental sustainability. As shown by their publication, *Governing for the future* (SDC, 2011a), which outlined their strategy, they saw this as involving influence on policy but also looking for outcomes in practice. SDC advisors worked within the Department for Education to develop the National Framework for Sustainable Schools, which was intended to 'reframe sustainable development as a positive opportunity for children and young people' but also to convey a 'simple message that was understandable by teachers and built on what they were already doing' (SDC, 2011a: 28). The importance of activities and action within schools themselves is conveyed by the identification of 'the school as an engine of social change' (SDC, 2011a: 29).

The SDC publication goes on to note some of the practical action occurring in schools linked primarily to education for environmental sustainability, but which are relevant to any conception of the city school as an environmental and social good. These include the production of travel plans and obtaining recognition for being 'healthy schools' or 'eco-schools'. Similar ideas, but with more detail of 'how to' and examples of good practice are to be found in the Ofsted publication *Taking the first step forward … towards an education for sustainable development* (2003).

The recurring themes are of the physical school premises being used as a starting point or exemplar, which can then be extended through the collaborative effort of the student body to influence the local neighbourhood and community (Clarke, 2012). So, for instance, the Ofsted publication provides examples of school action to 'successfully enhance their quality of life by improving the school environment' (Ofsted, 2003: 17). One urban school initiated a community action day to clean up an adjoining space to become 'a secluded nature reserve within this area of dense housing' (Ofsted, 2003: 17), while in another school profits from selling vegetables grown within the school grounds go to a local charity working with homeless people. Although these initiatives seem squarely located in an environmentalist conception of justice, there is sometimes an underlying suggestion of enhancing participation and recognition, as in the link to homeless people in the last example. Even where such sentiment is not immediately obvious, as in the transport related initiatives that often link explicitly to improving health, it is possible to see a potential for more critical ideas about justice. This could come though emphasising that walking and cycling produce environmental and health benefits, but are also 'affordable, accessible and inclusive forms of travel' (SDC, 2011b: 42).

Open Futures in urban schools

The next set of practical examples of city schools effecting change is taken from an initiative that is not explicitly one of education for sustainable development, and is not therefore linked to environmentalist conceptions of justice. In fact, the programme in question appears to accept the liberal justice premise of trying to provide environmental benefits to balance environmental burdens within city schools. However, as will be shown, within the schools involved, changes occurred that may be understood as enhancing local recognition and participation in important ways.

The schools are part of Open Futures (http://www.openfutures. info), an initiative that was evaluated as it developed over the period from 2006–13 by the Research Centre for Learning and Teaching at Newcastle University (CfLaT). Open Futures is a skills and enquiry based learning programme for primary schools, which intends to facilitate change in pedagogy and curriculum. There are four integrated strands: growit; cookit; filmit; and askit (Philosophy for Children: P4C), and it is the growit gardening strand that spearheads the development of school growing and the use of the outside space. However, an important aspect of the Open Futures approach, and one that we have linked to its particular success, is the way that the developments of curriculum and organisation, school space and culture are mutually interdependent (Woolner and Tiplady, 2014).

The most recent expansion of the programme was into a number of schools located in economically disadvantaged urban areas in Manchester, Hull, Birmingham and East London. As in previous waves, the schools got involved for various reasons, with differences across the schools over which of the strands they found most appealing or closest to previous initiatives in their schools. The programme has clear requirements for initial action, however, including appointing staff as strand leaders, releasing staff for training and adapting space for growing and cooking activities. Schools are helped by expert partners for each strand and, in the case of growit, the advice of the Royal Horticulture Society (RHS) experts has been particularly useful in establishing growing areas. Even where school outside space is very limited or, as is often the case in city schools, virtually all hard surfaces, the RHS has helped schools find solutions through container gardening, raised beds built on playgrounds and suggesting appropriate plants for small or awkward spaces. A noticeable side effect of the resulting 'unlikely gardens' is that they are often located in very visible spots, which ensure they are particularly accessible for all pupils and obvious to parents and the wider community (see Figure 3.2). This last point is important because the majority of the recently recruited schools hoped that the programme would help them in enhancing relationships with parents and developing community links.

As Open Futures develops in a school, the initial changes both embed changed practices but also enable further development. This is seen both in terms of tangible change such as use of the space and time given, but also in less tangible alteration to cultures of learning and social relationships. Staff and students explain how working collaboratively in a non-academic setting produces different, more equal relationships between children and with staff. This seems to combine very productively with the skills for critical thinking and listening that are explicitly developed through the askit (P4C) strand to enable change to teaching and learning practices, so more independent and enquiry learning is possible. Such approaches are in marked contrast to the 'minimal competency' learning and narrowed curriculum that high stakes testing systematically produces in schools serving poor and minority communities (Berliner, 2011).

Open Futures is a complex programme where concurrent developments in organisational structures, teacher and learner roles and the resulting culture of education all work together to embed

Figure 3.2 An 'unlikely' school garden that is very visible to school users and the community

Source: the author

Open Futures in the life of the school. The particular role of the physical school setting in this process is worth specific consideration, however. At the most basic level, having made room for gardening or cooking or any other practical activity, a school will tend to try to use that space. As one head teacher from an earlier wave of Open Futures explained, "If you've got that infrastructure, you can use it and you want to use it, don't you?" The influence of the physical school setting is more powerful than this suggests, however, if harnessed appropriately. Sometimes this draws on how finding space for an initiative conveys value and confers a certain position, which will be understood within the school but also in the wider community beyond. In one of the Hull schools, the allocation of a particular space to the filmit strand demonstrated the value the head teacher placed on these skills and learning activities. Furthermore, having a particular environment available makes more likely not just the obvious activities it was designed to accommodate but also supports inventiveness and innovation. In one of the London schools within the fairly small, but very visible, garden there are plant labels in French (see Figure 3.3), placed by the language coordinator who was not otherwise involved in school gardening.

Figure 3.3 Using the garden to support French language learning

Source: the author

It seems clear that an initiative on the scale of Open Futures can positively alter the cultures of learning and living within and, sometimes, beyond the school, potentially redressing injustices in a way that develops beyond redistribution. Although it might not be realistic to suggest implementing it in every urban school, and many schools would indeed not appreciate such a directive, the experience of the programme does concur with the proposal that the school in the city can be a force for positive change and perhaps suggest some ways to make this happen.

Emerging practice in North East schools

The final set of examples is more disparate, but possibly reflects more realistically what is possible and likely across the diverse range of Newcastle schools. Within our region, there are examples of schools with outdoor learning spaces, school areas for growing and gardening and, sometimes linked to this, schools which use their premises as exemplars of aspects of environmental sustainability.

When Creative Partnerships (CP) was active in school-based projects, a significant number of these focused on developing the outside space for learning. This can be seen as a sensible response to restricted indoor teaching and learning space, as well as having benefits in itself. An example taken from a number of local projects evaluated by CfLaT is that of Farne Primary. This school is located within Newcastle in a part of the city that is not a classic inner city environment but is economically disadvantaged and suffers from many of the environmental problems of city living. In educational terms, this is suggested by the rate of free school meals at the school, which is consistently around twice the national average.

Over three years, CP practitioners worked with staff, pupils and parents at the school on various initiatives focused on enhancing mathematics learning. A central component of this was the development, in collaboration with the pupils, of the outside space. Maths trails have been developed for each key stage and outdoor learning has become an integral part of the maths curriculum. This has changed pupil perceptions of the outside space from 'somewhere to play' to 'somewhere to learn' but their comments also reflect their enjoyment of being outside, enjoying the space and fresh air. Teaching practices and relationships also seem to have been changed through involvement in a collaborative project, engaging with the ideas of the CP practitioners and making use of the resulting changes to the physical environment. The head teacher suspects that a recent improvement in numeracy skills in the early years pupils may be a direct result of using the outdoor space to bring mathematical skills to life for the children. Overall, the school considers that the project, 'has added to and enriched the experiences of staff and children in school and has inspired us to reach out to our community'. It would appear that a project initially conceived in terms of distributive justice, redistributing access to useful learning space, and so maths achievement, but enacted in a somewhat participatory manner, did begin to address recognition towards the members of the local community.

In contrast to this example of a school making progressive changes to its existing environment, the next examples are of two schools that were completely rebuilt under the Labour government's spending programmes for school buildings (Building Schools for the Future, BSF; the Primary Capital Programme). One is a secondary school and one a primary, but in both there was a common intention among senior staff to spearhead a change of culture and teaching approaches. Although such expensive rebuilding is currently off the agenda, the experiences of these schools are worth considering for what they tell us about understandings of social and environmental justice applied to the built environment of the city school.

Jesmond Gardens Primary School serves an economically disadvantaged community in Hartlepool, a large town, which may be characterised as 'post-industrial'. The school was formerly Jesmond Road Primary School and housed in a two-storey brick 'board school' opened in 1902, but in September 2010 opened on a neighbouring site in completely new premises. The head teacher explained that they couldn't continue in the existing building and that the new build was essential to underpinning the changes they wanted to make. She summed these up as being about 'valuing children', and the school is built to high design and environmental standards. It is a consciously modern building and set within a varied landscape of playground and gardens, making it quite distinct from the closely packed rows of houses nearby as well as offering some protection from urban environmental hazards such as noise and air pollution. Within school, there has certainly been cultural change and the building offers the pupils a sense of an alternative, but it remains to be seen how successful the school can be in providing a resource to the wider community.

The outcomes for the secondary school that attempted a similarly dramatic shift in learning culture, underpinned by a building designed to facilitate a more active approach to learning, were less positive. With colleagues, the author has written elsewhere about the work done with students and staff to discover their existing ideas about learning and teaching, and to suggest how they might be adapted within the new context (Woolner et al, 2012; Woolner et al, 2014). The most recent of these publications explores how the enthusiasm for change of many staff struggled against the preference of some staff and students for less dramatic change, but was ultimately defeated by pressures from beyond the school. Following the suggestion of researchers in the UK and US contexts (Hargreaves, 2002; Thomson et al, 2009), the paper links this outcome to the lack of autonomy allowed to schools in less affluent areas under a regime of standardised testing and narrow expectations (Woolner et al, 2014). This is an important aspect for urban schools, and clearly relates to the wider injustices of the existing education system explored in Chapter 12 in this volume. However, as a demonstration that schools might need to be cautious, but not despairing, the current section finishes with two examples of city schools using their premises as exemplars of sustainable living.

The first was also a new build secondary school under the BSF programme. Washington School is located within the new town that overlaid a number of ex-mining villages in County Durham and was formerly housed in a collection of buildings, some dating from the 1920s, but mostly of light-build 1960s construction. For the new premises, there were various innovations relating to teaching, community facilities and the social side of school. A further intention was to follow certain principles of sustainable design and, specifically, to showcase visible aspects, such as an extensive 'green' living roof. This was pursued through the lengthy planning and consultation phases, and successfully achieved as an integral part of the new building. In some contrast to this very demonstrative approach to utilising the premises to educate about sustainability, the staff of a central Sunderland primary school have made adaptations and additions to unexceptional premises built in the 1980s. The school is located in a city location of dense housing and serves a community where people tend to be either white working class or have Bangladeshi family connections. Their houses often have yards not gardens, and they are not generally in a position to install environmental devices or generate sustainable energy. The school, on the other hand, has been able to invest in microgeneration, with meters that the children can read, and has developed its grounds in various ways. This includes space for allotment gardening but also improvements to the playground space, such as simple shelters, used by parents when collecting their children (see Figure 3.4). These enhance community cohesion but also ensure that walking, as a means of transport is a pleasant experience. In both of these schools, attempts to ameliorate the problems of the school setting that include the addition of sustainability features suggest an environmentalist conception of justice, perhaps developing into enhanced recognition of people within their communities.

Figure 3.4 Infrastructure for walking, an 'affordable, accessible and inclusive form of travel'

Source: the author

Conclusions: minimising the ills of the school in the city and making it a force for good

This chapter has considered the environmental burdens of the typical city school and noted how these may well be compounded or amplified by wider environmental injustice as well as by the social injustices found within education. However, the author has then investigated how the school in the city might instead be a force for good. The initiatives discussed vary considerably in scale and ambition, but all centre on desires to improve the immediate physical environment of the school. These environmental improvements variously aimed to provide students with more access to natural settings, use the outdoors for learning or to counteract local or global environmental problems. In passing, it should be noted that sometimes improvements aimed at learning have environmental benefits and vice versa: gardens developed as a learning resource may protect the school from noise and air pollution, while meters recording sustainable energy generation can be a useful teaching aid.

As has been argued, reaping the full benefits of such changes for school, students and the wider community means going beyond ameliorating the environmental negatives or distributing environmental goods more fairly using the physical school as a base. Each example considered demonstrates just one possible way of approaching the development of city school premises, but the mix of approaches suggests the myriad ways such initiatives might develop. The wider issue is how these developments might be understood in terms of conceptualisations of justice that reach beyond liberal notions of distribution. It is striking that the initiatives considered tend to have an educationally participatory aspect (for example, the involvement of students and teachers in planning at Farne Primary or Open Futures' appeal across teachers, other staff and students) and the discussion developed additionally suggests that an understanding of justice based on recognition and participation may be needed to see how the school in the city can contribute to increasing fairness.

Essentially, the argument hinges on the idea that developing city schools in this way, using them to improve the distribution of environmental goods and ills, could have effects beyond the school, but this depends on emphasising the recognition and participation sides of justice. As has been noted, the SDC appealed to the power of schools in accelerating sustainable development, and it seems possible that the important position of the school enables it to go further: the school could help to change, rather than embed, patterns of distribution of environmental, economic and social disadvantage. Yet this depends on participation. Within education, ideas about 'student voice' (Fielding, 2001; Flutter, 2006) and conceptualisations of change processes (Fullan, 2007; Priestley et al, 2011) suggest the necessity of genuinely participatory approaches, developing shared understandings and partnerships. This understanding parallels the proposal of justice scholars that participation and recognition are key aspects of a more complete understanding of justice. Could the democratic schools advocated by Fielding (2001) provide in microcosm the 'inclusive, participatory decision-making institutions' that Schlosberg puts 'at the centre of environmental justice demands' (2004: 522)? Should the city school aim to cultivate the 'full participants in social interaction ... full citizens' that Davoudi and Brooks (2012: 12) propose recipients of welfare must be to ensure just distribution?

These are weighty responsibilities, however, and a lot to expect of a Newcastle school in the current UK educational and social climate. Certainly, the later Ofsted publication on education for sustainability (Ofsted, 2008) suggests limited development nationally. The Ofsted survey found that understanding of sustainable development was fragmented, with few coordinated whole school approaches and that schools had travel plans but ignored them. Primary schools tend to be more successful than secondaries in reducing energy and water consumption (Ofsted, 2008: 18) and in using their grounds for learning about sustainability (Ofsted, 2008: 21). This tendency for primary schools to innovate is perhaps also suggested by the examples chosen for this chapter. Furthermore, the issue of 'earned autonomy' (Hargreaves, 2002: 206) being allowed only to more socially and economically fortunate schools seems particularly to restrict secondary schools, where league tables are arguably more pressing and potential spirals of decline more likely. Although this chapter has shown a coherence in understanding of the situation and of what is required, it is important not to underestimate the forces working against the schools in our city when we discuss the clear potential for them to address justice issues and increase fairness.

References

Bakó-Biró, Z., Clements-Croomea, D.J, Kochhara, N., Awbia, H.B. and Williams, M.J. (2012) 'Ventilation rates in schools and pupils' performance', *Building and Environment*, 48: 215-23.

Bennett, N., Andreae, J., Hegarty, P. and Wade, B. (1980) *Open plan schools*, Windsor: Schools Council Publishing/NFER.

Berliner, D. (2011) 'Rational responses to high stakes testing: the case of curriculum narrowing and the harm that follows', *Cambridge Journal of Education*, 41(3): 287-302.

Bronzaft, A.L. and McCarthy, D.P. (1975) 'The effect of elevated train noise on reading ability', *Environment and Behavior*, 7(4): 517-27.

Clarke, P. (2012) 'Sustainable cities, sustainable minds, sustainable schools: Pop-Up-Farm as a connecting device', *Improving Schools*, 15(1): 37- 44.

Clift, S., Hutchings, R. and Povey, R. (1984) 'School-related attitudes of 11-year-old pupils in spacious and space-restricted classrooms', *Educational Research*, 26(3): 208-12.

Davoudi, S. and Brooks, E. (2012) *Environmental justice and the city: full report*, Newcastle: GURU, Newcastle University.

Davoudi, S. and Brooks E. (forthcoming) When does unequal become unfair? Judging environmental justice claims, *Environment and Planning A*.

Durán-Narucki, V. (2008) 'School building condition, school attendance, and academic achievement in New York City public schools: a mediation model', *Journal of Environmental Psychology*, 28: 278-86.

Evans, G.W. and Maxwell, L. (1997) 'Chronic noise exposure and reading deficits. The mediating effects of language acquisition', *Environment and Behaviour*, 29(5): 638-56.

Facer, K. (2011) *Learning futures: education, technology and social change*, Abingdon: Routledge.

Fielding, M. (2001) 'Students as radical agents of change', *Journal of Educational Change*, 2: 123-41.

Flutter, J. (2006) '"This place could help you learn": student participation in creating better learning environments', *Educational Review*, 58(2): 183-93.

Fullan, M. (2007) *The New Meaning of Educational Change* (4th edn), New York/Abingdon: Routledge.

Haines, M.M., Stansfeld, S.A., Job, R.F.S., Berglund, B. and Head, J. (2001) 'Chronic aircraft noise exposure, stress responses, mental health and cognitive performance in school children', *Psychological Medicine*, 31: 265–77.

Hargreaves, A. (2002) 'Sustainability of educational change: the role of social geographies', *Journal of Educational Change*, 3: 189–214.

Kumar, R., O'Malley, P.M. and Johnston, L.D. (2008) 'Association between physical environment of secondary schools and student problem behaviour', *Environment and Behavior*, 40(4): 455-86.

Maxwell, L.E. (2003) 'Home and school density effects on elementary school children: the role of spatial density', *Environment and Behavior*, 35: 566–77.

NUT (England) (1974) *Open Planning: A report with special reference to primary schools*, London: NUT.

Ofsted (2003) *Taking the first step forward … towards an education for sustainable development*, London: HMI.

Ofsted (2008) *Schools and sustainability: A climate for change?*, London: HMI.

Priestley, M., Miller, K., Barrett, L. and Wallace, C. (2011) 'Teacher learning communities and educational change in Scotland: the Highland experience', *British Educational Research Journal*, 37(2): 265-84.

Rosen, K.G. and Richardson, G. (1999) 'Would removing indoor air particulates in children's environments reduce rate of absenteeism – a hypothesis', *The Science of the Total Environment*, 234: 87-93.

Salame, P. and Wittersheim, G. (1978) 'Selective noise disturbance of the information input in short term memory', *Quarterly Journal of Experimental Psychology*, 30: 693–704.

Schlosberg, D. (2004) 'Reconceiving environmental justice: global movements and political theories', *Environmental Politics*, 13(3): 517-40.

Smedje, G. and Norback, D. (2001) 'Irritants and allergens at school in relation to furnishings and cleaning', *Indoor Air*, 11: 127-33.

Shield, B and Dockrell, J. (2003) 'The effects of noise on children at school: a review', *Building Acoustics*', 10: 97-116.

Shield, B. and Dockrell, J. (2004) 'External and internal noise surveys of London primary schools', *Journal of the Acoustic Society of America*, 115: 730-38.

Stansfeld, S.A. and Matheson, M. (2003) 'Noise pollution: non-auditory effects on health', *British Medical Bulletin*, 68: 243–57.

Sustainable Development Commission (2011a) *Governing for the future*, London: SDC.

Sustainable Development Commission (2011a) *Fairness in a car-dependent society*, London: SDC.

Sutherland, R., Sutherland, J., Fellner, C., Siccolo, M. and Clark, L. (2014) 'Schools for the future: subtle shift or seismic change?', *Technology, Pedagogy and Education*, 23(1): 19-37.

Thomson, P., McGregor, J., Sanders, E. and Alexiadou, N. (2009). 'Changing schools: more than a lick of paint and a well-orchestrated performance?' *Improving Schools*, 12: 43-57.

Uline, C.L., Tschannen-Moran, M. and DeVere Wolsey, T. (2009) 'The walls still speak: the stories occupants tell', *Journal of Educational Administration*, 47: 400-26.

Woolner, P. Clark J., Laing K., Thomas U. and Tiplady L. (2014) 'A school tries to change: how leaders and teachers understand changes to space and practices in a UK secondary school', *Improving Schools*, 17(2): 148-62.

Woolner, P., Hall, E., Wall, K., Higgins, S. and McCaughey, C. (2007), 'A sound foundation? What we know about the impact of environments on learning and the implications for Building Schools for the Future', *Oxford Review of Education*, 33(1): 47-70.

Woolner, P. and Hall, E. (2010) 'Noise in schools: a holistic approach to the issue', *International Journal of Environmental Research and Public Health*, 7(8): 3255-69.

Woolner, P. and Tiplady, L. (2014) 'Adapting school premises as part of a complex pedagogical change programme', [online] ECER, 2–5 September, Porto, Portugal. Available at: http://www.ncl.ac.uk/cflat/news/Conferencepapers.htm [accessed January 2016].

FOUR

Transport poverty and urban mobility

Roberto Palacin, Geoff Vigar and Sean Peacock

Introduction

This chapter focuses on the concept of fairness in the city in the context of transport and mobility. Social exclusion in transport is double edged (SEU, 2003):

- Mobility and accessibility are unevenly given in society and this is, arguably, reinforced by policy and investment that favours certain modes and speed for the few over accessibility for all.
- The choices of the 'hyper-mobile' impact disproportionately on the less mobile, that is poorer sections of society are more likely to be subject to the harmful consequences (for example air pollution, road crash, noise and so on) associated with the disproportionate use of powered vehicles by 'kinetic elites' and others.

For reasons of space and data availability, we focus on the former of these two dimensions but are alive to the need to study the latter element. For both elements, there are surprisingly few studies that ground social exclusion and transport to specific places. In this context, we use secondary data to investigate transport poverty in Newcastle upon Tyne. This data reveals that the interrelated processes of social disadvantage, transport disadvantage and transport poverty are experienced by certain groups in the city, but evidence is thin. A key conclusion in this respect is the need for systematic research at and below the city scale into transport poverty, the scale of potential injustice and the effects of this on the wellbeing, cultural and economic life of the city and certain groups of residents in particular. Given the changing regulatory landscape for transport service delivery; the implications of government austerity post 2008, particularly in relation to local government finance; the considerable diminution of urban regeneration initiatives; and, the continuing closure of many local shops and services, this is an urgent research need.

This chapter addresses these concerns through first reviewing the literature on transport poverty and related concepts. It then focuses on two dimensions related to transport poverty, car ownership and bus services, and finishes with a conclusion. Illustrations from Newcastle, our 'ordinary city' are weaved into the discussion in the latter two parts.

Conceptualising mobility justice and transport poverty

This section explores how transport, mobility, immobility and social disadvantage interplay to cause transport poverty. It enables us to define the concept, consider the dimensions of transport poverty and fairness in an urban context, and investigate the relationship between transport poverty and other critical indicators of social inequality.

It is recognised that transport disadvantage – the lack of available, accessible or affordable transport – can act as a key barrier to accessing employment, education, training, healthcare and social networks and can cause and reinforce social exclusion (Kenyon et al, 2002; SEU, 2003). Lucas develops this in arguing that transport disadvantage and social disadvantage interact to create **transport poverty** (Lucas, 2012). While it is possible to be socially excluded but enjoy good access to transport, or be transport disadvantaged but be highly socially included (Currie and Delbosc, 2010), it is the interactions that cause transport poverty to occur – where 'inaccessibility to essential goods and services, as well as "lock-out" from planning and decision-making processes, can result in social exclusion outcomes' (Lucas, 2012: 106) and can create further social and transport inequalities.

The consequence of transport poverty is the inability to access key services, social networks, life chances and decision-making processes (Lucas, 2012), which ultimately has implications for social justice. The concept is associated with social and distributive justice, with access to transport linked to debates over the right to the city (Farmer, 2011; Attoh, 2012).

The interaction of transport disadvantage and social disadvantage as 'transport poverty' has been suggested both conceptually (see Figure 4.1) and demonstrated in a variety of national contexts (Gleeson and Randolph, 2002; Zou et al, 2008; Lucas, 2013; Martens, 2013; Velaga et al, 2013).

Transport poverty is recognised as a 'multidimensional concept' underpinned by various factors that cause or exacerbate such disadvantage, including location (distance from employment and

Figure 4.1 The relationship between transport disadvantage, social disadvantage and social exclusion

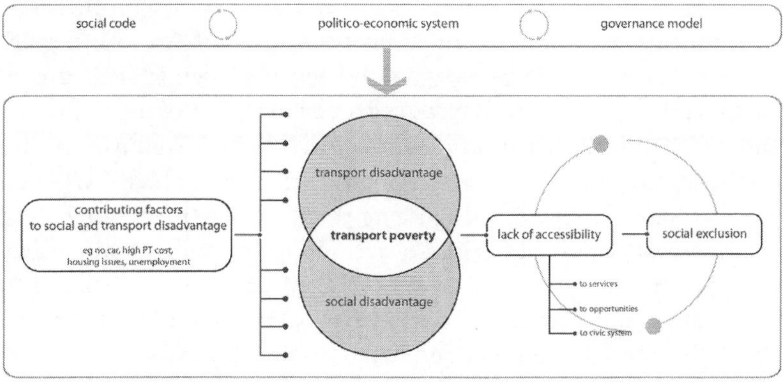

Source: Adapted from Lucas, 2012: 107.

essential services), mobility (ease of access) and membership of a particular societal grouping (for example, the young or non car owners) (Delbosc and Currie, 2011a: 171). Similarly, Betts cites three forms of disadvantage in relation to transport: locational, 'when there is very little or a complete absence of publicly funded transport choices, or its scheduling is not frequent enough to meet needs'; personal, 'when a person's mobility is affected by age (including youth), disability, frailty, poor health or language barriers'; and economic, 'when cost prohibits access to available transport' (Betts, 2007: 161). Pickup and Guiliano (2005) identify three factors in the causes of social exclusion where transport policy has a direct influence: poor access to services; feelings of hopelessness, where barriers such as ill health, lack of transport, low skills or few local jobs inhibit full participation in society; and polarised and fragmented communities, exacerbated by the concentration of socially disadvantaged groups and their 'entrapment' in remote suburban or rural areas. Betts conceptualises social disadvantage in terms of economic stress – 'where an unreasonable proportion of household income is absorbed by transport costs' (Betts, 2007: 161).

The literature has also tended to frame transport disadvantage in the context of social exclusion (for example Delbosc and Currie, 2011a; Stanley et al, 2011a; Lucas, 2012). Research consistently demonstrates that transport poverty restricts access to social and economic activities, lowering quality of life and exacerbating social exclusion (Delbosc and Currie, 2011b). While there is little agreement on a sole definition of social exclusion (Currie and Delbosc, 2010; Preston and Rajé, 2007), a lack of participation in activities considered normal in society

71

emerges as a consistent theme (for example, Stanley et al, 2011b). The proliferation of social exclusion is intrinsically linked with transport disadvantage, and problems of accessibility can both cause and result in social exclusion (Martens, 2013). Thus, academics and policy makers often refer to social exclusion as a holistic set of problems that should be tackled in unison (Levitas et al, 2007). A landmark in this consideration in the UK was the Social Exclusion Unit's (SEU) 2003 report *Making the connections*. This report did much to raise awareness of the issue and promoted the idea of accessibility planning in UK policy and planning as a way of mobilising local government in particular to think about and have better information to tackle transport poverty. Accessibility planning was underpinned by modelling work, which was then used to inform local transport plans. However, the translation of the results of this work into policy, finance and practice was variable at best, with little real change on all but a few exemplar areas (Lucas, 2012). Subsequently, the links between accessibility planning as an idea and local transport planning appear to have diminished further and the austerity of the period 2008–14 is likely to have exacerbated transport poverty. Specifically, the severe cuts to local government funding in the UK have had large impacts on bus services following subsidy withdrawal, while they have also, through staff cuts, undermined the inter-agency partnerships necessary to tackle transport poverty (Atkins, 2012).

Dimensions of transport poverty

This section looks at car ownership and public transport service issues as two key elements that can highlight the existence of transport poverty. It lays out the key themes from the literature incorporating secondary data from Newcastle. As Bell and Davoudi indicate in Chapter 1, Newcastle can be seen as an 'ordinary city'. It does, however, have a number of characteristics that set it apart from others. In common with many 'post-industrial' cities it displays relatively high levels of deprivation and widespread disparity in such levels. In Newcastle, 11 Lower Super Output Areas (LSOAs) in Gosforth, Jesmond, Kenton and High Heaton (north and east of the city centre), are counted amongst the 10% least deprived across England, while Cowgate (a housing estate some one and a half miles west of Kenton), is ranked the 87th most deprived LSOA of 32,844 in England. Another six LSOAs in Walker, Byker and Benwell are among the 1% most deprived in England; in total, 43 out of 173 Lower Super Output Areas (LSOAs) in Newcastle are counted among the 10% most deprived wards in

England. Weighted for population, Newcastle is the 67th (of 433) most deprived authority in the UK (DCLG, 2010). Newcastle also experiences a lower than average economic activity rate (68.4%, compared with 77.3% nationally) and a higher unemployment rate, 10.8%, compared with 7.8% nationally (ONS, 2013).

Experiences of social exclusion on Tyneside have been well documented, particularly as a result of a succession of urban regeneration initiatives. For example, an article in *The Guardian* newspaper investigating social exclusion on the Cowgate estate, suggested that the cost of transport and urban form play a role in perpetuating social exclusion – 'in Cowgate, parents keep their children off school because they do not have £2.40 for the bus fare' – and that the experience of social exclusion on the estate is compounded by the insular nature of the estate with 'only two ways in and two ways out' (Elliott, 2007).

Car ownership

Studies of transport disadvantage in relation to social exclusion have often focused on the impact of being unable to own or operate a car (Currie et al, 2010; Martens, 2013; Mattioli, 2013) as the ability to operate or own a car is regarded as a basic social and economic necessity in a hyper-mobile society like the UK (Lucas et al, 2009). Car ownership can increase opportunities to access employment, essential services and social networks and reduce social exclusion (Mattioli, 2013; Audrey and Langford, 2014). Low income households without a car exhibit more dimensions of social exclusion than low income households with a car, with individuals more likely to be unemployed, possess the lowest incomes and have access to less social support if they did not have a car (Currie and Delbosc, 2009). Nationally, 22% of households do not have a car, and this rises closer to 50% in urban areas. While being car free in London is considered by many to be a blessing, in other UK conurbations it may be problematic.

Many thus conclude that car ownership is 'the main transport factor in the social exclusion of low income households and other marginalised groups' (Lucas, 2003: 12). There is evidence that high entry costs to ownership, alongside the potential to communicate, offered by improving mobile technologies, are leading to lower interest in car ownership among younger people, although it remains unclear as to whether this effect is predominantly linked to the high cost area that is London.

A 2011 report by the Sustainable Development Commission (SDC) titled *Fairness in a car-dependent society* highlights that of the poorest 20% of adults, less than half hold a driving licence, while of the richest 20% of households, half own two or more cars (SDC, 2011). Those who are in the top income quintile were also found to travel two and a half times further by all modes than those in the bottom income quintile, and three times further by car. The findings of the SDC mirror earlier findings that note that low income people without cars make less than half the number of trips per year than high income people with cars (SEU, 2003). This reinforces the idea that car ownership, or lack thereof, remains intrinsically linked to transport disadvantage and is likely to indicate social disadvantage; and that transport poverty has not diminished in the first decade of the 21st century in the UK.

Excluding London boroughs, Newcastle has the fifth lowest car ownership rate of any local authority in England, at 58% of households, compared with comparator cities such as Leeds (68%) (ONS, 2012a). A comparison with the 2001 census reveals that while car ownership has increased by 3% over 10 years, these increases can be attributed to households owning two or more cars; the proportion of households that own just one car has remained constant (ONS, 2012b; Know Newcastle, 2013). Taking this at face value, this may suggest that poorer households that cannot afford a car have remained poor, while wealthier households that already owned a car have become wealthier. An analysis of 2011 census data also reveals that in deprived wards such as Walker and Elswick almost two thirds of households have no access to a car or a van. This is in stark contrast with some of the most affluent wards such as Parklands, West Gosforth and Dene, where less than a fifth of households have no access to a car or van. To illustrate this disparity even more, the average number of cars per household in Parklands (at 1.3) is almost three times that of Walker (at 0.44).

Less evidently, low income groups may still experience transport disadvantage in spite of owning a car. Evidence from the US, the UK and Australia indicates poverty is experienced as a result of being forced to own a car, in spite of their ability to afford one, as often no other transport options are available or affordable (Dobbs, 2007; Currie et al, 2009). Furthermore, household car ownership does not imply that it is available to all in the household at all times, with other household members often left without its benefits (Hamilton and Jenkins, 1989). Indeed, in this, and in other ways, gender remains an issue with second cars in a household often being needed to access employment opportunities and overcome social isolation even where such ownership reinforces poverty in other life areas (Dobbs, 2007).

Public transport services

The quality of public transport service can compound transport disadvantage. For households who do not own a car, public transport might be the only option. It is therefore critical that services are reliable, frequent and affordable (Beirão and Cabral, 2007). Poor access to public transport disproportionately affects those on low incomes and groups typically excluded from society (Wu and Hine, 2003), and many low income households depend upon an effective public transport service for access to resources, employment and services. Without this, extant conditions can contribute towards exclusion from many aspects of society and reinforce inequality (Welch, 2013; Desjardins and Drevelle, 2014). An explanation for this is that low income households are often confined to the urban periphery, poorly connected to employment centres, which increases travel time to work and also cost (Venter, 2011; Blair et al, 2013). This experience of transport disadvantage may also be compounded by being forced to work multiple jobs or requiring travel at off peak times, contributing towards a state of temporal exclusion (Cass et al, 2005; Blair et al, 2013). Part time work can also be hard to accommodate where travel times may be high, especially as women, who make up the bulk of part time workers, often remain responsible for care in or near the home (Dobbs, 2007).

In many urban contexts, the provision of bus services in the urban fringe is problematic; demand is often sporadic, dispersed across low densities and in some cases in competition with the more attractive proposition of travelling by car, stretching the availability of services (Mulley and Daniels, 2012). The SEU identified this problem in housing estates on the urban periphery of many UK cities, with specific reference to a lack of services at off peak times (SEU, 2003). Low income households may increasingly rely on jobs located on the suburban periphery, most of which are difficult to access without a car, or where services are infrequent.

In this regard, the deregulation of buses and subsequent commercialised restructuring has been shown 'to have a negative impact on areas where car ownership is low and deprivation relatively high' (Blair et al, 2013: 192). The privatisation of public transport has resulted in operators pursuing profitable routes while neglecting peripheral or rural routes where demand is lower (Cass et al, 2005). Given the dependence of low income households on public transport, this makes them most vulnerable to cuts in services and most at risk of experiencing transport disadvantage. Where services may exist, there may also be hidden barriers such as accessibility problems in getting on them, for example due to disability or the need to accommodate pushchairs.

Low income groups are also disadvantaged by excessive and sometimes prohibitive fares. It is recognised that transport costs consume a larger share of income of poorer households than richer households – in spite of transport expenditure being higher among the latter (Olvera et al, 2003; Venter, 2011). Ventner argues that low income households living on the urban periphery disproportionately pay higher fares as a result of longer travel distances to the centre (Venter, 2011), and Lucas argues that this perpetuates a 'culture of worklessness' where those living on the periphery of urban centres are 'locked out' of employment as they cannot afford to access the jobs available to them (Lucas, 2011: 1331). Loader and Stanley found that amalgamating bus fare zones and offering fare discounts on weekends enabled groups exhibiting signs of transport poverty to travel more often, in addition to increasing bus patronage and utilising excess bus capacity on services where demand from commuters was low (Loader and Stanley, 2009). There is also considerable evidence that low fares widen the spatial search patterns of the unemployed and draw people into training (for example, Goodwin, 1985).

A lack of information on transport options further contributes to the perpetuation of transport disadvantage. Currie and Delbosc suggest that a lack of information on the availability of pubic transport services or the opening times of different facilities is a commonly cited concern among transport disadvantaged groups (Currie and Delbosc, 2011). Indeed, in a recent study of public transport users in Greece, 37% of respondents noted that a lack of information for bus schedules and lines discouraged them from using public transport, with higher percentages for women (Tyrinopoulos and Antoniou, 2013).

Research into the advent of personal technology (for example, smartphones) in facilitating journeys and transfers by public transport is in its infancy. However, of future concern is the ability of socially excluded groups such as those on low incomes, the elderly and those with language barriers to confidently navigate this technology, particularly if such new systems become the norm and/or public transport authorities move towards phasing out older systems (for example paper timetables).

While crime on public transport is rare, the fear of crime is also a significant factor that inhibits its use. This particularly affects women, people with disabilities, people of low income and minority groups (Hine, 2012; Jones and Lucas, 2012). This manifests as an unwillingness to use stations or interchange facilities after dark or an avoidance of making a trip altogether (Hine, 2012). There are typically gender, age and racial dimensions to such disadvantage. Mahmoud and Currie found a particularly pressing concern for young people living on the urban fringe as a result of longer wait times and walks to public transport (Mahmoud and Currie, 2010). They also argue that infrequent and/or low quality public transport services are linked to greater concerns over personal safety, with higher frequencies and busier services at evenings and weekends seen to reduce these concerns as a result of shorter wait times and increased surveillance (Mahmoud and Currie, 2010). Migrant communities also appear to suffer in this regard and this is often compounded by a lack of information about services, cultural issues associated with using unfamiliar systems, and racism from passengers and sometimes staff (Miciukiewicz and Vigar, 2013).

Transport poverty in relation to public transport service in Newcastle has not been documented systematically in recent times. A broad-brush study of the North East as a whole (IPPR, 2005) noted the impact of declining bus patronage on low income households between 1988 and 2003. The report argues that blaming this on increasing car ownership does not acknowledge the possible existence of transport poverty among households forced to own a car 'due to the ineffectiveness of public transport networks' and the 'very serious' impact of this on the poorest households (IPPR, 2005: 10). The report also argues that the deregulation of buses has led to fare increases disproportionally greater than the costs of running a car, which has 'compounded economic injustice, particularly in the North East' (IPPR, 2005: 12).

A broader survey of Tyne and Wear bus passengers indicates that 90% are satisfied with their journey, the highest of any Integrated Transport Authority (Passenger Focus, 2014). However, cost is an issue with 63% stating that their journey represented value for money, with some operators scoring lower – for example, Arriva who operate many services across Newcastle scoring just 49%. Similarly, while fear of crime on buses is low during the day, with 99% of users feeling safe, only 56% did so at night. Overall, 81% of bus passengers felt safe at their nearest bus stop but this is likely to hide spatial variations as well as variations in safety perceptions among different genders and racial groups.

As such, a qualitative study of transport related social exclusion on Tyneside conducted in 2001 for the now defunct Newcastle West Gate New Deal for Communities partnership did provide evidence of deep transport poverty in one part of the city (Moore and Lilley, 2001). Out of 380 respondents, 43% had problems using public transport, which was found to limit access to shops and services and visits to friends and family. 57% of respondents in the peripheral communities of Newburn, Westerhope, West Denton and Lemington felt that public transport dictates the places they can visit, compared with 47% in the inner city areas surveyed. This confirms the SEU evidence earlier that peripherality from the central city exacerbates transport poverty. Service frequency and reliability were the most commonly cited problems, mentioned by 22% and 21% of respondents respectively. Across the sample, the cost of transport was considered to be less of a concern, as was personal safety. Nevertheless, the limited frequency of services at off peak times, the limited number of non-radial routes inhibiting the destination and activity choice of respondents and the lack of direct transport options to supermarkets and hospitals were found to be the greatest concerns. However, when respondents were broken down by ethnicity, black and minority ethnic communities were significantly more concerned about transport costs and transport information. It is thus reasonable to suggest that concentrated deprivation and language barriers experienced by these particular communities may be contributing factors. Given the increases in bus fares and cuts to services since 2001, a more recent update to this report is vital to inform the development of public policy, and in particular the development of 'quality contracts' as public transport in the conurbation acquires a degree of [re]regulation (see Nexus, 2013).

Conclusion

In ordinary cities such as Newcastle 'poor access to transport' is typically recognised as a cause of social exclusion and the spatial dimensions of it are recognised, 'exclusion is concentrated among people in poorer neighbourhoods' (Newcastle City Council, 2008: 6). The Local Transport Plan regards improving access to services as 'crucial in addressing social exclusion, particularly for disadvantaged groups and the most deprived communities' and aims to contribute to 'equality of opportunity' by enabling lower income groups to access jobs, training, healthcare, fresh food and open space (Tyne and Wear ITA, 2011: 80). This relates to the central rhetorical themes of fairness and justice that frame the document: one of its goals is to 'create a fairer Tyne and Wear, providing everyone with the opportunity to ... access a wide range of employment, training, facilities and services' with the aim of 'making sure the transport system ... is fair to all users' (Tyne and Wear ITA, 2011: i–ii).

To some extent, these useful overarching aims are carried through in terms of practical action. For example, the plan proposes a number of small-scale interventions, including improved walk/cycle access to business parks, the installation of talking signs at key locations for blind people, improved transport information at the MetroCentre bus interchange in Gateshead and audits of cycle facilities at Metro stations. But these do little to address the deep-seated issues portrayed earlier in this chapter. A future plan aim is to 'investigate whether high frequency feeder bus services can be provided between residential areas and the nearest relevant public transport interchange point, including during off peak times' to 'enhance the accessibility opportunities for many people in reaching key destinations' (Tyne and Wear ITA, 2011: 80-81). But there is very little in the LTP that directly targets transport poverty in the neighbourhoods where it is most common. There appears to be a missing level of action, at a meso-level between the strategy rhetoric and small-scale interventions, where action that might directly tackle transport poverty could occur. There is also no recognition that the choices of the 'hyper-mobile' impact disproportionately on the less mobile. Thus, for example, the wide variation in child casualty rates in road crashes between richer and poorer parts of the city remains unacknowledged and unaddressed.[1]

Thus, within Newcastle, as in all 'ordinary cities', transport poverty is an everyday reality. The interrelated nature of transport poverty and social exclusion implies there are concentrations of transport poverty within most cities, certainly in the UK. While such issues are acknowledged in policy material, there are few systematic responses. In part, this relates to a lack of policy levers, especially in a context of deregulation and privatisation of transport services, but also in a post-2008 era of individual and public service austerity.

Our examination has also uncovered an urgent need for more evidence of the effects of some of these trends on the long-standing issue of social exclusion and transport's role within it. Place-focused and alive to the diverse nature of many (potentially) disadvantaged communities, such research could provide the foundations to tackle a problem of great significance and yet one hidden from the everyday eyes of the majority of urban citizens and under the radar of many politicians and policy makers. For, just as the hypermobility of the ordinary citizen is 'normalised and unremarkable' (Bondi and Christie, 2000: 340), so the problems of transport poverty remain largely unrecognised and unaddressed.

Note

[1] Thirty five per cent of all road casualties in Walker in 2013 were children (0-15 age bracket) while in the affluent wards of East Gosforth and Parklands there were no casualties (0%) for this age group during the same period (North East Regional Safety Resource, 2014).

References

Atkins (2012) *Accessibility planning policy: evaluation and future directions. Final report.* [online] Available at: https://www.gov.uk/government/publications/accessibility-planning-policy-evaluation-and-future-directions [accessed January 2016].

Attoh, K.A. (2012) 'The transportation disadvantaged and the right to the city in Syracuse, New York', *Geographical Bulletin - Gamma Theta Upsilon*, 53(1): 1-19.

Audrey, S., and Langford, R. (2014) 'Dying to get out: young drivers, safety and social inequity', *Injury Prevention*, 20(1): 1-6.

Beirão, G., and Cabral, J.S. (2007) 'Understanding attitudes towards public transport and private car: a qualitative study', *Transport Policy*, 14(6): 478-89.

Betts, J. (2007) 'Transport and social disadvantage in Victoria: a government perspective', in G. Currie, J. Stanley and J. Stanley (eds) *No way to go: Transport and social disadvantage in Australian communities*, Clayton, Vic.: Monash University ePress, Chapter 12.

Blair, N., Hine, J. and Bukhari, S.M. (2013) 'Analysing the impact of network change on transport disadvantage: a GIS-based case study of Belfast', *Journal of Transport Geography*, 31: 192-200.

Bondi, L. and Christie, H. (2000) 'The best of times for some and the worst of times for others? Gender and class divisions in urban Britain today', *Geoforum*, 31: 329-43.

Cass, N., Shove, E. and Urry, J. (2005) 'Social exclusion, mobility and access', *Sociological Review*, 53(3): 539-55.

Currie, G. and Delbosc, A. (2009) *Car ownership and low income on the urban fringe – benefit or hindrance?* Clayton: Monash University

Currie, G. and Delbosc, A. (2011) 'Transport Disadvantage: a review', in G. Currie (ed) *New perspectives and methods in transport and social exclusion research*, Bradford: Emerald Group Publishing, pp 15-26.

Currie, G., Richardson, T., Smyth, P., Vella-Brodrick, D., Hine, J., Lucas, K. et al (2010) 'Investigating links between transport disadvantage, social exclusion and well-being in Melbourne – updated results', *Research in Transportation Economics*, 29(1): 287-95.

DCLG (2010) *English indices of deprivation 2010.* [online] Available at: https://www.gov.uk/government/statistics/english-indices-of-deprivation-2010 [accessed January 2016].

Delbosc, A. and Currie, G. (2011a) 'Transport problems that matter – social and psychological links to transport disadvantage', *Journal of Transport Geography*, 19(1): 170-78.

Delbosc, A. and Currie, G. (2011b) 'The spatial context of transport disadvantage, social exclusion and well-being', *Journal of Transport Geography*, 19(6): 1130-37.

Desjardins, X. and Drevelle, M. (2014) 'Trends in the social disparities in access to jobs by train in the Paris region since 1975', *Town Planning Review*, 85(2): 155-70.

Dobbs, L. (2007) 'Stuck in the slow lane: reconceptualising the links between gender, transport and social exclusion', *Gender, Work and Organization*, 14(2): 85-108.

Elliott, L. (2007) 'No place like home: Larry Elliott on child poverty in Newcastle's Cowgate estate', *The Guardian*, 29 June.

Farmer, S. (2011) 'Uneven public transportation development in neoliberalizing Chicago, US', *Environment and Planning A*, 43(5): 1154-72.

Gleeson, B. and Randolph, B. (2002) 'Social disadvantage and planning in the Sydney context', *Urban Policy and Research*, 20(1): 101-7.

Goodwin, P.B. (1985) *Some recent developments in understanding travellers' motivations in mode choice.* Round Table 68, European Conference of Ministers of Transportation, Paris.

Hamilton, K. and Jenkins, L. (1989) 'Why women and travel?', in M. Grieco, L. Pickup and R. Whipp (eds) *Gender, transport and employment: the impact of travel constraints*, Aldershot: Avebury, pp 17–45.

Hine, J. (2012) 'Mobility and transport disadvantage', in G. Margaret and J. Urry (eds) *Mobilities: new perspectives on transport and society*, Farnham: Ashgate, pp 21-39.

IPPR (2005) *At the crossroads?: Transport and social exclusion in the North East.* Newcastle upon Tyne: IPPR.

Jones, P. and Lucas, K. (2012) 'The social consequences of transport decision-making: clarifying concepts, synthesising knowledge and assessing implications', *Journal of Transport Geography*, 21: 4-16.

Kenyon, S., Lyons, G. and Rafferty, J. (2002) 'Transport and social exclusion: investigating the possibility of promoting inclusion through virtual mobility', *Journal of Transport Geography*, 10: 207-19.

Know Newcastle (2013) *Know your city: A profile of the people living in Newcastle, part two: factors that shape the lives of people living in Newcastle.* [online] Available at: http://www.knownewcastle.org.uk/GroupPage.aspx?GroupID=62 [accessed January 2016].

Levitas, R., Pantazis, C., Fahmy, E., Gordon, D., Lloyd, E. and Patsios, D. (2007) *The multidimensional analysis of social exclusion*, Bristol: University of Bristol.

Loader, C. and Stanley, J. (2009) 'Growing bus patronage and addressing transport disadvantage – the Melbourne experience', *Transport Policy*, 16(3): 106-14.

Lucas, K. (2003) *Transport and social exclusion: A G7 comparison study.* Annual European Transport Conference. Strasbourg: Act Travelwise.

Lucas, K. (2012) 'Transport and social exclusion: where are we now?', *Transport Policy*, 20: 105-13.

Lucas, K. (2013) *Modelling the relationships between transport poverty and social disadvantage.* Rio De Janiero: World Conference of Transport Research 2013.

Lucas, K. and Currie, G. (2012) 'Developing socially inclusive transportation policy: transferring the United Kingdom policy approach to the State of Victoria?', *Transportation*, 39: 151-73.

Lucas, K., Tyler, S. and Christodoulou, G. (2009) 'Assessing the 'value' of new transport initiatives in deprived neighbourhoods in the UK', *Transport Policy*, 16(3): 115-22.

Mahmoud, S. and Currie, G. (2010) *The relative priority of personal safety concerns for young people on public transport.* Canberra: Australasian Transport Research Forum.

Martens, K. (2013) 'Role of the bicycle in the limitation of transport poverty in the Netherlands', *Transportation Research Record*, 2387: 20-25.

Mattioli, G. (2013) 'Where sustainable transport and social exclusion meet: households without cars and car dependence in Great Britain', *Journal of Environmental Policy and Planning*: 1-22.

Miciukiewicz, K. and Vigar, G. (2013) *Encounters in motion: considerations of time and social justice in urban mobility research*, in D. Henckel, S. Thomaier, B. Könecke, R. Zedda and S. Stabilini (eds) *Space-time design of the public city*, Dordrecht: Springer, pp 171-85.

Moore, C. and Lilley, S. (2001) *Transport and social exclusion in the west and outer west of Newcastle upon Tyne.* Newcastle upon Tyne: Newcastle West Gate New Deal for Communities.

Mulley, C. and Daniels, R. (2012) 'Quantifying the role of a flexible transport service in reducing the accessibility gap in low density areas: a case-study in north-west Sydney', *Research in Transportation Business and Management*, 3: 12-23.

Newcastle City Council. (2008) *Building strong and inclusive communities: social inclusion strategy 2008-2011*. [pdf] Available at: https://www.newcastle.gov.uk/wwwfileroot/legacy/cxo/equality/SocialInclusionStrategy.pdf

Nexus (2013) *Proposal for a quality contracts scheme in Tyne and Wear*. [online] Available at: http://www.nexus.org.uk/busstrategy/consultationdocument/qcsproposal [accessed January 2016].

North East Regional Road Safety Resource (2014) Available at: http://www.gateshead.gov.uk/ne-roadsafety/Home.aspx [accessed January 2016].

Olvera, L.D., Plat, D. and Pochet, P. (2003) 'Transportation conditions and access to services in a context of urban sprawl and deregulation. The case of Dar es Salaam', *Transport Policy*, 10(4): 287-98.

ONS (2012a) *2011 Census: Key statistics for England and Wales, March 2011: car or van availability*. [online] Available at: http://www.ons.gov.uk/ [accessed January 2016].

ONS (2012b) *2001 vs 2011 Census – car ownership*. [online]. Available at: http://www.ons.gov.uk/ [accessed January 2016].

ONS (2013) *Newcastle upon Tyne: Key figures for economic deprivation, Apr 12–Mar 13* [online]. Available at: http://www.neighbourhood.statistics.gov.uk/ [accessed January 2016].

Passenger Focus (2014) *Bus passenger survey: autumn 2013 report*, London: Passenger Focus.

Pickup, L. and Giuliano, G. (2005) 'Transport and social exclusion in Europe and the US', in K. Donaghy, S. Poppelreuter and G. Rudinger (eds) *Social dimensions of sustainable transport*, Aldershot: Ashgate, pp 38-49.

Preston, J. and Rajé, F. (2007) 'Accessibility, mobility and transport-related social exclusion', *Journal of Transport Geography*, 15(3), 151-60.

Social Exclusion Unit (2003) *Making the connections: transport and social exclusion*, London: Office of the Deputy Prime Minister.

Stanley, J.K., Hensher, D.A., Stanley, J.R. and Vella-Brodrick, D. (2011a) 'Mobility, social exclusion and well-being: exploring the links', *Transportation Research Part A: Policy and Practice*, 45(8): 789-801.

Stanley, J., Hensher, D.A., Stanley, J., Currie, G., Greene, W.H. and Vella-Brodrick, D. (2011b) 'Social exclusion and the value of mobility', *Journal of Transport Economics and Policy*, 45(2): 197-222.

Sustainable Development Commission (2011) *Fairness in a car dependent society*, London: Sustainable Development Commission.

Tyne and Wear ITA (2011) *LTP3: The third local transport plan for Tyne and Wear, strategy 2011-2021*, Newcastle upon Tyne: Newcastle City Council.

Tyrinopoulos, Y. and Antoniou, C. (2013) 'Factors affecting modal choice in urban mobility' *European Transport Research Review*, 5(1): 27-39.

Velaga, N.R., Beecroft, M., Nelson, J.D., Corsar, D. and Edwards, P. (2013) 'Transport poverty meets the digital divide: accessibility and connectivity in rural communities', *Journal of Transport Geography*, 21(0): 102-12.

Venter, C. (2011) 'Transport expenditure and affordability: the cost of being mobile', *Development Southern Africa*, 28(1): 121-40.

Welch, T. (2013) 'Equity in transport: the distribution of transit access and connectivity among affordable housing units', *Transport Policy*, 30: 283-93.

Wu, B.M. and Hine, J.P. (2003) 'A PTAL approach to measuring changes in bus service accessibility', *Transport Policy*, 10(4): 307-20.

Zou, W., Zhang, F., Zhuang, Z. and Song, H. (2008) 'Transport infrastructure, growth, and poverty alleviation: empirical analysis of China', *Annals of Economics and Finance*, 9(2): 345-71.

FIVE

Food justice and the city

Jane Midgley and Helen Coulson

Introduction

The food system, the means by which food is produced, distributed and consumed, has for centuries shaped our cities and the way we live within them (Steel, 2009). Today, we have witnessed a growing interest in the food system, its interconnections and concern for its outcomes (cutting across health, economic, ecological, cultural and political issues), on both global and local scales. This has resulted in continued challenges to the capitalist industrial agri-food system that has dominated the late 20th and early 21st centuries (often referred to as the 'conventional' food system). This is happening at the same time as greater pressure is being placed on cities as they attempt to meet the demands and needs of their ever changing populations. Consequently, cities and their governance arrangements are at the very heart of the 'new food equation' (Morgan and Sonnino, 2010), as a complex array of individuals and organisations interact to challenge the pressures and problems that they perceive should be addressed if a more just food system is to be achieved.

This chapter is about 'food justice', broadly how different aspects of social and environmental justice interrelate with food. For those new to the topic, Gibb and Wittman provide a helpful summary and characterise food justice as 'ensuring that food system benefits and burdens are shared fairly; ensuring equal opportunities to participate in food system governance and decision making; and ensuring that diverse perspectives and the ways of knowing about the food system are recognised and respected' (Gibb and Wittman, 2013: 3).

This chapter is also about food justice and the city, in particular, our focus is on the city of Newcastle upon Tyne in North East England to complement the other contributions to this edited volume. This adds to the growing literature on food justice and translates the concept into a British context.

The chapter is organised as follows. In the first section we explore the concept of food justice in more depth and critically review published literature from interdisciplinary food studies authors and food activists, drawing primarily on the foundational North American sources. We focus particularly on how food justice has emerged as an organising concept for contemporary society, and the explicit political debates that have informed the term's development and its adoption. As such, food justice has the potential to capture a range of issues within its remit. Considering the varied activities that different actors are undertaking enables us to think through food justice in practice within Newcastle. Our analysis is exploratory, and none of the projects or activities we discuss within the context of Newcastle's food system have explicitly stated a food justice claim. However, given the diversity of organisations and communities involved in food related issues in Newcastle (and other British towns and cities) it is apposite to start to think through the application of justice in relation to urban food systems. We argue that without radical reform of the institutional arrangements and practices in this and other urban food systems, the pervading structural inequalities and injustices will remain.

What is food justice?

Food justice is a concept that possesses an organising capability that has been powerful in unifying social and political grassroots movements, particularly in North America, and has aligned a diverse range of food advocacy groups and organisations in an effort to transform the food system in more socially just ways (Agyeman and McEntee, 2014). Social movements involve a collective 'group of people with a purpose which will bring change that is different to the established order in which it originated' (Shortall, 1994: 286) and many historic examples found globally have a connection with food (see for example, Shortall 1994; DeLind and Ferguson, 1999). Given foods' multifaceted nature and central importance to everyday life, food justice has 'the potential to link different kinds of advocates, including those concerned with health, the environment, food quality, globalisation, workers' rights and working conditions, access to fresh and affordable food, and more sustainable land use' (Gottlieb and Joshi, 2010: 5). Indeed, food justice is argued to connect a diverse range of stakeholder interests in the food system that other movements have not previously been able to achieve (Wekerle, 2004).

The phrase 'food justice movement' has been cited to signify the coalescing of myriad food, environmental and social justice activists who not only engage in local 'alternative' food projects and campaigns of resistance against the industrial agri-food system, but also additionally forge and reform networks and associations that connect various issues and scales, both within and outwith the city. It is argued that the ideals of sustainability and social and environmental justice are embodied by food practices that are 'alternative', and oppositional, to the perceived corporate, industrial, global and unsustainable practices of the conventional food system. Alternative food system practices frequently aim to challenge food system relations by embedding behaviour in social and ecological practices, recognising place specificity, and redistribute economic value, the latter often being achieved through creating new forms of market governance alongside new networks of political and economic association (Goodman, 2003; Whatmore et al, 2003; Watts et al, 2005). However, it is argued that some alternative practices such as organic food and farmers' markets have been captured by policy and/or the conventional agri-food system (Guthman, 2004). Attempts to overcome this may account for the similarity between the aims of the food justice movement and the reassertion of alternative food qualities and their attributed practices.

Despite food justice's coalescing potential, Gottlieb and Joshi suggest that unifying the words 'food' and 'justice' into a new concept is problematic, and:

> does not by itself accomplish the goal of facilitating the expansion and linkage of groups and issues. Nor does it necessarily create a clear path to advocating for changes to the food system or point to ways to bring about more just policies, economic change, or the restructuring of global, national, and community food pathways. (Gottlieb and Joshi, 2010: 5)

Food justice is a broad, multifaceted concept open to multiple interpretations (Gottlieb and Joshi, 2010; Sbicca, 2012). While this breadth and openness can appeal to, and help engage, a range of actors and interests in food justice and its political organising, it does also mean that 'the "justice" in food justice varies according to the author' (Bedore, 2010: 1422). Consequently, scholars have begun to engage with ideas of justice in relation to the food system from a range of different perspectives, including race and class, drawing on long-standing pre-existing North American civil rights movements (Alkon and Agyeman, 2011; Agyeman and McEntee, 2014), democratic engagement of citizens in the food system (Hassanein, 2003; Levkoe, 2006) and food sovereignty. Food sovereignty is a social movement that attempts to achieve a more democratic, rights-based approach to the control of resources throughout the food system in the global north and south, and which is primarily framed[1] as a challenge to food security discourses (see *Journal of Peasant Studies*, 2009). Rights-based approaches to food system reform, such as food sovereignty and food justice, advocate the 'right to food' as a basic human right, encouraging participation and empowerment of consumers in the food system (rather than reliance on ad hoc charitable and/or emergency provision such as food banks) and have demonstrated how food is a deeply political issue (Rideout et al, 2007). Rights-based approaches are also one means to ensure that social justice concerns are not overtaken by sustainability or food localisation issues in attempts to reform food systems (Morgan, 2014). This is illustrated by actions within the US where food insecurity has been reframed as a community based problem, rather than an individual responsibility. This reframing provides the potential to link food insecurity and its effects on marginalised communities with other food system matters such as sustainable agriculture and health education (Allen, 1999; Bellows and Hamm, 2002; Kortright and Wakefield, 2011). This is now being taken forward through a food justice framing[1] (Wekerle, 2004; Morgan, 2014).

Significantly, food justice is often employed by activists in ways that reflect their sociohistorical context, and it is suggested that by exploring particular narratives of what food justice means to individuals, would help others to see the social and political situations, constraints and experiences of injustice (Dixon, 2014). This enables a region's economic, political and social history to contextualise and shape the specific food justice frames used by its advocates (Sbicca, 2012). But this 'shared' associative background can be problematic as food justice 'has been largely championed by those who have a stake in defining health, good food, and justice in ways that are comfortable to them and they bring all sorts of assumptions based on their own cultural histories' (Guthman, 2014: 1155). Thus, what conceptions of justice underpin the food justice movement remain unexamined. For example, we note the tension between distributive and procedural justice, and the gaps concerning age, gender, sexuality, (dis)ability and religion in cultural notions of food justice as other groups are privileged in debates. Understandings of the food justice concept are diverse and shaped by each individual's positionality, but this apparent weakness may also be its strength, as increasingly the food justice movement is inspiring activists and scholars to embark on connecting the various components. For example, the publication of *Food Movements Unite!* by Holt-Gimenez

(2011) attempts to connect food justice, food sovereignty and food democracy approaches to provide a powerful synergy to move towards a fairer food system.

One major influence on the food justice discourse has been the environmental justice movement (Alkon and Agyeman, 2011). This movement highlighted the disproportionate exposure of economically and racially marginalised people to environmental burdens and thus attempted to champion equal protection from environmental harms and improve procedural justice. Environmental justice has helpfully drawn attention to the fact that certain communities experienced disproportionate lack of access to healthy foods (Alkon and Agyeman, 2011). Despite this, and the work of Gottlieb and Fisher (1996) documenting an environmental justice approach to community food security almost two decades ago, environmental justice scholars have paid little attention to food access (Alkon and Norgaard, 2009). Expanding the conceptualisation of environmental justice beyond a concern with environmental harms to focus on the associations between the condition of the natural world and the material experience of everyday life demands that attention is given to rethinking practices and institutional arrangements. Indeed, the food justice movement has been identified as an organisational group that directly aims to address both unjust practices and institutions in addition to unsustainable environmental processes in its attempt to transform people's relationship with the production, transportation, and consumption of food (Schlosberg, 2013). For Schlosberg, 'building new practices and institutions for sustainability' (Schlosberg, 2013: 48) that reconstitute and reconfigure the way communities source basic human needs from the environment – termed 'sustainable materialism' – can be demonstrated in practice by the way the food justice movement has sought to develop sustainable (and just) material relationships with both human and non-human environments.

A further element of the food justice debate has been to stress the nexus between citizenship, democracy and sustainability and expose the power relations of the food system. Food justice helps counter the tendency for individuals to be constructed solely as consumers rather than as active citizens (Levkoe, 2006). Levkoe states that:

> Participation in food justice movements encourages the development of strong civic virtues and critical perspectives along with the necessary experience for shaping policy makers' decisions. Food justice activism has the ability to

increase the confidence, political efficacy, knowledge, and skills of those involved. (Levkoe, 2006: 90)

In this sense, food justice potentially empowers citizens to engage in more 'radical critiques' (Sbicca, 2012: 457) of the food system from an environmental perspective and challenge pervading institutional arrangements such as capitalism and racism. This transformative potential resonates with Schlosberg's concept of sustainable materialism. Schlosberg argues that we need to 'create new counter-institutions and practices, and, crucially, embrace a more sustainable relationship between just communities and a working environment' (2013: 49).

While the majority of food justice literature originates from North America, the concept has begun to take purchase in the UK, notably with the Food Ethics Council's (FEC) Food and Fairness Inquiry report, *Food justice* (2010). The FEC is a charitable organisation that works for a fairer food system and its report is orientated towards social justice and concedes that in the UK there has been a 'relative neglect of social justice in public debate about food policy' (Food Ethics Council, 2010: 9). Furthermore, the report documents the extent of social injustice in the food system within the UK and globally, with recommendations to the (then) UK government to change the existing 'unjust' policy trajectory. More recently in the UK, following independent approaches by different local authorities and partner organisations, a range of initiatives under the 'Sustainable Food Cities'[2] programme of charitable funding has created an alliance of organisations to address social, economic and ecological pressures facing different UK towns and cities and their communities. Even though it is not explicitly framed as such, this alliance and its activities can be taken as representative of a food justice movement emerging within the UK (Morgan, 2014). We discuss some of the Newcastle based activities of the alliance later in this chapter.

Inspecting the food system through the lens of justice provides a normative framework that evokes the notions of social equity and fairness (themselves open to contestation) in which inequalities in the agri-food system are identified and challenged. These range from low wages, zero hour contracts, and poor working conditions for food workers throughout the food chain to the existence of food deserts, food insecurity, and malnutrition in marginalised, low income communities. Increasing equity and challenging the injustices of the prevailing food system operating at various scales is thus a central priority for the food justice movement.

Notably, food justice writers and activists advocate for 'locally grounded alternatives to global food systems based on visions of a more just society' (Wekerle, 2004: 381) that aim to empower the most vulnerable by creating alternative local food networks. However, critical scholarship continues to question the presumed virtue of local food projects, highlighting the danger of equating certain spatial scales (the local) with a more just and equitable food system (Born and Purcell, 2006; Allen, 2010). Born and Purcell caution against the 'local trap'; this refers to 'the tendency of food activists and researchers to assume something inherent about the local scale. The local is assumed to be desirable; it is preferred a priori to larger scales' (Born and Purcell, 2006: 195). Thus, while local food systems may enhance the quality of life for many people 'they do not automatically move us in the direction of greater social justice' (Allen, 2010: 306), nor do they ensure material or process equity in their practice. The scalar restructuring of production and consumption on its own cannot address inequalities based around race, class, and gender. Therefore, discussions of 'reflexive localism' have sought to integrate notions of social justice (DuPuis and Goodman, 2005). By understanding the complexity of scale and placing emphasis on social justice considerations, local grassroots initiatives may possess the ability to challenge forces of oppression, exploitation and control. Thus, while the local is never neutrally evoked and deployed it is 'precisely at the local level that completely new economic forms that prioritise equity can be imagined, piloted and evaluated' (Allen, 2010: 298).

Food justice activism has purported to foster a 'new language of social change in the food arena' (Gottlieb and Joshi, 2010: 5). This builds upon 'ideologies that critique the structural oppression responsible for many injustices throughout the agri-food system' (Sbicca, 2012: 455). Indeed, at its heart and as noted earlier, the concept of food justice has sought to highlight how food insecurity and urban hunger are not individualised problems but are expressions of structural inequality that act to reproduce marginalisation in disenfranchised communities, frequently distinguished by race and class (Heynen, 2006; Alkon and Agyeman, 2011; Alkon and Mares, 2012; Heynen et al, 2012). In addition, the food justice movement has been critical of the white privilege that tends to permeate the local/alternative food movement (Slocum, 2007; Guthman, 2008) as well as raise concern over the green gentrification of communities (Morgan, 2014). Issues associated with food, therefore, have profound implications for power relations, health outcomes, and sustainability.

Increasingly, a food justice frame is being utilised to explore the notion of a 'just urban food system', which recognises the central role that cities play in the food system (Bedore, 2010; Morgan, 2014). Just urban food systems can be characterised as an 'ideal' type that addresses the many challenges facing the current food system at the urban scale. Background pressures include:

- the global financial crisis and the consequent austerity measures;
- the reduction in state welfare and increasing role of third sector[3] organisations in meeting emergency food needs;
- rising food prices;
- growing polarisation between the rich and poor;
- obesity epidemics and other nutritional health problems;
- climate change and ecological pressures.

However, one aspect that sets just urban food systems apart from past approaches is the co-governance between citizens, local state and non-governmental actors in responding to these pressures in their local/urban area (Morgan, 2014).

This review suggests that food justice is a nebulous concept, yet its role is to facilitate connections and unify a range of what at first glance can appear to be disparate issues, communities, and interests concerning the food system. We can trace the momentum of the movement from North American debates on structural inequality and the reproduction of socioeconomic and political disenfranchisement of particular urban communities, primarily on the grounds of race and class. Thus, we can see an associated political standpoint that promotes the empowerment of citizens and community participation in food systems and urban governance, most recently in conceptualising just urban food systems. Food justice proponents argue that it is at the local scale that the most potent challenges to injustice can be performed by responding to specific local concerns. It is also evident that food justice activism promotes a decoupling from the conventional agri-food system and its institutions, although how total and radical this argument is can vary.

We now turn to explore some of the different actions and activities that have occurred to date (July 2014) in Newcastle, as an example of how an 'ordinary' city is responding to the background pressures noted previously. We focus on food access practices to explore whether these have the capacity to unify diverse groups and interests in Newcastle, engage citizens in co-governance, and potentially transform the city's food system.

Newcastle: the potential and problems of food justice in practice

In 2012 a survey of Newcastle residents identified that on average 18% agreed with the statement that they had difficulty paying for food, this differed by ward (local administrative area) from between 3% to 38% of residents (NCC, 2014a). Moreover, charitable responses to food poverty and insecurity have seen noted clusters of food banks emerging in particular parts of the city, notably towards the east and west, which have historically been home to Newcastle's low income communities (Newcastle CVS, 2012). In Newcastle in 2013, 14.5% of children aged 4–5 years and 25% of children aged 10–11 years were obese compared to the English average of 9.5% and 19.2% respectively; this places Newcastle's childhood obesity rates in the worst national quartile (Chimat, 2013). These are just some of the stark health and socioeconomic realities facing residents, third sector organisations, local authority and public sector agencies as they begin to engage with food as a political issue and variably organise around this.

This section provides examples of activities occurring within Newcastle, which aim to improve food access and promote co-governance in the city. Our intention in using these examples is to critically consider food justice in practice, and not to specifically criticise any organisation or activity depicted. The examples are not a comprehensive list of all activities in the city. The material used in this section is drawn from publicly available documents and from previous research undertaken by the first author with third sector organisations during 2009–10 (see Midgley, 2013, 2014).

We begin by focusing on food access and the issues of social justice and sustainability highlighted by surplus food redistribution activities in Newcastle as one response to community and household food insecurity, more usually termed food poverty in UK debates (Midgley, 2014). Food poverty and waste are symbolic of the inequalities and the inefficiencies in the food system and the redistribution of surplus food that remains fit for human consumption is argued to increase food access and reduce environmental harm. This 'win-win' situation presents itself through the opportunity to prevent surplus food from becoming waste and its associated environmental costs into a valued economic resource that can feed those in need. This may be done as a statement of political and community activism (Edwards and Mercer, 2013). Thus, a manager of one local youth charity in the city who received surplus food to encourage client contact with its services commented:

'... I think it's a really, really good thing [surplus food redistribution]. Because when you see it on the telly and they have all these supermarkets dumping all this stuff and you think: Why? ... When you think of all the people that could take it.'

However, working with surplus food requires third sector organisations to insert themselves into local and regional food systems and their associated infrastructures (for example, what products food manufacturers and retailers would be willing to donate as well as deliver). Thus, as explained by the manager of a surplus food redistribution charity this was problematic in the context of Newcastle and the wider region.

'But one of the problems we've had is variety of food. Because there's a lack of food providers and producers in the North East, so that's had an impact on giving projects access to the variety of food ... you don't know what you're getting from one week to the next, it can be feast or famine.'

The uncertainty of supply was reiterated by the youth charity manager: "We'll get the best, but it's just, you know, we never know what's coming."

Research by Midgley (2014) has shown how surplus food and its material and relational qualities are reworked and made different by actors in the food system to enable its extraction from the market and traditional disposal methods. A key part of this practice relies on its recipients/consumers being made different or 'other' to ensure the surplus' donation. However, in doing so this does not mean that the access to food is free of market practices or provides unmediated access. For example, the introduction of a subscription fee by a national surplus food redistribution network had negative ramifications for access, discussed by the manager of a regional redistribution charity: "... the big organisations can afford that, little organisations cannot, so the ones that can't, that work with the more hard to reach groups, struggle."

This has implications regarding social justice and access to food by 'potentially compounding the existing inequalities experienced by vulnerable consumers' (Midgley, 2014: 1886). This feature is common to other forms of charitable and emergency food provision such as food banks where the access is denoted by the construction of an 'other' without the same consumer options or choices in the food system (Power, 2011).

Midgley (2014) highlighted how significant efforts were involved in managing the different qualities and values (cultural as well as economic) associated with the use of surplus food, in an attempt to overcome such constructions. Thus, a national food redistribution network manager commented:

'... some people have said in the past "providing second-hand food to second-hand people". Which is a terrible way of putting it, because first of all, it's not second-hand people. And the food we give out is of the highest quality, because otherwise, we wouldn't be getting it from the food industry.'

One element which links surplus food to justice issues is its 'facilitative quality' through changing not only food access in communities but by also attempting to provide longer-term support to different third sector organisations' activities and the intended wider social, economic and health outcomes for the varied user groups of this resource. This is in contrast to the emergency and transitory relief commonly associated with food banking (Midgley, 2014). Thus, one food cooperative manager working with surplus food stated: "But because of the ethos of the whole organisation, we're quite happy, you know making a difference to two or three families in a particular community, we've continued to do that."

However, any beneficial outcomes can only be achieved by negotiating and managing the different qualities of the food product, these pertain to the portrayal of end consumers and benefits of the resource's use, the risk associated with the product being misused (resale on the grey market or inappropriately prepared) or unused, the legal responsibility for public health, and the handling of branded goods and the economic power associated with them (Midgley, 2014). Surplus food redistribution practices may help alleviate food access issues. However, they function by inserting themselves into existing food and wider institutional systems (for example, welfare systems and waste regulation), which are the very same as those that give rise to the problems of food poverty and waste (Midgley, 2014). Consequently, without significant change these cannot resolve the social injustices inherent within the food system and wider institutional setting. Thus, surplus food redistribution undertaken by the third sector is heavily criticised for reducing the pressure on governments to respond to structural poverty and inequality (Poppendieck, 1998; Power, 2011).

We now return to the 'Sustainable Food Cities' alliance and discuss the recent development of a city food charter and the beginnings of a move towards co-governance of food system activities in Newcastle, using examples of food access activities wherever possible. The 'Newcastle Food Charter' is being taken forward by 'Food Newcastle' with a range of partners as part of the 'Sustainable Food Cities' alliance. Thus:

> Food Newcastle is a cross-sector partnership of organisations and businesses who jointly recognise the pivotal role food can play in driving positive social, economic and environmental change across Newcastle and beyond.
>
> Food Newcastle is committed to improving the health and wellbeing of people across the city by creating a healthier food culture and addressing locally important priorities related to food. (Food Newcastle, 2014)

The charter's publication encourages individuals, businesses and institutions in Newcastle to adopt the practices *it* recommends to reform the food system. For example, in the city council's open cabinet meeting on 'sustainable and affordable food' in June 2014, the council was clear that it supported the aims of the charter in a number of ways, specifically, its procurement practices and targeted health programmes in the east and west of the city (NCC, 2014b). Indeed, the fact that the city council chose to consider sustainable and affordable food as one key issue facing Newcastle in an open consultation meeting suggests a step, however tentative, to a more deliberative approach to food and its governance in the city.

Newcastle's 'Food Charter' forms the basis for a potential food policy council for the city (a feature common to North America (see Mah and Thang, 2013; Morgan, 2014)). The charter lists 10 objectives to achieve five priorities, the priorities are; 'good food for all', 'strengthen the local economy', 'fairness in the food chain', 'environmental sustainability', and 'strong community food culture' (Food Newcastle, 2013). This indicates a range of issues capable of capturing a broad constituency of interest. While some of the stated objectives are highly specific single issues, other objectives, particularly those concerning environmental sustainability involve multiple concerns. Many of the objectives make explicit the economic connections and impacts of the food system. This may be a way of attempting to empower food citizens and/or encourage buy-in from the city and wider region's food industry (producers, retailers, manufacturers, distributors and caterers) and/or reorganise the distributional effects of the food system. Interestingly, the charter often relates to the wider region recognising the interconnections and interdependency between the city and its surrounding area, as well as building on previous regional food producer and retail networks. Thus, while responsive to its context, the charter may not promote radical reform of the city's food system or its institutional arrangements. However, the potential of the charter may lie in its existence as a symbolic statement of intent to change the city's food system.

The actions of 'Food Nation', a social enterprise that aims to build healthier communities, show how some elements of the charter are being taken forward. 'Food Nation' has received funds to encourage healthy eating and other cooking skills to food bank customers from Newcastle City Council's Communities Service funding round in December 2013. Thus, this could be interpreted as taking forward two of the charter's priorities. The first priority of 'good food for all' ensures that everyone has access and knowledge to enable affordable and healthy food consumption, and to work closely with food providers to promote the wellbeing of the people they serve. And second, to help deliver a 'strong community food culture' by providing opportunities to learn about food and develop new skills. However, this assumes that to experience income poverty equates to a paucity of food knowledge, and adheres to long-standing cultural constructions of poverty in UK government policy and particularly food poverty discourses (Midgley, 2013). The work of the organisation has also expanded to include administering a proportion of public health funding, which aims to positively impact on local communities. Recent funding has focused upon food education with children and young people (including young adults who have experienced homelessness), as well as health and skills training with black and minority ethnic communities in different areas of the city (Food Nation, 2013). Together these activities suggest a reworking of existing power relations and institutional arrangements rather than substantive co-governance, and reproduce rather than challenge many of the structural inequalities that currently exist.

Concluding comments

Food undoubtedly often renders visible the inequalities and injustices in society. Food justice is a political and organising concept and may offer the opportunity for people to politically engage with food and in doing so become aware of wider structural injustices that currently permeate the urban food system (for example, unequal access to food and labour market inequalities). In turn, this may offer the potential for communities to come together and pursue transformative change. Moreover, food justice may have a role in coalescing various interests and actors in the food system. However, as the examples from Newcastle have shown, considerable difficulties are encountered when working within the parameters of the existing food system and governance arrangements to engender radical change. If practices simply rework existing relations and institutional structures, this prevents the formation of 'new counter-institutions and practices' (Schlosberg, 2013: 49), such as co-governance, that are required to truly transform and achieve a just urban food system (Morgan, 2014).

As we have identified, the food justice literature has tended to emphasise both class based and racial inequalities in relation to the food system, recognising its particular historic and political context. However, as noted, this leads to some social and cultural divisions (based on gender, age, (dis)ability, sexuality and religion) and issues (such as environmental justice, ecological health and sustainability) being less discernible in debates. Thus, we need to be aware of what lens we use to make visible different issues and experiences so that we recognise how food (in)justice is practised in diverse settings (Dixon, 2014).

We conclude by arguing that food justice and just urban food systems cannot be seen as the end point or outcome. Actions promoting justice that start with food may risk failure if they simply end with food. Attention must focus on challenging, rather than simply reworking existing practices and institutional arrangements, if structural inequalities and environmental problems associated with the food system are to be addressed in more just ways. As such, we would reiterate that food justice provides only one of many avenues in which structural inequalities reproduced by the food system can be understood and challenged.

Notes

[1] We and certain cited authors make reference to 'framing'. When used in relation to social movements, framing denotes an active interpretation and representation of an idea or event to help organise and guide action (see Snow et al, 1986). However, here we do not provide detailed analysis of the framing techniques and outcomes for the food justice movement.

[2] For further details see: http://sustainablefoodcities.org/about

[3] The third sector comprises charity, voluntary groups and social enterprises of different sizes and interests.

References

Agyeman, J. and McEntee, J. (2014) 'Moving the field of food justice forward through the lens of urban political ecology', *Geography Compass*, 8(3): 211-20.

Alkon, A.H. and Agyeman, J. (2011) *Cultivating food justice: Race, class and sustainability*, Cambridge, MA: MIT Press.

Alkon, A.H. and Mares, T.M. (2012) 'Food sovereignty in US food movements: radical visions and neoliberal constraints', *Agriculture and Human Values*, 29(3): 347-59.

Alkon, A.H. and Norgaard, K.M. (2009) 'Breaking the food chains: an investigation of food justice activism', *Sociological Inquiry*, 79(3): 289-305.

Allen, P. (1999) 'Reweaving the food security safety net: mediating entitlement and entrepreneurship', *Agriculture and Human Values*, 16(2): 117-129.

Allen, P. (2010) 'Realizing justice in local food systems', *Cambridge Journal of Regions, Economy and Society*, 3(2): 295-308.

Bedore, M. (2010) 'Just urban food systems: a new direction for food access and urban social justice', *Geography Compass*, 4(9): 1418-32.

Bellows, A.C. and Hamm, M.W. (2002) 'US-based community food security: influences, practice, debate', *Journal for the Study of Food and Society*, 6(1): 31-44.

Born, B. and Purcell, M. (2006) 'Avoiding the local trap', *Journal of Planning Education and Research*, 26(2): 195-207.

Chimat (2013) *Child health profile Newcastle upon Tyne*, [online] Child and Maternal Health Observatory. Available at: www.chimat.org.uk/resource/view.aspx?RID=152541 [accessed January 2016].

DeLind, L.B. and Ferguson, A.E. (1999) 'Is this a Women's Movement? The relationship of gender to community-supported agriculture in Michigan', *Human Organization,* 58(2): 190-200.

Dixon, B.A. (2014) 'Learning to *see* food justice', *Agricultural and Human Values,* 31(2): 175-84.

DuPuis, M.E. and Goodman, D. (2005) 'Should we go home to eat?: toward a reflexive politics of localism', *Journal of Rural Studies*, 21(3): 359-71.

Edwards, F. and Mercer, D. (2013) 'Food waste in Australia: The Freegan response', *The Sociological Review*, 60(S2): 174-91.

Food Ethics Council (FEC) (2010) *Food justice: The report of the Food and Fairness Inquiry*, Brighton: Food Ethics Council.

Food Nation (2013) *An evaluation of the funded projects 2012/13.* [pdf] Available at: http://www.foodnation.org/download/pdf-1394552905.pdf [accessed January2016].

Food Newcastle (2013) *Food charter.* [online] Available at: http://foodnewcastle.org/newcastle-food-charter/ [accessed January 2016].

Food Newcastle (2014) *About us.* [online] Available at: http://foodnewcastle.org/about-us/ [accessed January 2016].

Gibb, N. and Wittman, H. (2013) 'Parallel alternatives: Chinese-Canadian farmers and the metro Vancouver local food movement', *Local Environment,* 18(1): 1-19.

Goodman, D. (2003) 'The quality 'turn' and alternative food practices: reflections and agenda', *Journal of Rural Studies,* 19(1): 1-7.

Gottlieb, R. and Fisher, A. (1996) 'First feed the face: environmental justice and community security', *Antipode,* 28(2): 193-203.

Gottlieb, R. and Joshi, A. (2010) *Food justice,* Cambridge, MA: MIT Press.

Guthman, J. (2004) 'The trouble with "organic lite" in California: a rejoinder to the "conventionalisation" debate', *Sociologia Ruralis,* 44(3): 301-16.

Guthman, J. (2008) '"If they only knew': colorblindness and universalism in California alternative food institutions', *The Professional Geographer,* 60(3): 387-97.

Guthman, J. (2014) 'Doing justice to bodies? Reflections on food justice, race, and biology', *Antipode,* 46(5): 1153-71.

Hassanein, N. (2003) 'Practicing food democracy: a pragmatic politics of transformation', *Journal of Rural Studies,* 19(1): 77-86.

Heynen, N. (2006) 'Justice of eating in the city: the political ecology of urban hunger', in N. Heynen, M. Kaika and E. Swyngedouw (eds) *In the nature of cities: Urban political ecology and the politics of urban metabolism,* Oxford: Routledge, pp 129-42.

Heynen, N., Kurtz, H.E. and Trauger, A. (2012) 'Food justice, hunger and the city', *Geography Compass,* 6(5): 304-11.

Holt-Gimenez, E. (2011) *Food movements unite!: Strategies to transform our food system,* Oakland, CA: Food First Books.

Journal of Peasant Studies (2009) Special Issue 'Food sovereignty', 36(3): 663-706.

Kortright, R. and Wakefield, S. (2011) 'Edible backyards: a qualitative study of household food growing and its contributions to food security', *Agriculture and Human Values,* 28(1): 39-53.

Levkoe, C.Z. (2006) 'Learning democracy through food justice movements', *Agriculture and Human Values,* 23(1): 89-98.

Mah, C.L. and Thang, H. (2013) 'Cultivating food connections: the Toronto food strategy and municipal deliberation of food', *International Planning Studies,* 18(1): 96-110.

Midgley, J.L. (2013) 'Problematizing the emergence of household food security in England', *International Journal of Sociology of Agriculture and Food*, 20(3): 293-311.

Midgley, J.L. (2014) 'The logics of surplus food redistribution', *Journal of Environmental Planning and Management*, 57(12): 1872-92.

Morgan, K. (2014) 'Nourishing the city: the rise of the urban food question in the global north', [online] *Urban Studies*, Epub ahead of print Available at: http://usj.sagepub.com/content/early/2014/05/20/0042098014534902 [accessed January 2016].

Morgan, K. and Sonnino, R. (2010) 'The urban foodscape: world cities and the new food equation', *Cambridge Journal of Regions, Economy and Society*, 3(2): 209-24.

Newcastle City Council (2014a) *Residents survey 2012*. Cited in Open Cabinet Briefing Document, Newcastle City Council.

Newcastle City Council (2014b) *Delivering sustainable and affordable food briefing document. Policy Cabinet 11 June*, [online] Newcastle: Newcastle City Council. Available at: http://democracy.newcastle. gov.uk/ieListDocuments.aspx?CId=857&MId=5087&Ver=4 [accessed January 2016].

Newcastle Council for Voluntary Service (CVS) (2012) *Food for thought: Food bank provision in Newcastle*, Newcastle: Newcastle Council for Voluntary Service.

Poppendieck, J. (1998) *Sweet charity: Emergency food and the end of entitlement*, New York, NY: Penguin.

Power, E. (2011) 'Canadian food banks: obscuring the reality of hunger and poverty', *Food Ethics,* 6(4): 18-20.

Rideout, K., Riches, G., Ostry, A., Buckingham, D and MacRae, R. (2007) 'Bringing home the right to food in Canada: challenges and possibilities for achieving food security', *Public Health Nutrition*, 10(6): 566-73.

Sbicca, J. (2012) 'Growing food justice by planting an anti–oppression foundation: opportunities and obstacles for a budding social movement', *Agriculture and Human Values*, 29(4): 455-66.

Schlosberg, D. (2013) 'Theorising environmental justice: the expanding sphere of discourse', *Environmental Politics*, 22(1): 37-55.

Shortall, S. (1994) 'Farm women's groups: feminist or farming or community groups or new social movements?', *Sociology,* 28(1): 279-81.

Slocum, R. (2007) 'Whiteness, space, and alternative food practice', *Geoforum*, 38(3): 520-33.

Snow, D.A., Rochford, E.B., Worden, S.K. and Benford, R.D. (1986) 'Frame alignment processes, micromobilization, and movement participation', *American Sociological Review*, 51(4): 464–81.

Steel, C. (2009) *Hungry city: How food shapes our lives*, London: Vintage.

Watts, D.C.H., Ilbery, B. and Maye, D. (2005) 'Making reconnections in agro-food geography: alternative systems of food provision', *Progress in Human Geography*, 29(1): 22–40.

Wekerle, G.R. (2004) 'Food justice movements: policy, planning, and networks', *Journal of Planning Education and Research*, 23(4): 378–86.

Whatmore, S., Stassart, P. and Rentring, H. (2003) 'What's alternative about alternative food networks?', *Environment and Planning A*, 35(3): 389–91.

Spatial justice and the right to the city

Simin Davoudi and Derek Bell

> It would be a pity indeed if the busyness of political philosophers was to go completely unnoticed by spatial theorists and applied researchers. Equally, it would be a pity [...] if this essay were to stand alone as a review of implications of that busyness. (Pirie, 1983: 472)

These are the opening words of an article by G.H. Pirie, which seemingly for the first time used the term spatial justice. However, he knew that his interpretation of space was similar to the then 'familiar way as some kind of container, as an entity or physical expression made up of individual locations and their distance relations' (Pirie, 1983: 471). As we have shown in Chapter 1, this conceptualisation of justice and spatiality fails to recognise that injustices not only happen *in* space, but are also created, maintained and exacerbated *by* it. It is this recognition that is at heart of the three chapters that make up this section of the book. All three pay homage to Lefebvre's concept of 'the right to the city' and consider the city as a key site of politics. They argue that the right to the city is about having access to all aspects of urban life as well as the making of the city. It is about the city being shaped not *for* us but *by* us. The authors draw on their knowledge and experience of Newcastle (and Delhi in Chapter 6) to provide examples of the various ways in which the dialectical relationship between (in) justices and spatiality are played out in the everyday life of citizens and their experience in and of the city.

The section starts with Chapter 6 in which Suzanne Speak and Ashok Kumar show why we need to consider all cities as ordinary and distinct cities even if they are labelled differently as global cities or world cities. They show how seemingly very different cities, Newcastle and Delhi, share similar struggles for space, between economy and society, nature and development, the affluent and the poor. They argue that despite their perceived position on the urban hierarchy or typology, both cities are the sites of some common political contestations. While they acknowledge that the battle for access to physical territory is well documented within the literature on rights to the city, rights to land and rights to adequate housing, they argue for extending this debate to include the struggle for the right to occupy, alter and reform the perceived concepts of the city according to individuals' or communities' values. They draw on three formulations of the right to the city, the right to difference and the spatial dialectics of injustice to explore the ongoing control practices of urban elite in the two cities. Their observations provide a warning that the differences in the scale of injustices in the 'mega cities' of the Global South, such as Delhi, may lead us to overlook, or be complacent about, injustices in 'ordinary cities' of the Global North, such as Newcastle.

Chapter 7 by Lee Pugalis, Jon Swords, Michael Jeffries and Bob Giddings seeks to explore the right of a particular subculture – urban sports activists and specifically skateboarders – to produce space. They argue that although skateboarders (and other urban sports activists) are often represented by city authorities as 'unruly elements' that infringe the rights of consumers and damage the urban fabric, they are, in fact, producers of urban city space because they reimagine, use, consume and transform cities through the distinct spatiotemporal patterns of their practices. The authors show how the rights of skateboard activists can be undermined by those of economic consumers that city authorities across the world are seeking to entice through city rebranding and redesign. Through the case of Newcastle upon Tyne, or the 'Toon' in the local vernacular, they discuss the 'counter-practices' of skateboarders as they engage in an evolving, although not necessarily antagonistic, contest with city authorities as part of their spatiotemporal tactics to access the city centre and renegotiate city rights and, hence, contest neoliberal articulations of the city as profit seeking machine. The chapter also demonstrates the contribution of skateboarders to the remaking of the city through their regeneration of left over spaces that are ignored by global financial capital and remain largely barren outside its spatiotemporal cycles.

In Chapter 8, Teresa Strachan and Elisa Lopez-Capel draw on their engagement projects with young people in the east end of Newcastle to show how they create meaningful relationships with local open spaces and how significant these places are for their experience in and of the city. The authors demonstrate the disjuncture between the perception of open spaces by young people and by city planners. They argue that while others (including planners) might see the young people's selected open spaces as 'ordinariness' and 'despoiled', they themselves consider them as places where they build friendships, identities and a sense of place in society and the city. Their account presents a vivid example of the gap between what Lefebvre calls the conceived spaces of technocrats and the lived spaces of everyday life. They suggest that the absence of participatory processes, which can enable young people to exert influence over the decisions made about their valued places can explain why such a gap is so persistent and why young people experience a marginalisation of their political 'right to the city'. Through their photographic images and poems, we hear the voices of young people and see the city through their eyes when a busy dual carriageway becomes an 'Urban Horizon', a vista onto the south banks of the Tyne becomes 'Paris', and the back lanes of a typical Tyneside terraced street depicts 'Poverty'.

Together the contributions to this section of the book explore questions of spatial justice in relation to ordinary cities. Their detailed discussions of particular cases illustrate the very different contexts in which contests over city spaces – and their meanings – shape people's everyday lives. All three chapters draw on Lefebvre's concept of the 'right to the city' and together they demonstrate the usefulness of the idea for thinking about how people are marginalised by their cities and how they can respond to their marginalisation by reimagining city spaces. We see that any emancipatory politics necessarily involve not only a struggle for justice *in* space but also a struggle *for* spatial justice or the right to the city.

Reference

Pirie G.H. (1983) 'On spatial justice', *Environment and Planning A,* 15: 465–73.

SIX

Fit and miss-fit: the global spread of urban spatial injustice

Suzanne Speak and Ashok Kumar

Introduction

This chapter discusses justice and fairness in the two cities of Delhi, India and Newcastle upon Tyne, England. At first view these two cities may seem very different. Newcastle is a provincial city of a little over 280,000 people in an industrialised country and, as the title of the book suggests, might be thought of as just an 'ordinary city'. Conversely, Delhi is the capital city of what might still be considered as a 'developing country'. It is also, importantly, a mega city with a population estimated to be between 18 and 25 million. Its aggressive striving to be a 'world class city', as detailed in its master plan (Delhi Development Authority, 2005), conditions much of its urban policy.

However, it is these very differences that make the comparison between the two cities so valuable for a focus on justice and fairness in an 'ordinary city' for several reasons. First, much of the literature on urban injustice, especially in relation to urban planning policy and practice, focuses on the 'developing world', where stark examples of injustice are to be seen (see for example Watson, 2003; Fernandes, 2004). Second, injustice perpetrated in the cause of 'world city' status is also well documented (see for example Roy and Ong, 2011; Speak, 2013). Third, as Robinson (2006) suggests, the 'world city' status itself presents a limited understanding of the complexity of cities. A hierarchy of cities, which places some at the top as 'world cities', focuses attention on a small fraction of cities and the economic activities, policies and institutions that exist mainly in those cities and which might influence distributive justice. It emphasises the similarities between these 'world cities', overlooking the diversity of existence within them. Moreover, it places them in a category apart from other cities and in doing so diverts attention from the similarities they may share with smaller 'ordinary' cities lower down the hierarchy.

Regardless of their place in any perceived hierarchy or typology, in cities around the world, there exists a struggle for territory between economy and society, nature and development, the affluent and the poor. This struggle involves an overlapping of physical structures, memories and narratives as different groups or activities seek to occupy and exist within the same spaces. This sets up a battle for physical territory of the city, which is well documented within literature on rights to the city, rights to land and rights to adequate housing (Watson, 2003, 2006; Fernandes, 2004; Roy and Ong, 2011). These discourses explore the right to occupy the physicality of the city, to utilise, alter and reform its space. However, less well represented is the struggle for the right to occupy, alter and reform the concept of the city in line with an individual's or community's values, in effect, to challenge the very nature of 'urban'.

Faced with what Blinder (2006) refers to as the second and third industrial revolutions, borne of free market capitalism and globalised trade, it appears that the conflicts between different values and attitudes of urban populations are as strong as they were in Europe during the first industrial revolution. In this context of urban diversity, increasing urban poverty and social inequity similar to that of earlier centuries, many city authorities, particularly in the 'developing world', are striving to present an image of a contemporary urbane existence. In doing so, authorities prescribe a 'new orthodoxy of the urbane' (Speak, 2014) that is totally irrelevant to many of the city's inhabitants, and set up a conflict that is as much over behaviour as it is over territory. In short, they seek to forget, hide or eliminate those who 'don't fit' the urbane image.

The 'world city' narrative in developing countries is the most visible manifestation of this 'new orthodoxy'. It is an attempt to achieve cities of homogenous physical and social characteristics that are suited to economic growth at all costs. It is routinely played out through violent demolitions, evictions and displacements (Baviskar, 2006). Ignoring social and economic aspirations of more than half of their inhabitants, city and state governments are attempting to remake Mumbai in the image of Shanghai, and Delhi in the image of London (DuPont, 2011). These are cities hosting 'world class' commercial, residential, recreational and circulation spaces meant for high and middle income professionals working in high end knowledge industries.

The objective of planning under this rationale is the retention of the new urban elite and the setting up of the environment for the capture of international inward investment, leading to what Schuurman considers as 'a global, exploitative capitalism' (Schuurman, 2000: 10).

This requires demonstration of order and control in the public realm and the laying down of an internationally recognised and accepted form of 'urban normality' (Madanipour, 1998; Fernandes, 2004). The poor, and those whose values challenge the mainstream, are exiled or hidden, through political processes of institutional 'forgetting' (Fernandes, 2004) to make space for the world class cities and activities. This chapter questions both the fairness and the logic of this control.

Conceptualising urban injustice in Newcastle and Delhi

In order to develop a dialectical and comprehensive understanding of the control of behaviour and the remaking of political spaces, we have adopted the three formulations of the 'Right to the City', the 'Right to Difference' and the 'Spatial Dialectics of Injustice' (Lefebvre, 1996; Harvey, 2003, 2008). We now use these three conceptualisations of urban justice to explore the situation in our two cities.

Right to the city and struggles for the 'centrality'

The concept of 'rights to the city' opens up potential opportunities for all citizens to make claims about city spaces as per their desires and aspirations, rather than simply those within narrowly defined collectives based on certain social and economic criteria such as class, gender or caste. As David Harvey argues:

> The right to the city is far more than the individual liberty to access urban resources: it is a right to change ourselves by changing the city. It is, moreover, a common rather than an individual right since this transformation inevitably depends upon the exercise of a collective power to reshape the processes of urbanization. (Harvey, 2008: 23)

The 'right to the city' concept offers a challenge to normalised discourses, particularly those established to control collective power and demands for political change. For example, the normalised discourse on 'concentrated poverty' in America overlooks the fact that 'de-concentration' leads directly to the destruction and degradation of the political spaces that the urban poor have struggled to construct over decades (Samara, 2012: 39–40). In dispersing the poor to address 'concentrated poverty' their collaborative political challenge can be diluted and controlled. The need for control arises because political spaces have 'the potential to remake citizenship and to produce a new urban polity, both of these tasks being key components in the formation of a democratic form of counter-governance' (Samara, 2012: 40).

Lefebvre (1996) views the urban as a socio-spatial form of 'centrality'. Therefore, struggles to secure the right to the city equate to struggles to at least influence, if not control, the 'centrality'. It may be argued that the least acceptable urban behaviour is that likely to challenge the primary doctrine and destabilise the incumbent political authority. Such behaviour is growing in cities around the world where there are ongoing struggles for 'centrality'. Nevertheless, rights to the city are still being denied and struggles for 'centrality' are still being controlled spatially in our two cities.

In Delhi, under the Bhagidari (partnership) scheme, the state government set up an intermediate link between government and the general public through the establishment of new organisations called Resident Welfare Associations (RWA) at neighbourhood level. RWAs, whose members come mainly from middle and high income groups, mediate between 'the public', including members of low income groups and slum dwellers, and city authorities. Thus, the creation of an institution like the RWAs can be thought of as the gentrification of democracy and political association, which was once more fully open to the public (Ghertner, 2014: 201). In this we see a form of spatial injustice whereby opportunities for the urban poor to represent their claims and grievances directly to the city government have been controlled and foreclosed by being mediated through a different group of residents with different, and often conflicting, values and needs.

Newcastle, in North East England, is a city built upon the coal mining industry and was badly affected by the Tory pit closures in 1992. These were presented, ostensibly, as an act of economic logic as Britain pushed forwards into a new era of service sector and information economy. Many saw it as the more general demonising of old, industrial ways and very clearly, in favour of a specific form of contemporary urban existence and livelihood not represented by mining, miners or their pit villages, of which there were many within the Newcastle area (Milne, 2004).

However, in bringing an end to a traditional form of livelihood and way of life for entire communities over many generations, what Thatcher was really doing was punishing miners for their 1984-85 industrial action (Milne, 2004). In breaking the miners, the Tory government broke the unions, destroying the struggle for 'centrality' and a potential form of democratic counter-governance. The destruction of the unions, and the unity of mining communities more generally, destroyed the vehicle for solidarity through which communities around Newcastle, as well as many other 'ordinary cities' in the UK, might make their claims upon government, ensuring that they had no access to 'centrality'.

However, despite this 'elimination of the possibilities for the formation of political responses' (Dikeç, 2001: 1792), as Robinson (2002) notes:

> 10 years after the last pit closed – that community, that social cohesion, is celebrated on union banners, with slogans like 'Unity is Strength', 'United we Stand' and 'An Injury to One is Injury to All'. These, and other slogans on the banners – 'Through Struggle Comes Change' and 'Workers of the World Unite' may seem to belong to a distant, past world. In fact, they connect directly (and dangerously) with universal concerns... (Robinson, 2002: 331)

In both the mega city of Delhi and the ordinary city of Newcastle we can see that, by removing or diluting the mechanisms to support solidarity of the urban poor, governments can undermine the ability of communities or individuals to exert their claims on the 'centrality' and their rights to shape the city in a manner suitable for their needs.

The right to difference

The right to difference argues against the dominance or privileging of specific, predetermined classifications and groupings, especially those built upon class, ethnicity or culture, through which people might validate their rights to exert influence. As McCann (1999) notes, the right to difference is:

> [...] the right of every social group to be involved in all levels of decision making which shape the control and organization of social space. It is also the right not to be excluded from the spaces of the city center and segregated in residential neighborhoods. The right to the city is logically extended by the right to difference: the right to be free from externally imposed, pre-established classifications of identity. (McCann, 1999: 181)

The right to difference, in this way, complements the right to the city. Henri Lefebvre has conceived the right to difference in a manner which has connotations similar to being able to disagree and contest.

The right to difference stresses that people are able to refuse to be classified into categories determined by the 'homogenising powers'. To accept solidarities built around particularities imposed by dominant others would mean to accept marginalisation and remain entrapped in established categories. This right also implies that people have a right to resist the imposition of prescribed behaviour or lifestyles and create differential spaces, which best represent their own identities. This right, like the right to the city, is obtained through political struggles, which are manifest in concrete and material practices. For example, the right to difference can be seen in the construction of physical environments that represent an ethnic or cultural identity or way of life. Unlike the liberal view of multiculturalism, Lefebvre's right to difference is 'transformational-dialectical, not affirmative and deconstructive' (Kipfer et al, 2012: 120).

Translators of Henri Lefebvre's *Writings on Cities*, Kofman and Lebas (1996) further elaborate the relationship between the right to the city and the right to difference:

> The right to the city, complemented by the right to difference and right to information, should modify, concretize and make more practical the rights of the citizen as an urban dweller (citadin) and user of multiple services. It would affirm, on one hand, the right of the users to make known their ideas on the space and time of their activities in the urban area; it would also cover the right to the use of the center, a privileged place, instead of being dispersed and stuck into ghettos (for workers, immigrants, the 'marginal' and even for the privileged). (Kofman and Lebas, 1996: 34)

The dominance of neoliberal rationality is strongly represented by the spread of a globally recognised and accepted urban orthodoxy bringing so much social and physical change to cities around the world. It is manifest in the homogeneity of cities through international corporate investment, particularly in real estate, and the increasing privatisation of public space of the city (Madanipour, 1998). This homogeneity resists the demonstration of social, cultural and physical difference (see for example, Sandercock, 1998; Soja, 2010; Samara, 2012).

However, difference exists and is increasing. Watson (2006) refers to the 'deep difference' within the widening socioeconomic and cultural diversity in cities of the Global South. She identifies two main forms of difference. The first is between groups within society, generated by material, ethnic, religious or racial difference. The second is 'state-citizen' differences, referring to conflicts between the everyday needs of the population and the systems and processes of governance and management. Both of these differences alert us to the perceived problems of the fractured public interest (Bollens, 2004) and difference which, unless controlled and contained within and by urban policy, is perceived as dangerous.

The 'state-citizen' difference is often addressed by reconstructing the spatial locations of those differences, and those who inhabit them, as places and people of threat. Dikeç (2004) demonstrates that, in the first place, social injustice occurs by representing difference as dangerous, highlighting violent or dangerous incidents occurring in places that are constructed afresh in the public psyche, as places of menace and danger. Once this is done, places such as slums appear as reconstituted objects for policy interventions to address newly constructed or imagined problems and threats.

In Delhi, the right to difference of large swathes of the urban population is neither recognised nor respected. This is seen most clearly in evictions, relocations and control of the activities of the urban poor. Livelihood activities of the poor, and slum settlement in which many are undertaken, are represented by the authorities and media as unsightly, uncontrolled and potentially dangerous.

In support of action to evict urban informal settlers and stop their livelihood activities, environmental law cases in the high court have followed a similar trend in discourse, turning slums and informal settlements from poor but functioning residential areas, into sites characterised entirely by inadequate housing, environmental hazard, criminality and 'nuisance'. Nuisance is officially defined[1] as: 'obstruction to a public place or way, trades or activities hazardous to the surrounding community, flammable substances, objects that could fall or cause injury, unfenced excavations or wells, or unconfined and dangerous animals' (Ghertner, 2011: 26). The inclusion of 'trades or activities hazardous to the surrounding community' in the definition of nuisance, offers ample opportunity to control basic livelihood behaviour of the poor (Baskivar, 2003) or to vilify an entire settlement or community as dangerous.

One example of this control and prohibition of livelihood activity can be seen in Old Delhi. In 2006, the Delhi High Court, ruled in favour of a complete ban on handcarts and cycle rickshaws in the Chandni Chowk area of Old Delhi, near the historic Red Fort (Institute for Transport and Development Policy, 2006). The ruling was presented as a move to ease traffic congestion and begin the implementation of an alternative mass transport system[2] (which, at the time of writing a decade later, has not been introduced). Discourse on sustainability and environmental pollution was used to justify the action. However, handcarts and cycle rickshaws are the least polluting forms of transport and haulage available and there can be little logic in removing them in order to prioritise the motor vehicle. In doing so, the authorities were effectively destroying the livelihood activities of hundreds, possibly thousands, of people, removing them from sight and attempting to remake Old Delhi, with its rich traditional identity, into a more modern city.

Another example of the control of behaviour and remaking of identity is the redevelopment of a 50 year old slum settlement known as Kathputli Colony (Puppeteers' Colony). Near the increasingly affluent Shadipur neighbourhood of Delhi, Kathputli Colony is home to some 3,500 families. They are predominantly Rajasthani performers and include puppeteers, magicians, snake charmers, acrobats, singers, dancers, actors and musicians. The settlement is widely recognised as one of the largest communities of traditional performers and artisans in India, if not the world.

In April 2014 the Delhi Development Authority (DDA) began what it termed as a 'temporary relocation' of the Kathputli community into a transit camp, while it began demolishing the settlement to make way for luxury apartments and a shopping mall. The official intention is to return the original settlers to purpose built high rise apartments within the area which, the authority claims, will be a 'modern artistes community with facilities to nurture and showcase street art' (Bhowmick, 2014). However, Kathputli residents are opposed to this development, objecting to being forced into high rise apartments with little space. Their livelihood activities require outside space, freedom of movement, reciprocity and stimulation, which is developed within the organic form of an informal settlement built on shared interest and activities. One resident noted, "Our art dictates our lifestyle and our lifestyle is our identity; the lifestyle of a multi-storey building is not for us" (Bhowmick, 2014).

This imposition of DDA's blueprint for high rise housing in the city demonstrates a lack of understanding of how different sectors of society live and work. Moreover, it represents the desire to deny difference and superimpose a single, acceptable residential identity, and thus lifestyle, upon the city and its people (Speak, 2013).

While the commitment to improve the quality of life of Delhi's poor is laudable, this determination to force them to conform to a specific housing style is counterproductive and denies their rights to determine a different and more suitable lifestyle and residential form. It has already proved to have negative implications for quality of life.

In Newcastle also, we can see the denial and demonisation of cultural difference in the treatment of Gypsy and Traveller communities. In October 2011, around 20 Traveller families who had been evicted from their site in Dale Farm, Essex, parked their caravans and transit vans near to the headquarters of the Sage software company, in the Great Park area of Gosforth, a middle-class suburb of Newcastle. Local media reported the concerns of residents with comments such as these from residents of the Great Park residential estate:

> 'We have travellers that come back here every year at around the same time. The travellers usually stay for about three or four days, but I wouldn't be very happy if they were there for a long stretch.'

> 'It has been reported to the police that they are there. My husband called and we were told it is being dealt with.' (Wearmouth, 2011)

It is ironic in this case that the land on which the travellers rested was originally green belt land, protected from development. It was declassified to facilitate the development of a major new business park, primarily to accommodate the headquarters of Sage, the city's flagship international software company, and a subsequent major upmarket housing development. One might argue that the inappropriate activity to be controlled in this case is, in fact, the permanent development and business and not the cyclical, temporary travellers.

In a similar incident the *Northern Echo* reported the arrival of travellers at the Team Valley Trading Estate in Gateshead, just the other side of the River Tyne from Newcastle. In somewhat emotive language, the report noted 'Last week, *hundreds* of travellers *took over* Team Valley Trading Estate, in Gateshead. They brought with them around 30 caravans, cars, vans and *gas cylinders* after hundreds were evicted from Dale Farm ... ' (author's emphasis) (Davies, 2011).

What is interesting here is not only the reporting of somewhat spurious numbers but the importance of 'gas cylinders', presumably to emphasise the potential threat to the otherwise safe area. Given that the area hosts many small industrial and manufacturing units, using chemicals, gas and other potentially hazardous products, this seems an unrealistic concern.

The increasing 'privatisation' of public space, seen in both mega cities such as Delhi and ordinary cities like Newcastle, provides a backdrop against which difference is more starkly evident and uncomfortable in the urban realm. Much of the development within the public/ private realm is driven by corporate financial investment in real estate. Such investment needs to be protected and managed, not left open to manipulation or control by the general public (Madanipour, 1998). Thus, malls, plazas, gated estates must also be controlled and protected from activities and behaviour likely to diminish their capital value or returns. It is this protection of capital, as much as protection of the public, which drives the demonisation of difference and a demand for conformity.

Discussing the removal of urban difference in the expanding cities of the developing world, Sibley (1995), considers it as a politics of 'spatial purification'. In Newcastle, this purification can be seen in the case of the redevelopment of Eldon Square shopping centre. Until its redevelopment in 2010 the area of Old Eldon Square, in the very heart of the city was an open green area with a war memorial, which formed a barrier between two elements of the 1970s -build Eldon Square shopping centre. Given its prime location, the area was economically underproductive. However, it had for many years been a favourite meeting place for groups of young people who associated themselves with the 'Goth' movement and fashion.

The city's redevelopment plans for Old Eldon Square included opening up a thoroughfare across the square to enable easy access to new leisure and retail facilities along its edges and to the shopping centre. Any resistance to the plans was, no doubt, diminished by an incident in 2003 when a young man was burned in a clash between Goths and other local youths. In a news report entitled 'Fears over teen group rivalries', the BBC noted, 'The increasing animosity between Goths and Charvers[3] has drawn comparison with the Mods and Rockers clashes of the 1960s and late 70s' (BBC News online, 2003). As horrific as the event was for the young man involved, it was presented as being much more threatening to the general public than it was in reality.

Although examples from Delhi and Newcastle are manifest at different scales they show very similar demonization and denial of difference in support of economic policies and the pursuit of economic growth. They represent the privileging of one rationale – capitalist economics, over other, arguably equally valid, rationales of household livelihood or expression of self, or community identity. In both cases we see the overlaying of a predetermined blueprint for not only the physical design of the urban area, be it residential or commercial, but also the identities, activities and behaviour deemed acceptable within it. In both cases, to greater or lesser degrees, we see the representation of difference as deviance and threat.

Spatial dialectics of injustice

Our third conceptualisation seeks to understand urban injustice in a dialectical manner rather than in an essentialist causal way. In order to investigate spatial injustice Dikeç (2009) has developed two dialectically intertwined formulations. These are the 'spatiality of injustice' and the 'injustice of spatiality'. 'Spatiality of injustice' is based on the premise that justice has a spatial dimension to it, and that one can observe and analyse various forms of injustice manifest *in space*. 'Injustice of spatiality' shifts the focus from spatial manifestations of injustice to structural dynamics that produce and reproduce injustice through space. The focus, therefore, is not merely on the spatial manifestations of injustice, but equally importantly, on the spatial processes and practices that produce injustices.

Connecting these terms together, Dikeç (2001) has coined a third term, the 'spatial dialectics of injustice'. 'Spatial dialectics of injustice', he argues, range 'from physical or locational aspects to more abstract spaces of social and economic relationships that sustain the production of injustice' (Dikeç, 2001: 1792). He argues that these relationships and processes are evident in 'the organization of property markets, housing, rent, and tax policies, etc., which the notion of the injustice of spatiality tries to capture' (Dikeç, 2001: 1799).

In Delhi these processes are starkly evident in municipal slum relocation policy, which is justified, ostensibly, in the name of modernisation, economic development, adequate housing and environmental improvement. In 2002, the policy was directed towards 11 slums on the banks of the Yamuna Pushta River. Over the following decade the Municipal Corporation of Delhi (MCD) evicted the slum settlers and moved them to a relocation settlement at Bhalaswa Jahangir Puri, around 25 km from the original slums. The site is situated between a polluted lake on one side and a municipal rubbish tip on the other. Despite the discourse on environmental improvement and adequate housing used to justify the relocations, no housing or services were provided on the site. Households were simply leased a dwelling plot of between 12 and 18 m^2 (the size of an average bedroom in the UK) for 10 years at a cost of around Rupees 7,000 (£106). This is a considerable sum of money for the urban poor to pay.

At the time of writing, over a decade later, the environment of the site remains extremely poor. There is no functioning drainage and the area becomes waterlogged in the rainy season, when sewer water contaminates the ground. Standing water is a significant health hazard and MCD must fumigate frequently to kill malarial mosquitoes. Water, mainly brought in by tanker, is limited in supply and poor in quality. After some campaigning, taps were installed (one tap to 30 households, approximately 150 people), but groundwater remains contaminated by the adjacent landfill site. Energy is produced by each household using diesel generators. Food is cooked over wood fires or kerosene stoves.

Food security is the greatest priority for the urban poor. As no retail facilities were provided, the settlers tried to establish their own makeshift retail market, made of planks of wood erected on the roads around the site. These were destroyed by the authorities. The settlers come mainly from rural backgrounds and have good agricultural skills. When asked if they might be supported to use an area of wasteland in the settlement to grow some crops or keep small livestock, one MCD official noted "[Bhalaswa] is an urban extension, not a rural place, it's not appropriate, they can go to the market to buy their food, they don't need to grow it, beside, the land is not good" (personal communication to author 17/3/2009).

There is no possibility of employment in or near the site and the financial and time costs of travel to the city centre and back for work every day are prohibitive. Thus, men who work in the city must stay there. They sleep on the streets in the city in order to save money and return home when they can to bring money to the family. Ironically, this encourages street sleeping and pavement dwelling, types of behaviour reviled by the authorities (Speak, 2004). Despite the rhetoric of adequate housing and environmental improvement, it was clear from the start of the slum relocation that housing policy was being used as a structural tool to facilitate social engineering towards achieving their goal of 'world class city' status.

In Newcastle also, we see the wisdom of Dikeç's (2001) words clearly within policy on housing renewal, and especially in the emphasis on mixed tenure housing areas. For example, in 2002 the Walker Riverside regeneration scheme became part of the government's Housing Market Renewal Initiative (HMRI) (see for example, Cameron, 2003). The initiative was developed in response to increasing area abandonment in ordinary cities across the West Midlands and the North of England. HMRI had two aims: economically, it sought to deter the affluent from leaving the area, socially, it hoped to civilise and control such neighbourhoods, which are frequently represented as places of criminality, danger and civil unrest (see for example, Uitermark et al, 2007; Cameron, 2003).

Undoubtedly there was abandonment of many poorer neighbourhoods. However, the extent of outcry from residents of Walker, and other areas affected by HMRI, over the loss of community, identity and social ties, indicated that many people still viewed these areas and their housing as home and grieved for its loss (Robinson, 2005). The fact that the neighbourhoods were old and largely run down did not detract from their social value for many residents. Indeed, much of the controversy was over the fact that many homes were perfectly adequate and that demolition of them was neither economically nor environmentally logical.

Controversial from the start, some have argued that HMRI amounts to a political processes of social engineering or ethnic cleansing (Cameron, 2003). Moreover, Webb (2010) argues that, despite rhetoric about community involvement within the HMRIs, it was confined always to the delivery phase and communities were not allowed to challenge the logic or nature of the intervention itself. Webb notes, 'alternative realities, values and priorities represent a danger of distancing delivery from the HMRI rationality, they are a threat to the scientific nature of the HMRI, and must be risk managed' (Webb, 2010: 325).

In these cases in Delhi and Newcastle we can see Dikeç's (2001) 'spatial dialectics of injustice' played out in both its formulations. In both cases there is injustice *in space* of the systematic dismantling of functioning, stable, if poor neighbourhoods and communities. However, we can also recognise the processes, in this case processes of the market in relation to housing demolition and renewal, which produce and reproduce injustice *through space*.

Conclusions

The case studies presented in this chapter, from two ostensibly very different cities, clearly show that urban injustice and unfairness exists in both mega cities of the Global South and in the ordinary, provincial cities of the Global North, including the UK. The fact that the scale and form of that injustice might be different, at least to the outside view, presents a danger that we might overlook, or be complacent about, injustice in ordinary cities. This is especially the case for those ordinary cities of the Global North, where still, notwithstanding unemployment and the diminution of the welfare state, life for the majority of people is very far removed from, and materially better than, that of evicted slum dwellers in Delhi.

It is the very great difference in scale that makes the need for a conceptual framework for identifying and understanding urban injustice all the greater. The three conceptualisations presented here allow us to step back from scale or experience of urban injustice and see it in terms of the processes and practices which *use* the space of the city to perpetrate injustices *within* the space of the city, whether that city is seen as a mega city or an ordinary city. While subtly different in their framing of both the causes and manifestations of urban injustice, all their conceptualisations reveal similar key issues of denial of rights, demonisation of difference and manipulation of the populace. Moreover, in revealing the mechanisms and outcomes of unjust spatial practices, these conceptualisations of spatial injustice allow us to recognise that for those adversely affected, the mega city of Delhi is, actually, just an ordinary city too.

Notes

[1] Under Section 133 of the Code of Criminal Procedure 1973 of India.

[2] A decade later the only mass transit system in operation is the Delhi Metro, which does transport goods in the area and is of no use for moving around Old Delhi.

[3] Colloquial terms in the UK for a young, working-class person whose tastes and style are considered unsophisticated, vulgar or 'common'.

References

Baskivar, A. (2003) 'Between violence and despair: space, power and identity in the making of metropolitan Delhi', *International Social Science*, 55: 89-98.

Baskivar, A. (2006) 'Demolishing Delhi: world class city in the making', *Mute*, 2(3): 88-95.

BBC News online (2003) 'Fears over teen group rivalries', [online] Available at: http://news.bbc.co.uk/1/hi/england/tyne/3132291.stm [accessed January 2016].

Blinder, A.S. (2006) 'Offshoring: the next industrial revolution?', *Foreign Affairs*, 113-28.

Bollens, S. (2004) 'Urban planning and intergroup conflict: confronting a fractured public Interest', in B. Stiftel and V. Watson (eds) *Dialogues in urban and regional planning*, London and New York: Routledge, pp 209-46.

Bhowmick, N. (2014) 'The world's largest community of street performers is about to be torn apart', *Time.com,* [online] Available at: http://time.com/12073/india-kathputli-colony-of-street-artists-to-be-demolished/ [Accessed January 2016].

Cameron, S. (2003) 'Gentrification, housing redifferentiation and urban regeneration: "Going for Growth" in Newcastle upon Tyne', *Urban Studies,* 40(12): 2367-82.

Davies, K. (2011) 'Hundreds of travellers descend on Gateshead', *Chronicle Live,* [online] Available at: http://www.chroniclelive.co.uk/news/north-east-news/hundreds-travellers-descend-gateshead-1406327 [accessed January 2016].

Davis, M. (2006) *Planet of Slums,* London: Verso.

Delhi Development Authority (2005) *Draft master plan for Delhi 2021.* [online] Available at: http://www.dda.org.in/planning/draft_master_plans.htm [accessed January 2016].

Dikeç, M. (2001) 'Justice and the spatial imagination', *Environment and Planning A*, 33: 1785-1805.

Dikeç, M. (2004) 'Voices into noises: ideological determination of unarticulated justice movements', *Space and Polity*, 8(2): 191-208.

Dikeç, M. (2009) 'Space, politics and (in) justice', *Spatial Justice*, 33:1-14.

DuPont, V. (2011) 'The dream of Delhi as a global city', *International Journal of Urban and Regional Research*, 35(3): 533-554.

Fernandes, L. (2004) 'The politics of forgetting: class politics, state power and the restructuring of urban space in India', *Urban Studies,* 41(12): 2415-30.

Ghertner, D.A. (2011) 'Rule by aesthetics: world-class city making in Delhi', in A. Roy and A. Ong (eds) *Worlding cities: Asian experiments and the art of being global*, pp 279-306.

Ghertner, D.A. (2014) 'India's urban revolution: geographies of displacement beyond gentrification', *Environment and Planning A*, 46(7): 1554-71.

Harvey, D. (1996) *Justice, nature and the geography of difference*, Oxford: Blackwell.

Harvey, D. (2003) 'The right to the city', *International Journal of Urban and Regional Research*, 27(4): 939-41.

Harvey, D. (2008) 'The right to the city', *New Left Review*, 53: 23-40.

Institute for Transport and Development Policy (2006) *Position of ITDP on the recent Delhi High Court decision to ban cycle rickshaws on Old Delhi roads*, [online] New York: ITDP. Available at: https://www.itdp.org/position-paper-on-the-delhi-high-court-decision-to-ban-cycle-rickshaws-on-old-delhi-roads/ [accessed January 2016].

Kofman, E. and Lebas, E. (1996) 'Lost in transposition – time, space and the city', in E. Kofman and E. Lebas (eds) *Writings on cities*, Oxford: Blackwell, pp 3-60.

Lefebvre, H. (1996) *Writings on cities* (translated by E. Kofman and E. Lebas), Oxford: Blackwell.

Madanipour, A. (1998) 'Social exclusion and space', in A. Madanipour, G. Cars, and J. Allen (eds) *Social exclusion in European cities: Processes, experiences, responses*, London: Jessica Kingsley, pp 75-94.

McCann, E.J. (1999) 'Race, protest, and public space: contextualizing Lefebvre in the US city', *Antipode*, 3(2):163-84.

Milne, S. (2004) *The enemy within: The secret war against the miners*, London: Verso.

Robinson, F. (2002) 'The North East: A journey through time', *City*, 6(3): 317-34.

Robinson, C. (2005) 'Grieving home'. *Social & Cultural Geography*, 6(1): 47-60.

Robinson, J. (2006). *Ordinary cities: Between modernity and development* (4). Oxford: Psychology Press.

Roy, A. and Ong, A. (2011) *Worlding cities, Asian experiments and the art of being global*, Oxford: Wiley-Blackwell.

Samara, T.S. (2012) 'Citizens in search of a city: towards a new infrastructure of political belonging', in M.P. Smith and M. McQuarrie (eds) *Remaking urban citizenship: Organizations, institutions, and the right to the city*, London: Transaction Publishers, pp 39-56.

Sandercock, L. (1998) *Towards cosmopolis: Planning for multicultural cities*, Chichester: John Wiley and Sons Ltd.

Schmid, C. (2008) 'Henri Lefebvre's theory of the production of space: towards a three dimensional dialectic', in K. Goonewardena, S. Kipfer, R. Milgrom and C. Schmid (eds) *Space, difference and everyday life, reading Henri Lefebvre*, London: Routledge, pp 27-45.

Schuurman, F.J. (2000) 'Paradigms lost, paradigms regained? Development studies in the twenty-first century', *Third World Quarterly*, 21(1): 7-20.

Sibley, D. (1995) *Geographies of exclusion*, London: Routledge.

Soja, E. (2010) *Seeking spatial justice*, Minneapolis, MN: University of Minnesota Press.

Speak, S. (2004) 'Degrees of destitution: A typology of homelessness for developing countries', *Housing Studies* 19(3): 465–82.

Speak, S. (2013) 'Values as a tool for conceptualising homelessness in the global south', *Habitat International*, 38:143-49.

Speak, S. (2014) 'Desperation, delight or deviance: conflicting cultural landscapes of the urban poor in developing countries.' in M. Roe and K. Taylor (eds) *New cultural landscapes*, Oxford: Routledge, pp 136-52.

Stefan, K, Saberi, P. and Wieditz, T. (2012) 'Henri Lefebvre: debates and controversies', *Progress in Human Geography*, 37(1): 115-34.

Uitermark, J., Duyvendak, J.W. and Kleinhans, R. (2007) 'Gentrification as a governmental strategy. Social control and social cohesion in Hoogvliet, Rotterdam', *Environment and Planning A* 39(1): 125–41.

Watson, V. (2003) 'Conflicting rationalities: implications for planning theory and ethics'. *Planning Theory and Practice,* 4(4): 395–407.

Watson, V. (2006) 'Deep difference: diversity, planning and ethics'. *Planning Theory*, 5 (1): 31-50.

Watson, V. (2009) 'The planned city sweeps the poor away, urban planning and 21st century urbanization', *Progress in Planning*, 72(3): 151-93.

Webb, D. (2010). 'Rethinking the role of markets in urban renewal: the housing market renewal initiative in England'. *Housing, Theory and Society*, 27(4): 313-31.

Wearmouth, R. (2011) 'Travellers set up camp on Newcastle's Great Park', *The Journal online*, [online] Available at: http://www.thejournal.co.uk/news/north-east-news/travellers-set-up-camp-newcastles-4419224 [accessed January 2016].

SEVEN

Toonsformation: skateboarders' renegotiation of city rights

Lee Pugalis, Jon Swords, Michael Jeffries and Bob Giddings

Introduction

We live in an era when ideals of human rights have moved centre stage both politically and ethically. A great deal of energy is expended in promoting their significance for the construction of a better world. But for the most part the concepts circulating do not fundamentally challenge hegemonic liberal and neoliberal market logics, or the dominant modes of legality and state action. We live, after all, in a world in which the rights of private property and the profit rate trump all other notions of rights (Harvey, 2008: 23).

According to scholars such as Harvey, the rights of citizens are being displaced by the rights of the consumer. The renegotiation of rights can be related to the continuous process of spatial capitalist restructuring, which informs and is informed by social, cultural and democratic challenges including calls for 'justice' and 'fairness', however understood and interpreted. Urban activism has been foregrounded in the global public consciousness, with nok events including, the uprisings culminating in what is now referred to as the Arab Spring and anti-capitalist demonstrations initiated in New York ('Occupy Wall Street'), which subsequently spread around the world ('Occupy Movement').[1] The causes are complex and various, and the objectives diffuse, including revolts against political oppression, social exclusion, and the tyranny of economic liberalism and predatory capitalism. Such movements are helping to reframe the rights of citizens and reenergise debates, particularly at the city scale. They are concerned with spatial justice and fairness and expressed through notions such as the 'just city' (Fainstein, 2014).

Drawing inspiration from the renegotiation of the rights of global urban citizens and new theoretical deliberations (Soja, 2010; Fainstein, 2014; Marcuse, 2014), we seek to explore the right of a particular subculture – urban sports activists and specifically skateboarders[2] – to produce space. Skateboarders are often represented by city authorities (including politicians, local government officers, city centre managers, police officers and security guards) as 'unruly elements' (Harvey, 2008), which infringe the rights of consumers and do damage to the urban fabric. But, members of urban sports communities – urban sports activists – including skateboarders, free runners and BMX bikers – can also be perceived as producers of urban city space as they reimagine, use, consume and transform cities through distinct spatiotemporal patterns. Thus, we deploy the term 'activist' in the sense that they are actively producing and reproducing the city through everyday practices. Of particular interest are the rights of skateboard activists vis-à-vis economic consumers, which city authorities across the world are seeking to entice through city rebranding and redesign (Harvey, 1990).

Through the case of Newcastle upon Tyne, or the 'Toon' to invoke local vernacular, we observe the 'counter-practices' of skateboarders as they engage in an evolving, although not necessarily antagonistic contest, with city authorities as part of their spatiotemporal tactics to access the city centre and practise their right to change it (a right to produce space) (Lefebvre, 1991 [1974]). We provide a brief (and therefore partial) tracing of the transformation of Newcastle city centre over recent decades, drawing attention to the implications for skaters and examine the spatial tactics performed by urban sports activists as they attempt to renegotiate their removal from the contemporary neoliberal city. This helps us to generate new empirical insights of fairness and justice from the unique perspectives of skateboarders. Indeed, the subculture of skateboarders is largely neglected in discussions of spatial justice (although Borden's (2001) work is a notable exception) – and skateboarders are typically absent in formal policy debates about city roles and city futures; their voice silenced in elite governance forums and even initiatives such as fairness commissions.

A focus on the spatial practices of skateboarders is instructive as it helps to illuminate the spatiotemporal rhythms of a particular subculture. In particular, the chapter explores how the spatial performance of skateboarders is a tactic deployed to renegotiate city rights, thus remaking and contesting neoliberal articulations of the role of the contemporary city predicated on profit seeking values. In addition, the spatial performance of skateboarders generates constructive relationships with city authorities, consumers and other citizens as urban sports activists seek to access, be and participate in city life. In this way, skateboarders are key producers of city spaces: the regenerators of left over spaces often ignored by global financial capital (although sometimes co-opted) and the energisers of spaces that would otherwise be largely barren outside the temporal cycle of the capitalist working day.

The chapter begins by summarising the work of Henri Lefebvre and David Harvey, who have made significant contributions to theorising the notion of the right to the city. Section two provides contextual detail of how planning and commercial imperatives have altered the city centre of Newcastle and analyses the key implications for skateboarders. This is followed by our case study of the spatial performance of skateboarders in section three, which examines how this particular subculture produces space by accessing, being and participating in city life, before concluding with some brief reflections in the final section.

The production of space and city rights

The production of space is far from being an 'innocent' process as interests collide as they attempt to exert control over different versions of *their city* (Lefebvre, 1991 [1974]; Harvey, 2011; Rosen and Shlay, 2014). 'Control' is a contentious term in the context of urban space as multiple processes coexist and coevolve. Thus, instruments of control, such as land use regulations and legal rights of access, which have powerful effects on the nature and form of the city, are prone to challenge and renegotiation. Minton (2012) argues that recent decades have seen the control and stratification of urban space intensify to produce a neoliberal city and a celebration of privatisation (Lefebvre, 1976). Further, Harvey (2008) attests that the right to the city is increasingly strangled by the privileged few, as new forms of urban 'entrepreneurial' governance apparatus blur the boundaries between civic and commercial objectives, actors and practices (Pugalis and Bentley, 2014). Harvey's examination of spatial dispossession is instructive as it reveals that:

> Surplus absorption through urban transformation has an even darker aspect. It has entailed repeated bouts of urban restructuring through 'creative destruction', which nearly always has a class dimension since it is the poor, the underprivileged and those marginalized from political power that suffer first and foremost from this process. Violence is required to build the new urban world on the wreckage of the old. Haussmann tore through the old Parisian slums, using powers of expropriation in the name of civic improvement and renovation. He deliberately

engineered the removal of much of the working class and other unruly elements from the city centre, where they constituted a threat to public order and political power (Harvey, 2008: 33).

We would also add that the spatial fixing of capital through surplus absorption entails a demographic dimension as well as a class dimension: the rights of younger members of society are typically curtailed, the right to vote (or not) being a prime example. As we discuss below, street sport activists are more often than not categorised as 'unruly elements', which pose a threat to the extant capitalist order of city centres. Examples in Newcastle include attempts to remove, banish and ban skaters from the *public* grounds of Newcastle's cathedral, a *public* car park and a refurbished city centre *public* square. It is as if urban sports activists and other members of society depicted as being unruly are excluded from the broader public; their citizenship curtailed and rights removed. Nevertheless, it is important to note that what Harvey refers to as the 'darker aspect[s]' of urban transformation are not without challenge, exemplified by protest movements, but also more mundane acts, such as those performed by skateboarders, which we examine in the next section of this chapter.

We contend that the Lefebvrian concept of the 'right to the city' can be invoked to challenge hegemonic practices that seek to control urban space (Marcuse, 2014; Purcell, 2014). According to Lefebvre, urban democracy and the right to the city:

> Manifest [themselves] as a superior form of rights: right to freedom, to individualization in socialization, to habitat and to inhabit. The right to the *oeuvre,* to participation and *appropriation* (clearly distinct from the right to property), are implied in the right to the city. (Lefebvre, 1996: 174)

The concept cannot be confined to the right of accessibility – physically, mentally or symbolically – to what pre-exists, but entails a right to *change*: a social right to access, be and participate (Pugalis and Giddings, 2011). Our own reading of the right to the city, a concept that we consider to be crucial to debates concerning justice and fairness, seeps beyond the rights of ownership and access to embrace the progressive politics of 'use value', which is use in respect of active presence and appropriation, a 'right *to claim presence in the city, to wrest the use of the city from privileged new masters and democratize its spaces*' (Isin, 2000: 14, emphasis added). It is the right of all citizens (whether they are permitted to vote or not) to access, be and participate in urban space: a collective right 'to change ourselves by changing the city' (Harvey, 2008: 23).

To 'be' in the city emphasises the temporal aspects of producing space; accomplished through active presence, while the right to 'access' can present as well as constrain opportunities. Commensurate with the production of space, the right to the city requires collaboration and, potentially, contestation; social relationships 'between very different kinds of people' in order to produce a 'counter-space' (Lefebvre, 1991 [1974]: 383). The right to the city also includes aspects of the right to participation. In addition to the right to be, such as occupying urban space, the right to participate is to constitute the (social) production of new, differential spaces through a renewed right to urban life (see Speak and Kumar, Chapter 6, this volume). This helps to emphasise the point that rights are the product of continuous struggle and do not necessarily have a logical end point, which is particularly pertinent in the case of skateboarding. The right to the city is thus an 'active' process of continual struggle, negotiation and contestation.

Urban and city space, in particular, is a contested terrain as different groups and individuals seek to impose or practise their own spatial ideals in order to produce their own version of the city. Due to the finite nature of such space, it is alive with social tensions, relationships and exchanges. Inevitably, the rights of some to access, be and participate in city life, including shaping the contours of city transformations, are prescribed or curtailed by the visions, rules and activities of others. Therefore, such acts generate serious questions relating to spatial justice and fairness (see Bell and Davoudi, Chapter 1, this volume).

Urban sports activists: spatial representations and practices of skateboarders

Spatial tactics including social 'othering' and social 'ordering' have been deployed by city authorities to place particular individuals and groups as belonging to a particular place, such as a city square, or not. For those on the socio-spatial margins or those deemed to be 'out of place' (Shields, 1991; Cresswell, 1996), the implications can be profound. Urban sports activists are routinely regarded as problematic by public and corporate authorities whose representations of space dominate the governance, management and policing of the city (Woolley et al, 2011). In part, this is because urban sports activists are often portrayed as, at best, an unruly nuisance, or, worse still, an obstacle to the legitimate users, that is, consumers (Rogers and Coaffee, 2005). It is what Lefebvre refers to as the displacement of 'lived' and experienced spaces of representation by spatial abstractions (abstract space) and bureaucratic conceptions (conceived space) (Lefebvre, 1991 [1974]).

Skateboarders attract additional opprobrium because of concerns about the damage to street furniture and buildings, the perceived risk to other people from accidental collisions and the possible threat of legal claims in the event of injuries. The common civic responses in many cities, Newcastle included, are legal restrictions denoted with signage warning of fines for transgression, anti-skate obstacles added to street furniture and interventions by police and private security. At the extreme, revanchist forms of urban policy may be pursued as part of strategies to 'civilise the city' (Lees, 2014). In addition, skate parks or tightly-defined spaces permitting urban sport activists (that is, the right to access) may be built and/or designated to lure street sport participants away from prime commercial areas of the neoliberal city (Nemeth, 2006). Such purposeful acts of displacement and spatial dispossession, have often been lauded as 'good practice' by city management professionals, with little pause to consider whether street sport enthusiasts may consider this fair or whether democratic societies may consider this just (Rogers and Coaffee, 2005; Rogers, 2006).

Despite attempts by city authorities to remove street sport participants from city spaces, especially out of the glare of tourists and other consumers, there are moments when the perceived 'cool buzz' of urban sports activists is co-opted by city authorities. Critical interpretations of the co-opting of street sports may argue that these are only thinly disguised commodification endeavours: evidence that the privileged few, the '1%', have strangled the rights of the majority. David Harvey (2011) and Peter Marcuse (2009), for example, questioned 'whose city is it?'. This in turn raises crucial questions about the 'right to the city', when particular users, uses and activities are privileged over others.

Signifying more progressive patterns of urban policy is a pragmatic recognition by city authorities of the value of urban sport activists from a social-safety perspective. In some instances this has led to the redesign and modification of inhospitable places with the objective of producing spaces that are more conducive to street sports (that is, the right to be and to participate). Gateshead City Council, for example, invested £11,000 at the Five Bridges skate spot to enhance its skatability, based on the rationale that the active presence of skaters had a positive impact on the general public's perception of safety (Jenson et al, 2012). In this sense, urban sports activists are presented as the policy solution to tackling broader societal issues, such as antisocial behaviour and street crime. Although examples are relatively rare as well as being site or occasion specific, they help draw attention to a fundamental ambiguity of how city authorities represent urban sport activists: are they urban antagonists to be silenced, curtailed and/or displaced or are they urban energisers or even stewards of the urban environment to be celebrated?

The spatial performance of skateboarders is rather unique as they perceive city spaces in novel ways; envisaging alternative uses for what others may perceive as mundane architecture/urban artefacts. Steps, ledges, hand rails, curbs, walls and benches become challenges of balance, courage and skill. Nevertheless, not all parts of the city are accessible for these groups and it is important to understand the patterns of use, or appropriation, in time and space (see Lefebvre, 2004). Woolley and Johns (2001) identify four interlinking elements that generate places – or spots – conducive to skate. First, accessibility relates to the ease with which the majority of users can travel to and use a spot, with those near to other spots or public transport links preferable. Second, trickability refers to the number and variety of tricks that a spot facilitates. Generally, purposely-designed skate parks and plazas have the highest trickability. Third, the sociability of a spot refers to the opportunities for meeting friends and socialising. Finally, compatibility is the ease to which skaters use the place without conflict with other users. These elements vary by style, ability and mobility of a skater, and will change over the course of a day, year and life course of an individual.

Even 50 years after skateboarding broke out of California, and its enrolment into portfolios of global sports brands, enduring spaces for skateboarding in cities are rare in comparison with other sports. To some extent this is not necessarily an issue for skateboarders, as many skaters see themselves as urban explorers and revel in the challenge of creating new spots to skate. In this sense, the practice of skating can be conceptualised as producing new space: a small, but no less significant act of transforming the city.

Changing city roles and uses: the transformation of Newcastle

Newcastle provides a striking example of the interplay between the grand plans and paradigms of a city's civic authority and their impact on urban sports. In answer to Harvey's questions 'whose city is it?', we show how skateboarders have appropriated and altered their use of the city, exploiting opportunities unforeseen in the sweeping visions of regeneration plans and maintaining a presence even in the face of civic intolerance.

During the 1960s the aim was to zone the city by function and vertically segregate vehicles from pedestrians – much as Le Corbusier had suggested – which produced the type of abstract space that Lefebvre so vehemently critiqued (Lefebvre, 1991 [1974], 2014). The proposal was for the entire northern half of the city centre to be covered by a pedestrian deck, while vehicles would travel along smooth, straight, level roads on ground level, inspired by the Buchanan report (see Figure 7.1). Whilst all of these bold plans were not implemented, there was an extensive programme of road building dissecting the city centre as well as a complex network of urban walkways and some commercial schemes, which inadvertently provided an attractive space for urban sports activists to access and be (see Figure 7.2).

Figure 7.1 Road building and urban walkways

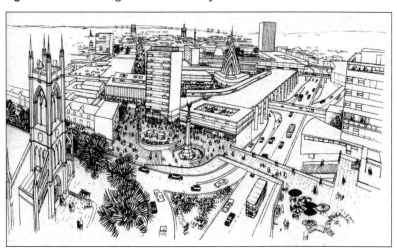

Source: Burns (1967). Illustration by Michael Evans.

By the end of the 1970s, very few residents remained in the city centre as the council determined that the city centre was primarily a place for work (and some leisure) (that is, a space of exchange values). In the 1980s, policy perspectives began to shift with a notable rise in the number of private sector apartments. Also an extensive programme of pedestrianisation commenced and a search for artefacts to utilise 'surplus space' ensued in the form of public art and street furniture, which provides urban sports activists opportunities to navigate the contemporary neoliberalised city with some ideal 'spots' for counter-practices as we discuss later in this chapter.

Figure 7.2 Preference for vehicles in cities

Source: Buchanan and Crowther (1963)

Since the early 1990s, the 'renaissance' of Newcastle (and Gateshead Quayside) has sought to 'open up' the city to developers as well as citizens more broadly, but particularly conspicuous consumers. Increasingly, modern landmarks started to project the values of commerce, including indoor shopping malls that produce the illusion of being public, but typically discriminate against particular publics (Giddings et al, 2005) and the majority ban the use of skateboards. Indeed, entire segments of the city have been privatised, whereby the public are granted access subject to particular codes and rules, including temporal restrictions. Inadvertently, the neoliberal city had generated ideal spots for urban sports activists. Much of the modernist architecture created plazas, blocks, walkways, slopes and gaps ideal for skateboarding (see Figure 7.3). However, their right to the city is a story of contestation and renegotiation as a combination of city authorities and commercial interests have sought to remove them from the consumer's gaze. Commercial interests perceived that the urban sports activists and young people generally were adversely affecting business, and city authorities were reacting to the perception that the safety of the city centre was deteriorating (Rogers and Coaffe, 2005). A variety of anti-skate measures were subsequently introduced across the city. For example, benches and steps in university campuses and public squares have been 'skate proofed' by adding metal attachments, which stop skaters from grinding on them. Also, by-laws have been introduced at Haymarket (the main city centre square) to prevent skating on and around the war memorial.

Figure 7.3 Unintended ideal skateboarding spots

Source: the authors

One policy response was the decision of the city council to provide a purposely designed skate park at the outer northern edge of the city centre, which was completed in 2004. While skateboarders are often seen to be cooperative during the skate park design process (Rogers, 2006), their interest can wane post-completion as they seek to reproduce the city in alternative ways. Atencio et al (2009), for example, suggest that skateboarders are particularly excited by finding unique and challenging spots to skate, which can be contrasted with the unvarying layout of skate parks (Thompson, 1998). This supports the notion of skaters as urban explorers. Indeed, Nemeth (2006) notes that bespoke skate parks can be perceived as token gestures by urban sports activists, and consequently they resist attempts to control them in tightly defined urban spaces.

Skaters' right to change space

For a brief period of time after it was built, skateboarders frequently accessed the purpose-designed Exhibition Park site (see Figure 7.4). However, it was subsequently appropriated by BMXers and scooterists, alongside skaters, and as a place for other young people to congregate. In this sense, a more diverse group of young people 'claimed' their right to the skate area of Exhibition Park. This draws attention to the nuanced complexity of rights between members of the same or similar subcultures but a detailed discussion of this is beyond the scope of this chapter. Coupled with its static layout, many skateboarders soon became tired of this urban space (Jenson et al, 2012) as they subsequently sought to reclaim a right to change the broader neoliberal city (Figure 7.5), of which four are described below.

The first one is The Law Courts (see Figure 7.6). Newcastle's Crown Court building on the Quayside might seem an unusual place to be appropriated by skaters, but its double set of eight steps with a convenient viewing space behind a rail make it a popular spot among the city's skateboarders. They are 'in session' when the court is not, usually in the evening and at the weekend. The second one is Old Wasteland in Shieldfield (see Figure 7.7) to the northeast of Newcastle city centre, which was once home to large factory buildings. Most had been demolished, but the base of some remains. For a long period of time, these spaces were commercially unattractive, but their large, flat concrete bases make for excellent skating and had been enjoyed by the skateboarders for a number of years. The Wasteland also had the advantage of being 'hidden' from the broader public, and so, its use remained undisturbed. In recent years, much of the area has been redeveloped and 'revitalised', necessitating the decampment of skateboarders from what is now termed the Old Wasteland, to an alternative site (known as the New Wasteland and described below), which is even further away from the city centre.

Figure 7.4 Exhibition Park

Source: the authors

Figure 7.5 Skateboarding spots across the city

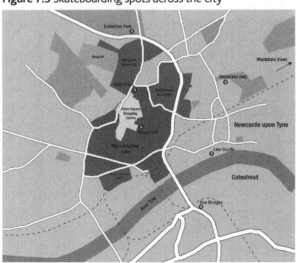

Source: the authors

Figure 7.6 The Law Courts

Source: Adam Thirtle. Reproduced with the author's permission.

Figure 7.7 The Old Wasteland

Source: the authors

The third one is Five Bridges (see Figure 7.8) and is located under a flyover in Gateshead. It has the advantage of high trickability, sociability and compatibility, and through repeated appropriation has become a council's recognised skate plaza (as distinct from skate parks, which usually feature bowls) with a growing national reputation, evidenced in its use by touring pro-teams for demonstrations. Despite its medium level accessibility, and in contrast to Exhibition Park, the journey is largely deemed to be 'worth it'. It is popular throughout the year, particularly during times of poor weather as the flyover provides some protection.

Figure 7.8 The Five Bridges

Source: the authors

The fourth site is New Wasteland (see Figure 7.9), which is 2.5 km east of the city centre and part of a factory site demolished in 2004. While it is near a metro rail station, its position beyond the residential area of Byker is perceived as distant – socially and geographically from the city centre. The site was first used by BMXers who adapted a step on the old factory floor by adding a concrete block. During the summer of 2012, skaters began to modify a different part of the site, producing *their space*.

Figure 7.9 The New Wasteland

Source: the authors

Utilising Woolley and Johns' framework sketched out below, Table 7.1 provides a summative analysis, demonstrating that city centre spots are still the most popular and score highly on nearly all the measures. However, in terms of compatibility with other users (as represented by private and public authorities), they are currently, virtually unusable. Despite its proximity to the city centre (albeit on the periphery), the purpose-designed site at Exhibition Park only scores medium on accessibility due to the lack of public transport options. In addition, it scores low for trickability, sociability and compatibility with other users, and is not popular with many of the skaters. The sites at the periphery score medium to high but are not as popular as the city centre. The New Wasteland scores medium for trickability and sociability but there are issues with accessibility, and safety as represented by compatibility. Its isolation and position adjacent to an area of urban deprivation are especially off-putting to younger skateboarders. The skaters themselves can be targeted by other youth groups (Jenson et al, 2012), and for younger participants, sites nearer to the city centre are viewed as both more accessible and safer. We will now analyse the rights of skaters to access and be in the city, followed by the right to participate and then the right to change.

Table 7.1 Analysis of skateboard sites using Woolley and Johns' (2001) framework, based on skateboarders' comments

	Accessibility	Trickability	Sociability	Compatibility
City centre, historic sites no longer skated				
Bank of England	High	High	High	Low
City Library	High	High	High	Low
Monument	High	High	High	Low
Haymarket	High	Medium	High	Low
Skate park				
Exhibition Park	Medium	Low	Low	Low
Periphery				
Law Courts	Medium	Low	High	Medium
Old Wasteland	Medium	High	High	High
Five Bridges	Medium	High	High	High
Distant				
New Wasteland	Low	Medium	Medium	Low

The right to access and be, or displacement and dispossession

Interviews with skateboarders indicate that they continue to be displaced from some of *their* favoured spots, supporting Harvey's (2008) broader observations of neoliberal tentacles spreading throughout the contemporary city, favouring commercial patterns of land use and property rights above all else. This is reinforced formally and informally by the public and corporate authorities who dominate city management, governance and decision making (Woolley et al, 2011). As already noted, some 'public' areas of Newcastle preclude skaters through legal restrictions and other parts of the city utilise interventions by police and private security.

Drawing on Lefebvre, Borden (2001) suggests public urban spaces can accommodate counter-cultural activities alongside other uses and claims to spatial rights. Nevertheless, in Newcastle most spots are only accessible at moments dictated by the temporal rhythms of commercial activity. For example, the Monument (a popular city centre square) can be skated at night and the Law Courts outside of business hours. Thus, the skateboarders are effectively excluded from accessing and being in the majority of the city centre unless informal arrangements are brokered, whereby skaters claim such spaces when commercial or institutional use is not active. In this way, a kind of time zoning for alternative uses could be established.

The Old Wasteland is perhaps the most obvious example of a space rejected by commercial interests and reproduced as a 'counter-space'. It had been skated for at least 20 years and skateboarders even raised money through entrepreneurial activities to pay for the construction of ramps and rails. It became a treasured spot, which was maintained and enhanced by skaters, while city authorities designated it as derelict. However, as corporate interests looked for profitable spaces for commercial building outside the city centre, it was acquired by developers. Construction encroached onto the skate floor and in March 2012 the site was excavated. Yet, even this neoliberal expansion into *the skateboarders' space* generated neither resistance nor protest, although skaters and BMXers paid fond farewells with 'sessions' and graffiti. Their displacement from the site had been anticipated by the skate community during 2010 when the initial fieldwork for this research was conducted. The situation was summarised by one participant, who said, "We'll just find somewhere else" (Skater B3). While it had provided an exemplary 'home' for several generations of skateboarders, the reaction of these urban explorers was to simply produce some new spaces. What this helps to demonstrate is the hardiness of skaters. Far from being perturbed by the trumpeting of capitalist values (Harvey, 2008), they display a remarkable resilience and appetite to explore and regenerate new spaces.

The right to participate or co-option

In parallel with pernicious as well as gentler acts of displacement, is the countervailing force of co-option. In 2012 and 2013, for example, Newcastle hosted an Urban Games involving skateboarders in the city centre with the support of the city council and NE1, the Business Improvement District company. The games were organised by Solar Learning, a company promoting entrepreneurial youth with a hope to transform the city into a more play-friendly environment, although the short-term nature of funding curtailed the longevity and sustainability of the programme. Importantly, this kind of engagement with the activists happens on the terms of those paying, in places and at times of their choosing. Once the spectacle is finished and the marketing done, it is not uncommon for urban sports activists to be once again rendered a visual nuisance and public inconvenience, and subsequently displaced.

Co-option is but one form of skateboarders' engagement and participation in broader city policies and initiatives. There has also been less cynical engagement in other locations. For example, Five Bridges was reconfigured to accommodate jumps and ramps to encourage the active use by skaters in order to serve broader policies, including combating antisocial behaviour, as discussed above. This pragmatic recognition can also be seen in the relationship between skaters and the police after younger users of Five Bridges sought police help when being bullied in the area:

> The youngsters who use the Five Bridges skate park in Gateshead were harassed by gangs who picked on younger members of the group. Neighbourhood Beat Manager Steve Purnell found out and acted to stamp out the trouble. 'I asked them what we could do to help. The main thing was that they could skate without problems ... most of the kids have my phone number and can ring if they need anything.' (Ford, 2009)

However, this recognition tends to be rare and site specific, and is highly contingent on individual personalities, which suggests that the scope for urban sports activists to participate in city management process is more limited.

The right to change: a revolution or compliance

Urban sports such as skateboarding have often been posited as direct challenges to authority (for example, Beal, 1995 and Landers, 2012), but our research found instances of direct, purposeful contestation are uncommon: "People think [skaters] want to go and destroy stuff. We don't. We just want to skate and have a good time. It's hard because everyone thinks we're just hooligans" (Skate 7/14).

There are instances where skaters have campaigned against changes to treasured sites, such as action at London's South Bank (Jones, 2014), but these are rare and no such campaigns have been waged in Newcastle. The alternative is demonstrated by the compliant move of skateboarders from the Old to the New Wasteland. Again, a former factory site, the spot offers some advantages and has undergone similar transformation to the Old Wasteland, at the hands of the skateboarders. Perhaps its greatest virtue is that users are shielded – out of sight – due to a high wall around the site. However, as already explained, there are a number of downsides. In this sense, the New Wasteland symbolises the production of a counter-space, but the concept of a new right and a respatialisation of justice is significantly compromised by the notion that the location is third choice to the city centre and periphery because of difficult accessibility and concerns about safety.

Over time and in a general sense, skateboarders in Newcastle have developed a mutual understanding with those charged with managing and policing the city, which can be a negative or positive experience:

> '… when we were skating down there [in the city centre], we just sit down to eat, security guard comes out, swears at you and all sorts, telling you to move along. And that same day we went down the Quayside [Law Courts] and we met one of the nicest security guards you could ever meet, he had a proper conversation with me, he said he wouldn't mind us skating here but we gotta move you on because my supervisor wants me to.'

The relationship with the broader public is equally complex with reported abuse and celebration of performances in equal measure. Yet, in Newcastle, skateboarders are not consciously contesting the neoliberal city. Rarely do they seek conflict and our observations indicate that they prefer to avoid such spatial disputes through their distinct spatiotemporal performances, which are highly adaptive to changing patterns of city development. This tempers perspectives, especially those propounded by some radical scholars (exemplified by those readings of the 'right to the city' that emphasise its revolutionary potency), that urban sports activists are actively transgressing neoliberal market rules and directly challenging dominant, consumption-orientated images of the 'civilised city'. Through the case of skaters in Newcastle, we have found that the spatiotemporal performance of this urban youth subculture searches out the path of least resistance. This tends to result in the production of new skate spaces in the interstices of the neoliberal city. Nevertheless, we would stress that the civic-legal constraints and behaviour of security staff, combined with the outlook of the sports' activists, result in a wholly asymmetric power relationship between city authorities and skateboarders. This raises the questions: Is this just? Is it fair?

Concluding observations

The power structures within urban cityscapes are by no means fair, but this chapter, through the empirical case of urban sport activists and, specifically, skateboarders in Newcastle has examined how they renegotiate city rights through their unique spatiotemporal performances. We have invoked the concept of the 'right to the city' originally developed by Henri Lefebvre and subsequently deployed in modified forms by a succession of critical urbanists, to help us to structure an analysis of the methods and tactics utilised by skateboarders to change and produce space. Our research findings indicate that skateboarders are not necessarily seeking to be permitted rights to skate across all areas of the city centre at any time, much preferring to be out of the gaze of the broader public. Their requests are much more practical and prosaic. Ultimately, they call for respect and the ability to be left alone. As one of them remarked, "What I don't like even when we've been skating along and we're just a bit tired and we sit down and have a drink and we get asked to move along ... Can we finish our food at least? 'No, you've got to move along'" (LBM). In this sense, this particular group of skateboarders are seeking to comply with broader patterns and modalities of city rights, for example, by way of iterative negotiations – seeking to renegotiate momentary rights at particular timespaces that do not explicitly clash with or are not necessarily devised to challenge the temporal rhythms of commercial activity. Such a compliant renegotiation of momentary rights, exemplified by skateboarders' preference to avoid spatial disputes, is a valuable research finding, as much Lefebvrian-inspired research tends to emphasise the revolutionary and, arguably, more antagonistic potency of the right to the city.

This chapter has helped to demonstrate how urban sport activists acknowledge normative, legal and habitual city rights and roles. In the case of Newcastle, the role of urban sports activists in producing counter-spaces, however fleeting or innocuous, is much more amicable than popular opinion may suggest. Whether such acceptance of city relationships is unique to this location, is not entirely clear. This warrants further research to explore the vigour and manner to which urban sport activists contest dominant city roles, rules, conventions and practices in other places.

It needs to be recognised that no single group, whether those pursuing counter-practices or not, is able to claim exclusive right to the city, and there is potential for conflict within the urban sports community, as well as with other user groups. It may be for this reason that city authorities have been antipathetic to urban sports. Yet, by grappling with the issue of *social justice for all*, it should be possible to explore how the design of public spaces in the city centre could mitigate conflicts and enable the accommodation of different kinds of users including skaters who, contrary to common assumptions, can energise space, improve the perception of public safety, and deter antisocial behaviour.

A key implication of this research is that the fairness of city rights and city roles is deeply situational. Returning to David Harvey's opening quotation, which lamented the inadequacy of 'the ideals of human rights' that do little to penetrate everyday life and alter spatial practices, it may be that fairness is often a very simple request. As one participant said, "All I want is somewhere nice I can sit with my friends" (BMX3).

The overall pattern is that increasingly, to avoid conflict (the antonym of compatibility) skateboarders are searching for and producing new skate spaces further from the city centre and the purview city authorities, with adverse effects on accessibility, trickability and sociability. Already displaced from the Old Wasteland, Gateshead Council has plans to demolish the flyover, which would obliterate the Five Bridges spot; and a shift in policy could place the Law Courts site out of bounds. It appears unlikely, over the short term at least, that there will be a radical reconstitution of dominant perceptions of skateboarders and urban sports activists: one whereby this urban youth subculture will be acknowledged by city authorities and commercial interests as legitimate users (and producers) of urban space in the neoliberal city, perhaps precipitating a fundamental reorganisation of city life and promoting the values of spatial justice. Yet, the resilience of skateboarders would suggest that they will continue to explore, energise and regenerate spaces often deemed redundant at particular moments in timespace to the untrained eye. For this reason alone, urban sports activists are valued city makers and their right to the city should be acknowledged.

Notes

[1] Unified by the slogan 'we are the 99%', which draws attention to prevailing economic disparities via the wealth and power wielded by a minority (that is, the 1%).

[2] Although skateboarding is often perceived to be a teen pursuit (that is, city youths), the demographic profile of skateboarders is more diverse and while the scene is mainly male, it is not uncommon, as we have observed, for skaters to be in their 30s, 40s and 50s.

References

Atencio, M., Beal, A. and Wilson, C. (2009) 'The distinction of risk: urban skateboarding, street habitus and the construction of hierarchical gender relations', *Qualitative Research in Sport and Exercise,* 1: 3-20.

Beal, B. (1995) 'Disqualifying the official: an exploration of social resistance through the subculture of skateboarding', *Sociology of Sport Journal,* 12: 252-67.

Borden, I. (2001) *Skateboarding, place and the city: Architecture and the body,* Oxford: Berg.

Buchanan, C. and Crowther, G. (1963) *Traffic in towns: A study of long term problems of traffic in urban areas,* London: HMSO.

Burns, W. (1967) *Newcastle: A study in replanning at Newcastle upon Tyne,* London: Leonard Hill Books

Cresswell, T. (1996) *In place/out of place: Geography, ideology and transgression,* Minneapolis, MN: University of Minnesota Press.

Fainstein, S.S. (2014) 'The just city', *International Journal of Urban Sciences,* 18(1): 1-18.

Ford, C. (2009) 'Police help Gateshead skaters beat bullies' *ChronicleLive,* [online] 12 April. Available at: http://www.chroniclelive.co.uk/news/north-east-news/police-help-gateshead-skaters-beat-1452664 [Accessed January 2016].

Fuggle, S. (2008) 'Discourses of subversion: the ethics and aesthetics of Caporeira and Parkour', *Dance Research,* 26: 204-22.

Giddings, B., Hopwood, B., Mellor, M. and O'Brien, G. (2005) 'Back to the city: a route to urban sustainability', in M. Jenks and N. Dempsey (eds) *Future forms and design for sustainable cities,* London: Elsevier, pp 13-30.

Harvey, D. (1990) *The condition of postmodernity,* Oxford: Basil Blackwell.

Harvey, D. (2008) 'The right to the city', *New Left Review,* 53: 23-40.

Harvey, D. (2011) *'Whose City?', Whose City? Labor and the Right to the City Movements,* Santa Cruz, CA: Conference, 26 February.

Isin, E.F. (2000) 'Introduction: democracy, citizenship, and the city', in E.F. Isin (ed) *Democracy, citizenship and the global city,* Cambridge, MA: Blackwell, pp 1-22.

Jenson, A., Swords, J. and Jeffries, M. (2012) 'The accidental youth club: skateboarding in Newcastle-Gateshead', *Journal of Urban Design,* 17(3): 371-88.

Jones, A.J.H. (2014): *On South Bank: the production of public space,* Farnham: Ashgate.

Landers, F. (2012) 'Urban play: imaginatively responsible behaviour as an alternative to neoliberalism', *The Arts in Psychotherapy,* 39: 201-5.

Lees, L. (2014) 'The urban injustices of New Labour's "New urban renewal": the case of the Aylesbury Estate in London', *Antipode*, 46(4): 921-47.

Lefebvre, H. (1976) *The survival of capitalism*, London: Allison and Busby.

Lefebvre, H. (1991 [1974]) *The production of space*, Oxford: Basil Blackwell.

Lefebvre, H. (1996) *Writings on cities*, London: Blackwell.

Lefebvre, H. (2003 [1970]) *The urban revolution*, Paris: Gallimard.

Lefebvre, H. (2004) *Rhythmanalysis: space, time and everyday life*, London: Continuum.

Lefebvre, H. (2014) 'Dissolving city, planetary metamorphosis', *Environment and Planning D: Society and Space*, 32(2): 203-5.

Marcuse, P. (2009) 'From critical urban theory to the right to the city', *City*, 13(2): 185-97.

Marcuse, P. (2014) 'Reading the right to the city', *City*, 18(1): 4-9.

Minton, A. (2012) *Ground control. Fear and happiness in the 21st century city*, London: Penguin.

Nemeth, J. (2006) 'Conflict, exclusion, relocation: skateboarding and public space', *Journal of Urban Design*, 11: 297-318.

Pugalis, L. and Bentley, G. (2014) 'State strategies and entrepreneurial governance', in L. Pugalis and J. Liddle (eds) *Enterprising places: leadership and governance networks*, Bingley: Emerald/ISBE, pp 123-48.

Pugalis, L. and Giddings, B. (2011) 'A renewed right to urban life: a twenty-first century engagement with Lefebvre's initial "cry"', *Architectural Theory Review*, 16(3): 278-95.

Purcell, M. (2014) 'Possible worlds: Henri Lefebvre and the right to the city', *Journal of Urban Affairs*, 36(1): 141-54.

Rogers, P. (2006) 'Young people's participation in the renaissance of public space – a case study of Newcastle upon Tyne, UK', *Children, Youth and Environments*, 16: 105-26.

Rogers, P. and Coaffee, J. (2005) 'Moral panics and urban renaissance. Policy, tactics and youth in public space', *City*, 9: 321–40.

Rosen, G. and Shlay, A.B. (2014) 'Whose right to Jerusalem?', *International Journal of Urban and Regional Research*, 38(3): 935-50.

Shields, R. (1991): *Places on the margin: alternative geographies of modernity*, London: Routledge.

Soja, E.W. (2010) *Seeking Spatial Justice*, Minneapolis, MN: University of Minnesota Press.

Thompson, J. (1998) 'A good thrashing skateboard park design', *Landscape Architecture*, 8: 78–100.

Woolley, H., Hazelwood, T. and Simkins, I. (2011) 'Don't skate here: exclusion of skateboarders from urban civic space in three northern cities in England', *Journal of Urban Design,* 16: 471–87.

Woolley, H. and Johns, R. (2001) 'Skateboarding: the city as playground', *Journal of Urban Design,* 6: 211–30.

EIGHT

Young people and their experience of place in the city

Teresa Strachan and Elisa Lopez-Capel

> More and more the spaces of the modern city are being produced for us rather than by us. (Mitchell, 2003: 18)

Introduction

For many of us, a formative part of our childhood would have been time spent in a favourite outdoor open space. Drawing on the outputs of engagement projects in the east end of Newcastle upon Tyne, this chapter reveals how young people create meaningful relationships with local open spaces and how these spaces play an important role in their everyday lives. The chapter goes on to suggest that a young person's perception of open space is very different to how planning policy and practice perceives these components of the city's neighbourhoods. This may be due in part to an absence of any ongoing participatory process by which young people can exert influence over the decisions made about the places that they value. Using a Lefebvrian theoretical context, we suggest that these young people experience a marginalisation of their political 'right to the city' and that the policy impacting upon their 'corner' of the city remains the domain of adult decision makers (Lefebvre, 1996).

Children and young people comprise a significant part of Newcastle's population. While the United Nations define 'young people' as being between the ages of 15 and 24, the young people referred to in this chapter range in age from eight to 24 years old, thereby including a proportion of children within the study. Within Newcastle, the eight to 24-year-old age group makes up 28% of the population (although this figure includes a large student population). Within the three 'east end' wards of Byker, Walker and Walkergate, where the chapter's case studies were located, the same eight to 24-year-old age group comprises 22% of the population, which compares to the England

and Wales average of 21% (ONS, 2011). These are three of the most deprived wards in the city.

The open spaces referred to in this chapter include those that are green, or hard landscaped public areas, or a combination of both, and bear closest resemblance to the definition for open space as used by the Scottish Government (2008). The range of open spaces within these three wards includes small pockets of indistinct grassland, a long riverside corridor of 'natural and semi-green space' (Newcastle City Council and Gateshead Council, 2011) and a 'green flag' park (NCC, 2012). Other open spaces include 'amenity green space', 'urban farms', 'community gardens' and 'allotment gardens', contributing to Newcastle's portfolio of green infrastructure, which underpins to 'the quality of the natural and built environment and is integral to the health and quality of life of communities' (Newcastle Gateshead, 2014: 98). Figure 8.1 depicts what might be regarded as a 'stereotypical' open space within the city's green infrastructure provision. The distribution of open and green space in Newcastle can be seen in Figure 2.4 'Greenspace in Newcastle upon Tyne by category, 2011' in Chapter 2.

Figure 8.1 How planning policy and practice might perceive open space

Source: image courtesy of Elisa Lopez-Capel

The chapter will begin with a discussion of the Lefebvrian 'right to the city', followed by a reflection on the value of place and why open space holds such significance for young people. The engagement case studies are then discussed in relation to the chapter's theoretical framework. Finally, Newcastle's open space policy and practice is investigated, which leads to a number of conclusions in relation to young people, the open spaces that they use and their participatory rights.

Theoretical context

While Lefebvre's 'right to the city' is central to the framework of this chapter, the case studies consider young people's rights in a political rather than in a spatial sense (Lefebvre, 1996). The open spaces that form the basis of the discussion within this chapter are those that are familiar to young people in their own neighbourhood. Lefebvre recognises the importance of such spaces in the city in what he refers to as the 'ouvre', or 'the need for information, symbolism, the imaginary and play' (Lefebvre, 1996: 147).

As young people use open spaces in their local neighbourhoods they develop strong bonds with those places. We suggest that it is the young people's own perception of these spaces, rather than just their physical (function or appearance) or social purpose that gives them their true value. There is a clear disjuncture between how young people perceive these open spaces and how the city planners perceive them. With the absence of a participatory process that might involve young people in decisions that determine the future of these open spaces, the likelihood of them being able to secure their 'right to the city' remains remote.

The dearth of participatory opportunities for young people at the neighbourhood level is extensively discussed in literature relating to the planning of open space and green infrastructure (Hart, 1997; Frank, 2006; Roe, 2007; Percy Smith, 2010; Laughlin and Johnson, 2011). This theme forms a key framework for the chapter and overlaps into another debate relating to environmental justice. Walker (2012) recognises that 'procedural', along with 'distributive' justice is a component of environmental justice. In addition to this, 'environmental justice matters because it is a critical component of social justice' (Davoudi and Brooks, 2012: 4). The chapter therefore reflects upon the debate surrounding the extent to which young people have, or could have a say in the decisions that shape these open spaces and postulates as to whether or not the lack of opportunities for young people to participate might amount to environmental injustice.

The relationship with young people and open space is studied across several disciplines, including environmental psychology, geopsychology, sociogeography, town planning and urban design. Gibson (1977) used the term 'affordances' to describe the direct gains that benefit young people through their relationship with place. How these affordances vary from one age group to another is not clearly defined, but the concept's implications for urban design and planning policy making should not be underestimated. The value of open space to young people can be determined by its physical (function and appearance) and social (opportunities to meet people) characteristics, as well as what Laughlin and Johnson (2011) describe as a third element – what the young people themselves think of the place. This third element is considered to be a key factor in the discussion, where it is suggested that the lack of participation by young people in the planning process exacerbates the lack of understanding of the priorities for change (Laughlin and Johnson, 2011).

Access to open space not only varies according to the availability and distribution of those open spaces, but also according to the social class of the young people themselves. In such instances, options for travel to alternative recreational spaces may be limited by cost, or by cultural or social tradition (Ward and Golzen, 1978; Hart, 2002; Davoudi and Brooks, 2012). Furthermore, the use of open space can also be influenced by gender, race and ethnicity (Byrne and Wolch et al, 2009). Even within the broader definition of the term 'young person', different age groups can also determine levels of parental control over which places are used and when (Valentine, 2004). Territorialism and issues relating to fear and safety between different groups of young people can also influence their use of public open spaces (Day and Wager, 2010). Significant to this study, is the widely held view of the particular value of open and green space to residents of more deprived communities (Ward and Golzen, 1978; Hart, 2002; Day et al, 2011). This was found to be even more pronounced in terms of access by the younger elements of deprived communities, underlining the vital role that these places play within the lives of young people from deprived city neighbourhoods (Burt et al, 2013).

The type and quality of open space that young people might value also varies greatly. Ward and Golzen (1978) and Roe (2006) refer to the attachment that young people make with less formal open spaces and the value that these places hold in their everyday lives. They are also described as 'forgotten' and 'redundant' spaces (Matthews, 2003 in Hopkins, 2010), 'cool places' (Skelton and Valentine, 1998), 'slack space' (CABE, 2004), 'spaces in-between' (Atkinson, 2003) and, 'special places' (Roe, 2006). In addition to this, the level of provision of facilities within these open spaces can fluctuate and hence be perceived in different ways by a variety of users. In its Urban Green Nation report, The Commission for Architecture and the Built Environment (CABE) found that the 16 to 24 age group reported lower quality in all of its indicators on urban green space and were more likely to think that parks and open spaces are the aspect of their local area that needs the most improvement, (CABE, 2010). CABE attributes this figure to the higher use of these spaces by young people and hence their increased awareness and experience of them.

While the CABE report goes on to explain that, 'It could be that parks and open spaces are not being designed and managed to meet their needs' (CABE, 2010: 19), we suggest that it demonstrates that young people are able to speak on behalf of the community in knowing what might be best for the locality, because of their heightened local knowledge of a place (Hart, 1979; Frank, 2006). However, unlike other 'hard to reach' and often marginalised groups in the community, young people are 'relatively powerless to articulate their own views and environmental needs and to challenge adultist practices and processes' (Valentine, 2004: 104). Reasons for this might include the belief that young people cannot know what is best for them; that adults do know best and deal with young people's needs through a process known as 'othering' (Lahman, 2008); and that adults' natural authority would be undermined.

Embedding an effective method by which young people can take a meaningful part in the planning process is fundamental if 'tokenistic' consultation is to be avoided (Hart, 1992; Skelton, 2007). While considering what that process might amount to lies outside the scope of this chapter, the starting point in the discussion must be to gain an understanding of how young people perceive place in their neighbourhood and why they perceive it in the way that they do. The longer-term benefits of a generation of citizens who understand decision making and their role within that process will help to strengthen that relationship between people and place and the entire sustainable communities agenda. Severcan (2003) noted that as the young people that they were working with participated in 'place making activities', their feelings for and knowledge and understanding of their local area increased significantly at the local level. This is also significant in the quest for social justice, which 'refers primarily to the full participation and inclusion of everyone in a society's major institutions, and the socially supported substantive opportunity for all to develop and exercise their capacities and realise their choices' (Young, 1990: 173). Purcell develops this notion further in describing the public 'right to appropriation' as being not just participation, but the capacity to change and to shape the city (Purcell, 2008).

Case studies

The two case studies were undertaken with separate groups of young people in the east end wards of Newcastle. They emerged as engagement projects within bigger research programmes, which had their own distinct project aims and intended outcomes, which were led by staff from Newcastle University.

Case study one: 'growing places' project

'Growing places' was an 'art meets science' project that was aimed at engaging young people from hard to reach community groups in the east end of Newcastle. Focusing on the theme of sustainability, the project was designed to allow an artist and a scientist to work with community groups to create artworks reflecting young people's perception of their changing urban environment. It was offered to the young people as an opportunity for them to influence the future developments in their neighbourhoods. The project was based on research relating to the effect of urbanisation on green space within Byker. In turn, this research had built upon the previous, 'Vision of the Future', project, which had been inspired by the photographs taken by Sirkka-Liisa Konttinen (1983), documenting the 40-year transformation of the Byker community. Working with two groups of young people aged nine to 13 and 13 to 25 years, from local community groups, environmental scientist Elisa Lopez-Capel and poet Andrew McMillan delivered a range of creative writing workshops looking into the past, present and future of their estate. The young people were able to express their opinions about what they liked, what they would like to change, and what sort of place they would like the estate to be in the future. These open spaces mostly comprised an assortment of grassed areas that lay either between the estate's residential blocks or along its periphery. The engagement activities took place at local youth clubs and in a shop in the main street, where work was exhibited for the local community and the general public.

Even as the young people articulated their observations during the workshops about the open spaces within their local neighbourhoods and the social value that they gained from them (Laughlin and Johnson, 2011), it was clear that their comments stemmed from a strong sense of there being a disjuncture between what they would like to use the spaces for and what they could actually use them for. Young Person 1 reflected that there was "lots of green spaces, but the wrong type: nothing for kids to do", adding that they "can't play football, because residents don't want football outside their houses". The young people commented how few of the open spaces were flat and although they were nice to look at, they were not suitable for playing on (except, as they suggested, for sledging). They claimed that the dedicated football fields were probably empty because dogs foul there, but acknowledged that there was still an open space that could be used for football. Observations such as these emphasise the heightened local knowledge that young people can have of their local area; how they justify their use (or lack of use) of that open space; and how they make sense of others' behaviour in that open space (Hart, 1979; Frank, 2006; Day and Wager, 2010).

A young person's sensitivity to the needs of different elements of their young community and the territorialism that prevails also emerged from the project. For instance, when describing the different areas of open space, Young Person 2 distinguished between the "top, middle and bottom" open spaces, which they described as being "very territorial", and in another location, Young Person 3 describes the "small kids play parks" as being "quite territorial". Not only do they distinguish between the groups that use the different spaces, but they can also set themselves apart from the behaviour and the perceptions of those places held by those other groups. Recognising a degree of territorialism (Day and Wager, 2010) and associating their own identity with that place (Valentine, 2004; Hopkins, 2010) would appear to be a natural process for the young people in this project. In addition, the young people were able to recognise and value others' perceptions of that place and this was encapsulated in a poem, entitled 'Byker Wall' by one of the project's young participants:

There is a place called Byker
I like it like the ball
It isn't that nice
But don't care at all
My big brother says that it looks like a heart
My dad says like a jail
My mum likes discovering things just like Me
It may not be fantastic
You may not like the wall
But I think that it is clever
Because it is sliding like a worm
   (Young Person 4)

Young people are also aware of the health benefits associated with access to open spaces, and the sense of empowerment and identity the place potentially offers them. As an example, Young Person 5 refers to the 'City of the Future' as a place that "looks like a field of grass, not factories that produce gas", and a city where "I can hear, no pollution and no fear".

These young people recognised how places evolve over time (Mazzoleni, 1993) and relationship between the world as it is now and what it may become (Hart, 1979; Mallan and Greenaway, 2011). The project's poet, Andrew McMillan, assisted the young people in drawing together their writing about their estate in a poem entitled 'Roots, shoots and leaves'. The poem summarises the young people's understanding of the value that they and others attach to place and the hope that future change will bring.

> What someone thinks is monstrous
> Someone else can see as art as something wonderful
> Recycling our past retelling our stories
> Of how it's a funny place
> Of how it's lovely and quiet with the occasional fight
> Of how we've let it get run down
> Of how the Queen Mother came to launch a ship
> And stories mean something's worth saving
> And stories need retelling and anything can be rebuilt
> Given time if we start digging we'll find what we thought
>   was buried
> And watch it grow
>   (Andrew McMillan, reproduced with permission)

Although the 'growing places' project was envisioned as a science communication project for young people, it was also an unexpected educational project for the project's stakeholders on the potential power of young people's voice. The 'growing places' project provided evidence of the importance young people attribute to their local neighbourhood, the difference in perception between different members of the community and to that which was intended in the original design and layout of the estate. While there was clearly an abundant appreciation of the place and its open spaces, as they exist now, as well as a hope for how it will evolve into the future, there was no evidence that the young people had any means by which they could influence this process. The value of the engagement exercise as a means to voice those views was therefore an important outcome of the project.

Case study two: 'NE6 Voice' project

The second case study used visual methods to record the places that were important to a group of young people in their local neighbourhood. The inspiration for the project was the work of the artist, George Shaw, in his Turner Prize nomination exhibition, the 'Sly and Unseen Day' (2011–12), which was hosted by the Baltic Centre for Contemporary Art, in Gateshead. The artist recalled and painted the everyday places that he had encountered during his teenage years, growing up in Coventry. These painted images portrayed everyday scenes such as street corners, vacant shop units with their closed roller shutters and open spaces with their sparse trees and overgrown grass.

The case study formed part of a bigger research project to explore better methods of engaging young people in the planning process and was led by town planner, Teresa Strachan. Working with a group of 20 14- and 15-year-old GCSE geography students from a local secondary school, the young people were asked to take photographs of places in their neighbourhood that were important to them. The only limitation imposed on the exercise was that the photographs should not include people (which had also been a guiding principle of Shaw's painted images). The resulting narratives give an honest and poignant account of the young people's reflection on the places that they value. The project's young participants named the photographic collection 'NE6 Voice'.

Two of the young people's photographs are discussed in some depth, but other insightful observations can be made across the whole project. Some of the most revealing outcomes were the titles that the young people gave to the locations for the purpose of the exhibition about their local area. Two examples of their chosen locations are described later, but others include: a photograph of a busy dual carriage way from a bridge that overlooks it, which the young person described as 'Urban Horizon'; a street corner from where the young person could see the quayside on the south banks of the Tyne, was entitled 'Paris', as they had imagined that it was a view of Paris, when they were younger. Another was the view of the back lanes of a typical Tyneside terraced street, which the young person entitled 'Poverty'. This gives an indication of the diverse range of the open spaces that the young people consider to be important to their everyday lives and how they are attached to and create value for those places.

The open space in Figure 8.2 creates a 'buffer' between an extensive adjacent area of heavy industry and an expanse of 1950s semi-detached housing. Figure 8.2 presents an approximately rectangular shape,

Figure 8.2 Contrasting definitions of open spaces: 'Outdoor Sports Facility' (NCCGC, 2011); 'Recreation Ground' (Ordnance Survey, 2014); 'The Weekend' (Young Person 6)

Source: image courtesy of Teresa Strachan

displaying the typical characteristics of a 1950s designated municipal open space. The belt of scrubby trees along its boundaries offers a sense of semi enclosure around the grass field, while the goal posts provide for informal sports games. Its appearance is characteristic of this part of Tyneside, where regular shaped areas of green space break up the dense areas of industry and housing. It is described by Newcastle City Council as an 'Outdoor Sports Facility' (NCCGC, 2011), while an Ordnance Survey map from 2014, describes the space as a 'Recreation Ground'. Young person 6, who selected this open space for the project, named it 'The Weekend', indicating the significance it played in their everyday routines (Laughlin and Johnson, 2011).

Young Person 6 explained that they go to this place to "play football, have a laugh and relax", while acknowledging the value of the "greenery and the open space and the urban area too". They described it as their "back field", suggesting that its proximity to where they live is significant to them, that they have some ownership over it and gain identity from it as local residents (Hopkins, 2010). The young person described it as a "safe place". Although the term 'safe' does need further clarification, Valentine (2004) explains that it has become an increasingly recognised prerequisite for the suitability of open spaces by young people, both as stated by their age group and by their parents. The young person goes on to explain that because

Figure 8.3 Contrasting definitions of open spaces: 'Outdoor Sports Facility' (NCCGC, 2011); 'Recreation Ground' (Ordnance Survey, 2014); 'The Dene' (Young Person 7)

Source: image courtesy of Teresa Strachan

of the size of the field, they are able to use their little space and that "other people don't bother us", reinforcing the way in which young people can share spaces for different uses and users, while exerting a level of territorialism (Day and Wager, 2010).

The open space in Figure 8.3 is located within the same densely populated neighbourhood as Figure 8.2, where extensive areas of heavy industry still dominate the built environment. This is a more elongated site than that in Figure 8.2, containing both a playing field area and a small pavilion (not shown in the photograph). The rusting goalpost and the spoilt area of grass adjacent to it create an impression of a bleak and abandoned place. Nevertheless, and in spite of the fact that Young Person 7 admitted that that there was "nothing to do" and there was "just boredom", they had identified the place as being important to them and wanted it to form part of the collection of images for the project's exhibition.

Young Person 7 talked about having "happy memories" of the open space, but felt that others spoilt the place and that if it was to be tidied up those other users would "probably just do it again". This reflects the ways in which different groups use and create their own territories within the open spaces (Day and Wager, 2010). The comments also illustrate how young people make their own assessments of other elements of the community and can make sense of the broader world through their relationship with place (Hart, 1979; Mazzoleni, 1993). The young person did not level blame at anyone for the place not being tidied up, but was aware of how the other young people might respond, should it be tidied. They also suggested that the underlying cause for the vandalism and the repeated threat of antisocial behaviour could be due to the limited opportunities and the lack of things to do there. Their comments emphasised that the mess was made by only some, saying that people "think that we all do this sort of thing". This statement gives an insight into the wider sense of responsibility that young people can feel for their peers. So while Figure 8.3 may not conform to either a commonly held perception or previous experience of a local authority's typical 'Outdoor Sports Facility' (NCCGC, 2011), the everyday politics of the younger population with its much wider, and potentially longer-term implications, is certainly being played out in this place (Strife and Downey, 2009).

Policy and practice

The city's open space policy and practice initiatives (and bodies that influence these) sit at a range of different levels, from European, through to national legislation and down to joint planning policy with Gateshead Council (2014) and then to neighbourhood level. There are many different policy and guidance initiatives that might impact on the planning of open space, ranging from the 2014 bid for Green Capital to the 'Let's Talk' programme that promotes community dialogue as part of the Decent Neighbourhood Standards (DNS) in Newcastle's wards. Key open space policy vehicles have focused upon open space provision from an access, quality and quantity perspective (ODPM, 2002; NCC, 2004; Newcastle Gateshead, 2014), but over this time period, the nature of the process has changed from one of strategic open space provision and protection through careful consultation with the local community (ODPM, 2002), to one where open space is a strategic tool in supporting the regeneration of city-wide economy (Newcastle Gateshead, 2014).

The United Nations Convention on the Rights of the Child established a clear framework for young people to participate in matters that affect them and their environment in Articles 12, 24, and 31 (UNICEF, 1989), and the UK government is legally bound in international law to comply with the Convention. However, in spite of the international rhetoric, the subject of participatory justice for children and young people, particularly in relation to their environments, rarely crosses the national or local political agenda.

One exception to this lack of participation with young people was the development of the Heart of Walker Supplementary Planning Document (NCC, 2009), which was supported by the engagement charity, Planning Aid North. Generally, however, engagement with young people tends to take place outside of planning and focuses on other initiatives delivered at either the city or neighbourhood level. These have included 'Udecide' projects supported through the Neighbourhood Renewal Fund and the 'MyPlace' project, but these too have experienced severe cut backs in recent years.

As Newcastle's Youth Council gains momentum and because the City has signed up to the Children's Rights Charter, there is a degree of hope that young people will be able to establish a voice in the decision making process. In September 2013, Newcastle's Youth Council presented a report to the policy cabinet, following a city-wide consultation with young people, stating that the council should (among other things) 'ensure free, safe places for young people to go and cheap activities for them to do in their own neighbourhoods, so that young people can have rich experiences in their lives regardless of financial resources within their families or where they live' (NCC, 2013a: 5). However, for the young person using an open space in the east end wards, or indeed any other ward in Newcastle, the method by which they can make their voice heard about the places they use still remains ambiguous.

Conclusion

This chapter set out to offer an insight into how young people value the open spaces in their neighbourhoods. It is clear from the case study discussions that the young people from these deprived neighbourhoods positively engage with their environment and the open spaces within them, supporting the findings of Hart (2002), Day et al (2011) and Burt et al (2013). Not only do they determine the value of those spaces by their aesthetics, but also other factors such as functionality, the ability to meet friends, to feel safe and to have their own place, have equal if not more significance. Interestingly, the young people do not express their desire to access areas of open space elsewhere in the city, or indicate that they experience a worse 'open space deal' than young people in other parts of the city. Rather, they claim ownership of the open spaces in their local neighbourhoods and exert their expert knowledge over them.

This expert knowledge allows the young people to talk with confidence about the adequacy of the facilities within the open space, how others use/misuse the space and even how the wider community perceive their age group. So while the function and social value of open spaces are important, so is the role of the space in the way that it connects them with an identity and an understanding of the broader world, allowing them to 're-contextualise' their role within it (Mazzoleni, 1993; Hopkins, 2010; Mallan and Greenaway, 2011).

Moreover, the case studies have revealed that there is an obvious disjuncture between the perception of open spaces by young people and by the city planners. Despite what might be regarded as the 'ordinariness' and even 'despoiled' appearance of these open spaces, the young people in the projects have built friendships, identities and a sense of their place in society, through their relationship with those places. The current absence of the opportunity to participate in Lefebvre's 'right to the city' will only lead to a political marginalisation of this significant element of the community both now and as they progress into adulthood. In turn, the failure to build in a participatory process for young people in the places that they use and value on a daily basis will seriously undermine any move towards environmental justice (and through this to social justice).

The pursuit of the 'right to the city' at neighbourhood level with young people at its centre could also bring tangible benefits, allowing open spaces to be better planned and maintained by taking on board their heightened knowledge and experience of the area. Indeed, the open spaces themselves could be one such arena where meaningful participation with young people could be undertaken (Percy Smith, 2010). While some steps are being taken through Newcastle's emerging Youth Council, without a specific agenda to consult young people more broadly within their communities, as part of an ongoing plan-making and reviewing process, then such initiatives will only remain ad hoc, or tokenistic at best.

References

Atkinson, R. (2003) 'Domestication by cappuccino or a revenge on urban space? Control and empowerment in the management of public space', *Urban Studies*, 40: 1829-43.

Burt, J., Stewart, D., Preston, S. and Costley, T (2013) *Monitor of engagement with the Natural Environment Survey (2009-2012): Difference in access to the natural environment between social groups within the adult English population*, Natural England Data Reports, Number 003. Available at: http://publications.naturalengland.org.uk/file/4871615

Byrne, J. and Wolch, J.R. (2009) 'Nature, race, and parks: past research and future directions for geographic research', *Progress in Human Geography*, 33(6): 743-65.

Commission for Architecture and the Built Environment (2004) *Space and CABE education, what would you do with this space? Involving young people in the design and care of urban spaces*, London: CABE.

Commission for Architecture and the Built Environment (2010) *Urban Green Nation: Building the evidence base*, London: CABE. Available at http://webarchive.nationalarchives.gov.uk/20110118095356/http:/www.cabe.org.uk/publications/urban-green-nation

Davoudi, S. and Brooks, E. (2012) *Environmental justice and the city*, Global Urban Research Unit, School of Architecture Landscape and Planning, Newcastle University.

Day, L., Sutton, S. and Jenkins, S. (2011) *Children and young people's participation in planning and regeneration. A final report to the Ecorys Research Programme*, Centre for Research in Social Policy.

Day, R. and Wager, F. (2010) 'Parks, streets and 'just empty space': the local environmental experiences of children and young people in a Scottish study', *Local Environment*, 15(6): 509-23.

Driskell, D. (2002) *Creating better cities with children and youth: a manual for participation*, Sterling VA: Stylus Publishing.

Fainstein, S. (2010) *The just city*, New York: Cornell University Press.

Frank, K. (2006) 'The potential of youth participation in planning', *Journal of Planning Literature* 20(4): 351-71.

Gibson, J. (1977) *The theory of affordances*, USA: Hilldale.

Harland, D. (2010) *Byker, a vision for the future*. Available at: www.harch.co.uk/art-architecture/byker-vision-of-the-future/

Hart, R. (1979) *Children's experience of place*, Irvington.

Hart, R. (1992) *Children's participation: from tokenism to citizenship*, Florence: UNICEF.

Hart, R. (1997) *Children's participation: the theory and practice of involving young citizens in community development and environmental care*, London: Earthscan.

Hart, R. (2002) Containing children: some lessons on planning for play from New York City, *Environment and Urbanization* 14(2): 135-48.

Hart, R. (2008) 'Stepping back from "the ladder": reflections on a model of participatory work with children', in A. Reid, B. Jensen, J. Nikel and V. Simovska (eds), *Participation and learning: perspectives on education and the environment, health and sustainability*, Netherlands: Springer, pp 19–31.

Hopkins, P. (2010) *Young people place and identity*, London: Routledge.

Konttinen, S.L. (1983) *Byker*, Jonathan Cape.

Lahman, M. (2008) 'always Othered: ethical research with children', *Journal of Early Childhood Research*, 6(3): 281-300.

Laughlin, D. and Johnson, L. (2011) 'Defining and exploring public space: perspectives of young people from Regent Park, Toronto', *Children's Geographies*, 9: 3-4, 439-56.

Lefebvre, H. (1991) *The production of space*, Oxford: Blackwell.

Lefebvre, H. (1996) *Writings on cities*, ed. and trans. E. Kofman and E. Lebas, Oxford: Blackwell.

Mallan, K. and Greenaway R. (2011) 'Radiant with possibility': involving young people in creating a vision for the future of their community. *Futures* 43(4): 374-86.

Mazzoleni D. (1993) 'The city and the imaginary', in E. Carter, J. Donald and J. Squires (eds) *Space and place: theories of identity and location*, London: Lawrence and Wishart, pp 285-302.

Mitchell, D. (2003) *The right to the city: social justice and the fight for public space*, London: Guildford Press.

Newcastle City Council (2004) *Green spaces ... your spaces: Newcastle's green space strategy.* Available at: http://www.newcastle.gov.uk/wwwfileroot/legacy/ns/strategies/greenspaces/GreenSpaceStrategy.pdf

Newcastle City Council (2006) *Walker Riverside Area Action Plan.* Available at: https://www.newcastle.gov.uk/wwwfileroot/legacy/regen/ldf/Walker_Riverside_AAP.pdf

Newcastle City Council (2009) *Heart of Walker: supplementary planning document.* Available at: http://www.newcastle.com/wwwfileroot/legacy/regen/ldf/HeartofWalkerSPDFebruary2009.pdf

Newcastle City Council (2012) *Green capital bid to the European Commission.* Available at: http://www.thebiggreenpledge.org.uk/sites/www.thebiggreenpledge.org.uk/files/GreenCapital/Bid/NGC%20Bid%20-%20Section%201%20-%20complete.pdf

Newcastle City Council (2013a) '*Seeing Newcastle through young people's eyes.* Available at: https://www.newcastle.gov.uk/sites/drupalncc.newcastle.gov.uk/files/wwwfileroot/your-council/community_engagement/thinkabout_policy_cabinet_11_september_2013.pdf

Newcastle City Council (2013b) *Creating a greener Newcastle.* Available at: http://democracy.newcastle.gov.uk/documents/g4129/Public%20reports%20pack%2013th-Mar-2013%2016.30%20Cabinet.pdf?T=10

Newcastle City Council and Gateshead Council (2011) *Green infrastructure evidence base: final report.* Available at: https://www.gateshead.gov.uk/DocumentLibrary/Building/PlanningPolicy/Evidence/GI/GreenInfrastructureStudy-EvidenceBaseJanuary2011.pdf

Newcastle Gateshead (2014) *Draft One Core Strategy, submission document*. Available at: https://www.gateshead.gov.uk/Building%20 and%20Development/PlanningpolicyandLDF/LocalPlan/ GachteadandNewcastleJointDocuments.aspx

Office of the Deputy Prime Minister (2002) *PPG 17: Planning for open space, sport and recreation*, London: HMSO.

Office for National Statistics (2011) *Census Statistics*.

Percy Smith, B. (2010) 'Councils, consultations and community: rethinking the spaces for children and young people's participation', *Children's Geographies*, 8: 2, 107-122.

Percy Smith, B. and Matthews, H. (2001) 'Tyrannical spaces: young people, bullying and urban neighbourhoods', *Local Environment*, 6(1): 49-63.

Perkins, H. (2010) 'Green spaces of self interest within shared urban governance', *Geography Compass* 4(3): 255-68.

Purcell, M. (2008) *Recapturing democracy*, New York: Routledge.

Roe, M. (2006) 'Making a wish: children and the local landscape', *Local Environment: International Journal of Justice and Sustainability*, 11(2): 163-82.

Roe, M. (2007) 'Feeling "secrety": children's views on involvement in landscape decisions', *Environmental Education Research,* 13(4): 467-85.

Severcan, Y.C. (2003) *Children's attachment to public space in the context of urban regeneration: effects of children's involvement in planning and design activities*, Middle East Technical University, Dissertation.

Shaw, G (2011) *The sly and unseen day*, exhibition, Baltic Centre for Contemporary Art, Gateshead.

Skelton, T. (2007) 'Children, young people, UNICEF and participation', *Children's Geographies*, 5(1): 165-81.

Skelton, T. and Valentine, G. (eds) (1998) *Cool places: geographies of youth cultures*, London: Routledge.

Strife, S. and Downey, L. (2009) 'Childhood development and access to nature. A new direction for environmental inequality research', *Organization & Environment* 22(1): 99-122.

The Scottish Government (2008) *Planning Advice Note 65, Planning and open space*. Available at: http://www.scotland.gov.uk/Resource/ Doc/225179/0060935.pdf

UNICEF (1989) *UN Convention on the rights of the child*. Available at: http://unicef.org.uk/UNICEFs-Work/UN-Convention/

Valentine, G. (2004) *Public space and the culture of childhood*, Aldershot: Ashgate.

Walker, G. (2012) *Environmental justice, concepts, evidence and politics*, London: Routledge.

Ward, C. and Golzen, A. (1978) *Child in the city*, London: Architectural Press.

Wolch, J.R., Byrne, J. and Newell, J.P. (2014) 'Urban green space, public health, and environmental justice: the challenge of making cities "just green enough"', *Landscape and Urban Planning*, 125: 234-44.

Young, I.M. (1990) *Justice and the politics of difference*, Princeton, New Jersey: Princeton University Press.

Young, I. M. (2000) *Inclusion and democracy*, Oxford: Oxford University Press.

Participation, procedural fairness and local decision making

Derek Bell and Simin Davoudi

> There is a critical difference between going through the empty ritual of participation and having the real power needed to affect the outcome of the process... [Participation] without redistribution of power is an empty and frustrating process for the powerless. It allows the powerholders to claim that all sides were considered, but makes it possible for only some of those sides to benefit. It maintains the status quo. (Arnstein, 1969: 216)

People are concerned about more than the effects of local decision making on their lives. They also care about how those decisions are made. Procedural fairness and inclusive public participation in decision making are instrumentally and intrinsically valuable. They are instrumentally valuable because they allow people to defend their own interests in the decision–making process. If the decision making process unfairly excludes some people or unfairly limits their power to affect a decision, they are more likely to find that decision does not benefit them. As Arnstein suggests, a lack of procedural fairness makes it possible for some people to benefit at the expense of others.

However, the value of procedural fairness is not just instrumental. We are also independently concerned that decisions are made fairly. We care about *how* decisions are made as well as *what* the actual outcomes are (Frey et al, 2004). As Frey et al suggest:

> [People care] about how they are treated in the market place, in the public realm, or within hierarchies. The decision making procedures, or institutions, applied in these contexts may importantly affect people's well-being. Institutions express judgements about the people involved that may greatly influence their self-worth. (Frey et al, 2004: 378)

Institutions or decision-making processes that exclude some people or leave some people powerless to influence decisions fail to recognise those people as the political or moral equals of the included and powerful. This failure to show equal respect or equal recognition is itself an important form of injustice. So, for example, we may be unhappy with a decision because we were not properly consulted or included in the decision-making process even if we would have supported the decision that was reached (Frey et al, 2004: 377). Equally, we might accept a decision as legitimate even when we disagree with the outcome because we believe that the institutional arrangements for making the decision were fair and inclusive.

The importance of procedural fairness and public participation in local decision making is the focus of the two chapters in this section. In Chapter 9, Neil Stanley examines the land use planning process in cities in England, especially with regard to controversial developments or locally unwanted land uses (LULUs). He focuses on two questions: what causes public perceptions of unfairness in land use planning? How might planning processes be restructured to avoid public perceptions of unfairness? His discussion of the causes of public perceptions of unfairness emphasises both distributive and procedural justice. As he explains, opposition to a LULU is often based on a perception that one community is being asked to bear a greater burden or risk than other communities. However, this concern about distributive unfairness – or the unfairness of the outcome – is often exacerbated by concerns about the fairness of the decision-making process. Stanley argues that the development process in English cities is particularly likely to generate perceptions of procedural unfairness because public participation comes too late in the decision-making process and public voices are often constrained or marginalised by the institutional arrangements. So, people are unlikely to feel that they have had a 'fair say'. In the final part of his chapter, Stanley considers how land use planning processes for controversial developments might be improved through a critical discussion of a case study of one attempt by a city government to develop a consensus-based approach to planning for waste disposal. Stanley concludes by endorsing the Newcastle Fairness Commission's commitment to the importance not only of making fairer decisions but also of being seen to make fairer decisions.

In Chapter 10, David Webb asks to what extent can we assume that a commitment to fairness within the guiding principles of a city government will translate into fair forms of policy and decision making? Webb argues that the liberal approach to fairness, which has shaped contemporary debates in Newcastle, does not translate easily into practice. He makes his argument through a detailed case study of the development of Cherry Tree View, a new block of self-contained units designed for households facing homelessness. Webb argues that the Elswick area of Newcastle, where Cherry Tree View is located, suffers from inequalities of policy protection, which still remain despite the work of the Newcastle Fairness Commission. His detailed account of the development process highlights both distributive and procedural injustices. He points out that Elswick has a disproportionate share of the city's emergency accommodation for people facing homelessness. He also shows the powerlessness of the local community and the lack of transparency in the decision-making process. He argues that we can best understand the lack of protection for the Elswick area by examining the historical institutional context which has shaped the approach to neighbourhood management in Elswick. He concludes that political commitments to abstract liberal conceptions of fairness do not change the institutional culture of a city government. Instead, they reinforce the separation between political ideals and administrative practice, which allows fairness to be a rhetorical commitment rather than a practical reality. City governments can only make fairness and justice 'real' through administrative decisions rather than political commitments.

Together the contributions to this section of the book illustrate the importance and the difficulty of realising procedural fairness in local decision making in the city. As the critics of democratic proceduralism argue, procedural fairness is not enough to guarantee justice *in* or *of* the city. However, a just city is not possible without fair procedures for local decision making in the city. Designing – or remaking – institutions that can provide fair access to and voice in local decision making, especially with regard to controversial developments, is one key aspect of achieving justice in the city. Fairer and more inclusive democratic processes are not only more likely to deliver fairer outcomes; they also come closer to recognising the fundamental political equality of all citizens. Unfortunately, the chapters in this section show that fair processes are not easy to achieve: commitments by political leaders to abstract principles of fairness are unlikely to translate into fair administrative decision-making procedures without radical changes in the institutional culture of city governments. Moreover, the institutional culture of city governments is unlikely to change while the broader political economy in which they are located remains unchanged.

References

Arnstein, S. (1969) 'A ladder of citizen participation', *Journal of the American Institution of Planners*, 35: 216-24.

Frey, B., Benz, M. and Stutzer, A. (2004) 'Introducing procedural utility: not only what, but also how matters', *Journal of Institutional and Theoretical Economics*, 160: 377–401.

NINE

Public perceptions of unfairness in urban planning

Neil Stanley

Introduction

This chapter addresses the importance of public perceptions of unfairness in land use planning in a city context. We examine the psychological and institutional dimensions of planning that promote perceptions of unfairness among the public, especially the members of a community selected to 'host'[1] a contentious development proposal (otherwise known as a locally unwanted land use (LULU)). We draw attention to lessons that developers, professional planners, planning policy makers and planning decision makers might learn from one notable attempt by a local planning authority to use innovative methods to make, and be seen to make, a fair decision relating to a LULU. While the particular study of decision making we refer to is not located in Newcastle, it is city based, and a comparable Tyneside-based case does exist (see *Gateshead Metropolitan Borough Council v Secretary of State for the Environment* (1995)). Common examples of LULUs include: windfarms, mobile telephone base stations (masts), power stations, factories that discharge pollutants and waste incinerators.

Perceptions of unfairness, the Newcastle Fairness Commission and the planning system

Perceptions of unfairness in planning decision making is one aspect of the increasing levels of concern of western societies with the creation and distribution of risks, identified in Ulrich Beck's *Risk Society* (Beck, 1992). In planning, the fear generated, mostly in a host community, by a LULU, is formally known as 'public concern'. This concept has gained legal recognition as a 'material consideration' (see section 70(2) of the Town and Country Planning Act (TCPA) 1990) in the facility-siting decision stage of the planning system (Piatt, 1997). If public concern arises in the context of a planning application, it must be taken into account by a decision maker. The failure to have regard to a material consideration results in a flawed decision, which may then be the subject of a legal challenge. Detailed consideration of the concept of public concern in planning law is dealt with elsewhere (Stanley, 1998).

In regard to what the public perceive as fair or unfair we draw upon the important work of the Newcastle Fairness Commission (Newcastle Fairness Commission, 2012), which produced a number of fairness principles to guide decision making in the public sector.

The Commission, while recognising that 'fairness' is a contested concept, declined to define fairness and instead set out four key principles to guide fair decision taking based upon available evidence:

> **Fair share** – Where people can expect fair outcomes and a fair share of services, according to their needs.

> **Fair play** – Where people can have confidence that decisions are made in an even-handed, open and transparent manner, according to evidence.

> **Fair go** – Where people have opportunities to participate, and a chance to fulfil their aspirations for the future.

> **Fair say** – Where people feel included in their city, communities and neighbourhoods, given a fair hearing and an effective voice in decision making. (Newcastle Fairness Commission, 2012: 2-3)

A planning process that is perceived by the public as fair is important in two respects: in a practical context, it helps to garner support for proposed developments; and fairness is an important value in its own right (Newcastle Fairness Commission, 2012). Of particular significance in planning policy and planning decision making are the principles of fair play and fair say.

In regard to fair play (that is, procedural fairness) the Newcastle Fairness Commission report contains a telling observation '... the perception of fairness is as important as the substance of it' (Newcastle Fairness Commission, 2012: 33). It therefore matters a great deal that the public feel that they can trust the decision makers; that they believe that the decision process is fair, and that they can influence decision making at the local level. With this observation in mind the report recommended that local authorities seek consensus when making decisions, taking time to listen to the public, however challenging that experience might be. The report suggested that adopting this course of action would lead to 'better decisions, more cohesive communities and fairer outcomes' (Newcastle Fairness Commission, 2012: 33).

A key issue that the Newcastle Fairness Commission report addressed was how to deal with individuals or communities who felt unfairly treated, excluded or forgotten. Applying the Commission's fair play principle, the Commission stated that people must have confidence that decisions are made in an even-handed, open and transparent manner according to evidence. Not only must a decision process be fair but also people must perceive that the outcome of the decision process is fair.

The work of the Newcastle Fairness Commission in regard to 'fair say' reflects the conclusions that Sherry Arnstein came to in her seminal work on public participation (Arnstein, 1969). Arnstein studied the degree to which decision processes provided opportunities for citizen participation in important decisions that affect them, such as planning, and the degree to which citizens control the outcome of decision processes. Arnstein observed that, 'There is a critical difference between going through the empty ritual of participation and having the real power needed to affect the outcome of the process' (Arnstein, 1969: 216).

Arnstein devised a 'ladder' of participation to describe the extent of citizen power in determining the outcome of decision processes. Beginning with the lowest rung, the ladder comprises: 'manipulation, therapy, informing, consultation, placation, partnership, delegated power and finally citizen control' (Arnstein, 1969: 216). In regard to planning in England and Wales the relevant rungs are informing, consulting and placating. These forms of citizen participation are tokenistic. In consultation citizens are allowed by the power holders (the administrators of the decision system and decision makers) to have a voice but they lack the power to ensure that their views carry appropriate weight. In placation citizens advise the power holders but the power holders retain the right to decide the outcome of the decision process. Thus, while citizens are allowed an opportunity to have their say, for example in regard to a planning application, they have no power to affect the weight, if any, which a power holder will accord their inputs into the planning decision process. In such circumstances it is arguable that citizens have been unfairly denied an 'effective voice in decision-making' (Newcastle Fairness Commission, 2012: 3).

Why the public often perceive a decision to grant planning permission for a LULU as unfair

Public perceptions of unfairness, especially in a host community, are influenced by the extent to which development-related risks and benefits are equitably distributed (Stanley, 1998). It is patently unfair when a community is required to bear all the costs (that is, adverse impacts of a proposed development) but does not receive any compensatory benefits for hosting a LULU (Austin and Schill, 1994; Been, 1993). Expressions of concern, relating to perceived unfairness, are likely to be most acute when the distribution of costs and benefits involve the siting of a hazardous facility. When faced with a LULU, a host community will be more inclined to oppose the proposal if it believes that the planning system is unfairly imposing a hazard upon it (see *R v SoSTI, ex p. Duddridge and others*, 1996).

Perceptions that a LULU has been unfairly imposed upon a host community will be exacerbated by the lack of adequate consultation by the developer with a host community regarding the selection of the site for the LULU. The first real indication that a host community may have of an impending LULU is the posting of planning notices close to the site of the proposed LULU, giving brief details of the planning application. The failure of a developer to provide a host community with an adequate opportunity to comment upon the location of a LULU may understandably be perceived as a denial of 'fair say'.

In addition, the host community will have regard to any history or pattern of similar developments, which have, over time, been imposed upon it. The host community may feel that a pending decision to grant planning permission for yet another LULU is just another of a long line of decisions that unfairly locate LULUs in their community (see discussion of patterns of locating LULUs in disadvantaged communities in Chapter 10). In such circumstances it is understandable why a community would have little confidence that the outcomes of the planning system are fair.

In the US, developers have attempted to dodge this issue by attempting to site LULUs in industrialised areas in anticipation that local opposition will be muted (Farkas, 1980). This response to the problem of finding suitable sites for a LULU is known as 'the path of least resistance' (Morell and Magorian, 1982: 155). It is based on three assumptions:

1. Host community concern is likely to be muted where similar facilities already operate without any apparent problems.

2. The residents in these host communities are unlikely to organise themselves into an effective opposition.
3. Local planning policy may support the proposed type of development in an area that hosts similar development.

The major shortcoming of this approach is the realisation, by the host community, that it has been selected as the dumping ground for the types of developments that other communities do not want. Experience in the US illustrates the shortcomings of this approach: outrage at the intrinsic unfairness of such decisions and a sustained campaign to fight LULU dumping on disadvantaged communities (Bullard, 1994).

Individuals living in a host community may conclude that, when faced with the imminent imposition of a LULU, the planning system is operating unfairly. This perception only adds to the list of reasons that explain why a high level of public concern is to be expected.

Unfairness and 'public concern'

There are often fundamental differences in development-related risk perceptions between a developer, the local planning authority and members of a host community. This issue has been encapsulated in the following model: risk = hazard + outrage (Sandman, 1993) where 'hazard' is the risk that the developer and, arguably the local planning authority, pay primary attention to whereas 'outrage' comprises the wider range of threats that concern the host community. Developers and the local planning authority, in its regulatory role, assess risk using statistical risk assessments to calculate the probability of adverse outcomes (that is hazard) of siting a LULU in a particular location. Little, if any attempt, appears to be made to understand the process by which a host community assesses the risks of a LULU.

Sandman's 'outrage' model and the concept of public concern in planning law are complementary. Therefore, the planning system must address both 'hazard' and 'outrage' if it is to command the support of a host community and be perceived by that community as delivering fair outcomes.

Any attempt by the developer or local planning authority to 'educate' the host community and persuade it that their concerns are the wrong ones and that only 'hazard' (that is the identification and calculation of adverse outcomes based upon formal risk assessment) is relevant to the outcome of a planning application will only serve to reinforce the existing impressions of the host community that its concerns are:

- not being properly assessed
- being downplayed
- falling upon deaf ears.

Similarly, any attempt by developers, local authority planning officials or decision makers to dismiss expressions of outrage as ill-informed, irrational and selfish manifestations of NIMBYism (acronym – not in my back yard – implying that individuals support facility siting in principle but oppose it in their own neighbourhood on insupportable grounds – also see Devine-Wright, 2011) will only inflame opposition. It is a mistake for a developer to assume that the host community is only motivated by self-interest in objecting to a LULU. In addition to concerns relating to health, pollution, and local amenity, the host community is also concerned about the fairness of the planning process and its outcomes (the decision to grant/refuse permission for a facility).

The feelings of grievance experienced by a host community caused by:

- being talked down to by others; or
- having its concerns unfairly dismissed as ill-informed and/or irrelevant

will serve to reduce its ability to view any threat posed by a LULU with an open mind. Perceptions of unfairness in the host community are thus reinforced.

The frustration that the developer and the local planning authority experience when a host community does not appear to accept the logic of formal risk assessments that demonstrate the safety of a proposed LULU, could be reduced if the developer, the planners and the decision maker acquired a better understanding of how a host community assesses the threats posed by a LULU.

How the structure of the planning process can exacerbate public perceptions of unfairness

One reason why the public may perceive the planning system as operating unfairly concerns a systemic problem: sequential planning policy making, in which few members of the public are engaged, followed by the implementation of that policy in a decision to grant or refuse planning permission for a proposed development.

The planning system utilises a consultation-driven approach to the formulation of policy, which guides proposed development into appropriate locations (Moore and Purdue, 2012: chapter 10). Detailed planning policy is contained in a Local Development Framework (LDF), which each local planning authority drafts. Unfortunately, the formulation of LDF policy attracts minimal public interest and engagement. Often, only professional planners employed by a local authority to draft LDF policy content, and land owners whose future plans to develop their land holdings, which may be obstructed by unfavourable wording of LDF policy, engage with local planning policy formulation. Attempts to engage stakeholders, especially the public, in the design of local policy via the public screening of videos and presentations in school halls, and staffing information points in city centre locations, meet with little success in capturing an accurate set of public opinions.[2] Publicity in local newspapers advertising the location of premises where draft LDFs may be inspected, generally fails to engage the public with LDF policy content. Not only are LDF policies framed in 'planning speak' but it is likely that an individual will not perceive any benefit in responding to a consultation largely because, at the policy making stage of planning, there appears to be no threat to an individual's core interests.

The consultation-driven planning policy process is premised upon an assumption that the benefit to individuals of investing time in reading draft planning policy and providing feedback to the local planning authority is self-evident. In practice, the likelihood of an individual choosing to provide feedback is small. Only if the individual perceives some threat or advantage in the draft policy content to his/her self-interest might he/she provide feedback. The local policy formulation process is based upon the assumption that all individuals consume information as 'fact respecters'. Fact respecters are individuals who carefully analyse information before reaching a considered conclusion. Unfortunately, for the local policy process there are a variety of shortcuts that individuals use to balance the time and effort involved in analysing information against any anticipated benefit (O'Hare et al, 1983). Thus the design of the local policy process, premised upon the assumption that everyone is a fact respecter, will fail to elicit accurate insights into the opinions of well informed individuals.

The design of the planning decision system, which focuses upon an all or nothing win/lose outcome, compels each side to adopt polarised and entrenched positions. The development approval process usually commences with the submission of a detailed planning application by the developer and this may be interpreted by the host community as confirmation that the decision is a foregone conclusion and an example of a 'decide-announce-defend' decision process. The proposal is clearly 'not negotiable' and the host community is left to mount a rearguard action with limited hope of securing a rejection of the planning application. In these circumstances it is highly likely that a host community will perceive the manner in which the planning system and its decision outcomes operate as unfair.

We also note the restriction upon a decision maker's ability to fully reflect the concerns of a host community in a planning decision: the fact that the planning system operates in the wider public interest (Moore and Purdue, 2012: 1). Thus, the interests of a host community are not a paramount consideration in any planning decision. The host community's concerns, whether public concern (including perceptions of unfairness) or other material consideration, are just some of the many considerations that the decision maker must have regard to (see section 70(2) TCPA 1990).

Planning decision makers, in reaching their decision to grant/refuse a planning application are legally obliged to have regard to contents of the LDF and any other material considerations (section 70(2) TCPA 1990). Thus, only considerations that are relevant to planning law and relevant to the case before the decision maker are taken into account. Individuals in a host community must therefore be careful to base their objections to a proposed LULU upon only those issues that the system considers to be valid. The battlefield on which a planning application is fought is restricted by not only the contents of LDF policy, at the local level, but also national planning policy (for example, the National Planning Policy Framework). Without appropriate advice and guidance members of a host community, especially one which is disadvantaged, will be in a weak position to fight a LULU when compared to the ability of a developer to fund expert legal and planning advice. In a planning decision relating to a proposed LULU, a host community, especially one in a poor area, may fear that it will be 'outgunned' by the developer's legal and planning teams.

The tools available to developers, the local planning authority and planning decision makers to address inherent planning system weaknesses causing the perception of unfairness

In this section the use of mitigation, compensation, incentives and improved engagement with a host community is discussed. The first three of these measures may be deployed by developers and decision makers to address the adverse impacts, or 'costs' of a proposed LULU, while the final mechanism is helpful in avoiding the developer and host community adopting entrenched positions.

Planning decision makers have the power to mitigate some of the adverse impacts of a development. Planning permission is invariably granted subject to planning conditions and these can be framed in such a way as to mitigate harmful impacts of a proposed development, for example, limiting factory hours of operation in order to address noise concerns raised by nearby homeowners.

Despite the use of planning conditions (section 70(2) TCPA 1990; Moore and Purdue, 2012: ch 15) to address the direct 'costs' of development, currently the system does not fully mitigate the full range of adverse consequences of the grant of planning permission, and therefore resorting to compensation and/or incentives may be required.

The Environmental Protection Agency in the US supports mitigation measures in preference to compensation because it is financially efficient to proactively eliminate issues at the design stage rather than paying out compensation once a facility is operational (McMahon et al, 1982).

The planning system in England and Wales enables a developer, rather than the planning decision maker, to address the adverse impacts of its development proposal via the use of a planning obligation (see sections 106, 106A and 106B TCPA 1990). An obligation will run in tandem with a grant of planning permission for the development to which it relates. Obligations may be used to provide a range of gains, such as the funding of road improvements where congestion would arise from the proposed development. The use of obligations is tightly controlled by government planning policy (Circular 5/2005) and the Secretary of State desires that obligations should only be sought where they are necessary to the grant of planning permission, relevant to planning, relevant to the development permitted, directly related to the development, and fairly and reasonably related in scale and kind to the development and are reasonable in all other respects. Unacceptable development should not be granted permission merely because the developer offers planning gain, which is unrelated to the proposed development. Equally, an acceptable development should not be denied planning permission because the developer refuses to offer planning gain.

In 2010 the government introduced a further mitigation measure: the Community Infrastructure Levy (CIL) (section 205 Planning Act 2008; Moore and Purdue, 2012: ch 18). The CIL supplements the planning obligation system by securing additional gains. CIL is intended to provide a fair mechanism to secure contributions for infrastructure from developers and encourage planning for economic and housing growth by local and regional authorities. CIL funds must be spent by local authorities to support development in their area. CIL must be used to provide new infrastructure rather than improving existing infrastructure unless the need for improvement stems from the new development.

The government requires (section 115 of the Localism Act 2011) local authorities to allocate a proportion of CIL revenue, raised in a neighbourhood, to that neighbourhood. Any neighbourhood bearing the brunt of new development should receive revenue that will address the impacts associated with the new development. Infrastructure funded by CIL includes: transport, flood defences, schools, hospitals, health and social care facilities, play areas, parks, open spaces, sports facilities, district heating, police stations and other community safety related schemes. CIL is aimed at providing infrastructure for an area rather than an individual planning application. Planning obligations will continue to be relevant in mitigating adverse impacts of an individual planning application. CIL and planning obligations are therefore to have complementary roles. Currently, it is too early to assess the impact of CIL upon host community perceptions of unfairness.

In order to address the costs of siting a LULU in a host community, it is commonly thought that a host community will readily agree to community compensation as the acceptable price of a LULU and that an increased flow of community compensation increases the acceptability of the development to the affected public. Richard Cowell's work regarding compensation and the siting of windfarms reminds us that a host community will not necessarily accept a LULU just because a range of community gains are on offer, for example, the prospect of receiving a percentage of windfarm revenue (Cowell et al, 2011). This note of caution comes at a time when the government hopes to encourage community compensation provision as part of a strategy to increase investment in renewable technology. While the government has associated the rapid expansion of renewables in other countries with higher levels of public support where significant amounts of compensatory benefits are on offer, this ignores the particular circumstances in other countries that have led to such a rapid expansion. In other words, acceptability is not just a matter of the 'right' amount of compensation.

In the US, some states have chosen to compensate host communities via reductions in local property taxes. The New Jersey Major Hazardous Waste Facilities Siting Act 1981 makes provision for a 5% gross receipts compensatory tax. In contrast, the opportunity to provide compensatory benefits is much more restricted in England. The use of planning obligations by a developer to provide community gains, as noted above, is tightly controlled by central government policy

(Circular 5/2005). Community benefits that have little or no direct link with the development will carry little or no weight in a planning decision (see *Tesco Stores Ltd v Secretary of State for the Environment* 1995). Thus, although a developer could, via a planning obligation offer to provide the following compensatory benefits:

- establish a contingency fund to pay for any decline in property values due to the siting of its development within a host community;
- pay for regular health screening of members of the host community;
- pay for the cost of providing pollution monitoring equipment and training of community representatives so that the host community can ascertain whether the development is operating within safe limits;
- pay compensation for damage to community image,

it is very unlikely that the current planning decision system would take these compensatory benefits into account (see Circular 5/2005).

A community may still require an inducement to encourage it to host a LULU. The provision of incentives is not uncommon in the US, for example, the Massachusetts Hazardous Waste Facility Siting Act 1980, but their use is currently not permitted in England.

To address the sense of unfairness experienced by a community when it is not consulted upon the selection of the site of a proposed LULU, prior to the developer lodging a planning application, it is open to a developer to simply avoid relying upon the minimal formal consultation guaranteed by the current planning system. Frequent informal contact between the developer and host community is likely to be more productive of a win/win outcome in which the developer obtains planning permission, with the support of the host community, and the community is fully compensated for its losses. The developer should also avoid, in the early stages of the decision process, presenting the host community with a detailed planning proposal on a take it or leave it basis.

The requirement for developer–host community negotiations has been given formal legal recognition, but unfortunately not in England and Wales: see the Massachusetts Hazardous Waste Facility Siting Act 1980 (O'Hare et al, 1983). However, the planning system in England does not prevent negotiations taking place between developer and host community. One example of a developer going well beyond the current minimum planning system requirements to consult and engage the public is the Tidal Lagoon Swansea Bay plc application to construct a tidal lagoon power station in Swansea Bay (Tidal Lagoon Swansea Bay plc, 2013).

While the current design of the planning system is not conducive to a win/win consensual outcome, the host community does have a significant bargaining chip to play. A concerted campaign of opposition may persuade a decision maker to reject the LULU planning application, thereby forcing the developer to expend additional time and money in appealing the refusal. In return for hosting the developer's LULU, the host community will expect the developer to provide full compensation.

One local authority's attempt to address LULU-related challenges

We now examine a 'famous' case study involving a planning application for the siting of an Energy from Waste (EfW) incinerator in Hampshire (Petts, 1995). The public's vociferous opposition (see Sandman's 'outrage' model in the section about unfairness and 'public concern') to this particular LULU, forced the county waste planning authority to review its entire approach to developing local waste policy and implementing that policy by granting planning permission for a waste management facility.

In the 1990s, Hampshire County Council (the Council) realised that it was facing a waste crisis. The geology of Hampshire, comprised largely of chalk, was unsuitable for landfilling municipal solid waste. Waste incineration seemed the solution. The Council's waste policy (Hampshire County Council, 1989) included an incineration option.

In 1991 the Council, as the waste management authority for Hampshire, submitted a planning application for a 400,000 tonnes per annum EfW incinerator in Portsmouth. The application met with 'strong, well organised and concerted' (Petts, 1995: 524) opposition from a range of stakeholders, including Portsmouth City Council. Local protesters organised a 'Ban the Burner' campaign, and, backed by local media, produced a 22,000 signature petition opposing the application and over 500 letters of objection (Day, 2000).

The Council's reliance on the standard consultation-based formation of local waste planning policy failed to anticipate the host community's outrage. It was not difficult to anticipate why the concerns of the host community had surfaced at a late stage in the planning process – the facility siting stage. This was the stage at which the implementation of the Council's waste policy posed a major threat to the interests of the host community. Not only did the objectors oppose the incinerator, but they questioned the Council's waste policy priorities:

- an over-emphasis on waste disposal at the expense of recycling and waste minimisation;
- the need for such a large incinerator;
- incinerator's environmental impacts: pollution, visual intrusion, poor design, traffic issues and proximity to a residential area.

The Council was surprised when its planning application was rejected and was even more surprised at the level of opposition its proposal had generated. It was forced to consider the following:

- Why had its reliance on consultation-based policy formulation failed to attract support?
- Without sound support for its waste policy, how could it proceed with the facility siting stage of its strategy?

How did the Council tackle the problems it had identified by its failure to obtain planning permission for a city based, EfW incinerator? The Council commissioned a proactive community involvement programme to elicit information from a wide range of stakeholders. The Council wished to engage stakeholders in LDF policy and win the support of stakeholders for both LDF waste policy and its outcomes (that is, the implementation of LDF policy by applying for permission to build an EfW incinerator). The Council's programme hinged upon the establishment of three Community Advisory Forums (CAFs) in strategic locations within the county.

Realising the defects in its previous local waste policy: that citizens were consulted on LDF waste policy only after it had been drawn up, the Council intended that CAFs would encourage meaningful engagement with LDF waste policy. To be a worthwhile exercise, the Council desired that the CAFs:

- were allowed adequate time for discussion;
- would ensure that all waste management options were on the table;
- would ensure that CAF participants were placed in an equal position, especially in regard to access to information (that is, CAFs could request any information whether for or against a particular waste option); and
- that each CAF would aim to achieve a consensual outcome.

Efforts were made to ensure that a cross-section of stakeholders were represented on each CAF, but the company chosen by the Council to construct and operate its waste management facilities, observed but did not participate in CAF meetings. Each CAF was to examine all options to manage the Council's municipal solid waste and achieve a broad base of support for the strategy that emerged. The CAFs findings would then be fed into proposals for site specific waste treatment facilities. The Council published a draft waste strategy (County Waste Management Plan, 1989), which the CAFs used to facilitate discussion. The Council confirmed that its waste management plan would be amended in the light of the findings of the CAFs. The CAFs had an advisory function only: CAF discussions could not determine the direction and contents of the Council's waste policy.

The use of CAFs does have a number of benefits when compared to traditional consultation-driven policy making:

- CAF participants are brought up to a common level of understanding so that informed discussion takes place.
- Less articulate CAF members are allowed sufficient time to consider the available information before making contributions to discussions.
- Discussion occurs in a constructive environment.

The Council's CAFs did achieve a consensus among most stakeholders that an integrated waste management strategy was necessary and enabled stakeholders to understand the views of other stakeholders. The CAFs improved the credibility and trustworthiness of local authority waste disposal officers among CAF members. Council officers' and key elected members' understanding of public concern was enhanced. The use of CAFs demonstrated the value of slowing down the traditional policy process to allow opinions to be expressed and to revisit draft waste strategy. CAF use enabled the county to say that it had genuinely consulted its stakeholders (Stanley, 2000: 1231).

The use of CAFs did, however, have shortcomings:

- there was a dominance of expert one-way delivery of information (experts making presentations to CAF participants);
- the limited opportunities for CAFs to listen to contrasting opinions;
- the relatively short timescale within which the CAFs met for discussion;
- complaints by elected councillors that the CAFs undermined their role as democratically elected representatives of the public.

The council's CAF report confirmed likely public support for EfW incineration as one component of the council's waste policy. The report revealed CAF reservations regarding:

- the polluting impact of such a large incinerator;
- how to monitor the performance of an operational EfW incinerator.

The report contained a CAF proposal that the Council should provide increased support for waste reduction and waste recycling.

The objectives of CAF participants and the Council differed in important respects. The Council wished to raise the profile of waste management issues, to listen to the opinions expressed by CAF participants and to achieve a consensus that the Council's integrated waste management strategy was acceptable to stakeholders. In contrast, CAF participants desired to influence both the Council's waste policy and the planning decisions relating to the implementation of the Council's waste policy.

The Council subsequently applied for and was granted planning approval for an EfW incinerator located well away from Portsmouth. Relevant to the successful grant of planning permission were the following considerations, which underscore the importance of the issues addressed in this chapter:

- The permitted EfW incinerator was small scale and would only burn 60% of the waste arising in the area in which it was located.
- The site selected for the incinerator had previously been used for incineration and was compatible with adjacent land uses.
- The incinerator was designed to minimise visual impact.
- The Environment Agency had already issued an environmental permit, relating to the environmentally acceptable operation of the facility, before the planning application was granted.
- The facility would meet an urgent need.

This list of factors, which were instrumental in the success of the planning application, did not, however, address all the concerns of the host community.

Concluding remarks

In this chapter we have attempted to highlight the significance of public perceptions of unfairness in land use planning decisions in cities. In so doing, we aim to provide a pragmatic analysis of injustice in and of the city. In common with a number of contributors to this text, the author favours Fainstein's multiculturalist conception of justice (Fainstein, 2010) as opposed to Rawls' political liberalist theory of justice (Rawls 1972 and 2001). In focusing our analysis upon: the psychological and institutional factors that tend to promote host community perceptions of unfairness in planning decision making; the work of the Newcastle Fairness Commission; and a local planning authority's laudable attempt to address the challenges of siting a LULU with a consensus-based approach to planning practice, we hope to persuade developers, planning experts, planning policy makers and decision makers that significant improvements can be made in the current planning process. In particular, decision makers should strive not only to make fairer decisions but also be seen to be making fairer decisions.

Notes

[1] Hereinafter referred to as 'the host community'.

[2] The case study by Petts (1995), referred to in the final section, impliedly supports this contention in that the strong public concern and opposition to the proposed waste incinerator did not surface during the period in which public consultation regarding the County's waste management policy priorities was taking place.

References

Arnstein, S. (1969) 'A ladder of citizen participation', *Journal of the American Institution of Planners*, 35: 216-24.

Austin, R. and Schill, M. (1994) 'Black, brown, red and poisoned', in R. Bullard (ed) *Unequal protection: Environmental justice and communities of color*, New York, NY: Sierra Club Books, chapter 3.

Beck, U. (1992) *Risk society: Towards a new modernity*, London: Sage.

Been, V. (1993) 'What's fairness got to do with it? Environmental justice and the siting of locally undesirable land uses', *Cornell Law Review*, 78: 1001.

Bullard, R. (1994) *Unequal protection: Environmental justice and communities of color*, New York, NY: Sierra Club Books.

Circular 5/2005, issued by the Department for Communities and Local Government.

Cowell, R. Bristow, G. and Munday, M. (2011) 'Acceptance, acceptability and environmental justice: the role of community benefits in wind energy and development', *Journal of Planning and Management*, 54(4): 539-57.

Day, P. (2000) *Environmental law and legislation*. Presentation at Environmental Law and Legislation Conference 25/1/2000 University of Leeds.

Devine-Wright, P. (ed) (2011) *Renewable energy and the public: From NIMBY to participation* London: Earthscan.

Fainstein, S. (2010) *The just city*, Ithaca, NY: Cornell University Press.

Farkas, A. (1980) 'Overcoming public opposition to the establishment of new hazardous waste disposal sites', *Capital University Law Review*, 9: 542-54.

Gateshead Metropolitan Borough Council v Secretary of State for the Environment (1995) Environmental Law Reports 37.

Hampshire County Council (1998) *County waste management plan*, Winchester: Hampshire County Council

McMahon, R., Ernst, C. and Haymore, C. (1982) *Using compensation and incentives when siting hazardous waste management facilities: A handbook*, Washington, DC: EPA.

Moore, V. and Purdue, M. (2012) *A practical approach to planning law*, Oxford: Oxford University Press.

Morell, D. and Magorian, C. (1982) *Siting hazardous waste facilities*, Cambridge, MA: Ballinger.

Newcastle Fairness Commission (2012) *Report of the Newcastle Fairness Commission,* [online] Newcastle upon Tyne. Available at: www.ncl.ac.uk/socialrenewal/engagement/fairnesscommission/ [accessed January 2016].

O'Hare, M., Bacow, L. and Sanderson, D. (1983) *Facility siting and public opposition*, New York, NY: Van Nostrand Reinhold.

Petts, J. (1995) 'Waste management strategy development: a case study of community involvement and consensus-building in Hampshire', *Journal of Environmental Planning and Management*, 38(4): 519.

Piatt, A. (1997) 'Public concern - a material consideration?', *Journal of Planning and Environment Law*, 397.

R v Secretary of State for Trade and Industry, ex parte Duddridge and others (1996) *Environmental Law Reports*, 325.

Rawls, J. (1972) *A theory of justice*, Oxford: Oxford University Press.

Rawls, J. (2001) *Justice as fairness, a restatement*. Cambridge, MA: Harvard University Press.

Sandman, P. (1993) *Responding to community outrage: Strategies for effective risk communication*, Fairfax, VA: American Industrial Hygiene Association.

Stanley, N. (1998) 'Public concern: the decision-maker's dilemma', *Journal of Planning and Environment Law*, 919-34.

Stanley, N. (2000) 'Contentious planning disputes: an insoluble problem?', *Journal of Planning and Environment Law*, 1226-39.

Tesco Stores Ltd v Secretary of State for the Environment (1995) *Journal of Planning and Environment Law*, 581-604.

Tidal Lagoon Swansea Bay plc (2013) *Consultation strategy in support of the Statement of Community Consultation*. [pdf] Available at: http:// tidallagoon.opendebate.co.uk/files/TidalLagoon/160513_TLSB_ consultation_strategy_FINAL.pdf [accessed January 2016].

Legislation

Localism Act 2011: Part 6, Chapter 2.

Massachusetts Waste Facility Siting Act 1980.

Planning Act 2008.

Town and Country Planning Act 1990.

TEN

The importance of the past: cultural legacy and making fairness real

David Webb

Introduction

The deployment of fairness within the discourse of local government implies that this concept has both political value and practical effect, and yet the complexities of and constraints on local government suggest that governing fairly is unlikely to be straightforward. Fairness in Newcastle entails the overlaying of a particular framework of principles onto established practices for governing locally. This chapter deals with two questions which arise from this:

- Is this framework sufficient?
- To what extent can we assume that a commitment to fairness within the guiding principles of an organisation will translate into fair forms of policy and decision making?

These questions are pursued through a case study of an approach to on-the-fly policy making, which raises difficult questions about what fairness means in practice and in the context of competing priorities. The events discussed took place partly prior to the discussions around fairness in Newcastle, although they raise issues around the fair stewardship of neighbourhoods, which have still not been addressed three years on from the publication of the Fairness Commission report.

This chapter makes three arguments in response to the questions above. First, it is argued that the Elswick area, in which the case study is based, suffers from inequalities of policy protection, which have been highlighted by residents but unfortunately still remain in spite of the work of the Fairness Commission. Second, the chapter argues that the potential consequences of these inequalities are exacerbated by a history of unfair treatment that has been felt by the residents of Elswick and should be taken into account in discussions about how to promote fairness in the future. Finally, it is argued that these inequalities of policy protection and historical treatment can be explained to a large extent by the institutional context that has shaped the approach to neighbourhood management in Elswick, and that this attention to the culture of local government is a blind spot in the way Newcastle has approached fairness. To make these arguments, this chapter begins by providing a contextual description of local politics in the city and a discussion about how fairness is understood within the headline statements of aspiration of the two local parties. The chapter's argument is then situated within established critiques of liberal approaches to fairness, before turning to the case example and finally to the wider issues it illustrates.

The political context in Newcastle

Newcastle is a city that benefits from a strong tradition and level of electoral support for left wing politics. The past three decades have been dominated by Labour and the Liberal Democrats, with the latter gaining control in 2004 but losing it back to Labour in 2011. Fairness has been a recurrent theme of the local political discourse throughout the last decade, although the Liberal Democrats have tended to emphasise inclusivity ahead of redistribution. In their 2004 manifesto, the Liberal Democrats set out seven principles, two of which were to:

• be an open, accountable, listening, responsive council;
• put the customer and citizen at the heart of everything we do, delivering services in a caring and sensitive manner. (Newcastle Liberal Democrats, 2012: 2)

Likewise, at a national level, fairness became a prominent term used by the Liberal Democrats to describe their attempts to ameliorate Conservative-led budget cuts.

The post 2011 Labour administration has been accompanied by two successive and interrelated attempts to encapsulate the values the party seeks to advance. A wave of fairness commissions were established by Labour local authorities in the early years of the coalition government. These emphasised the importance of greater income equality in society, and in doing so, challenged the limited definition of fairness within national politics as a smoothing of austerity measures. They also responded to the need to define a local agenda that could take up the coalition's challenge of devolving responsibility through localism. The same challenge also frames Newcastle's membership of the Cooperative Councils network, which promotes active citizenship and externalised forms of not-for-profit service delivery, but which seeks to combine this with strategic leadership aimed at an equitable distribution of local services.

The cooperative agenda, and the Liberal Democrat principles set out above, can be seen as attempts to throw off Newcastle City Council's reputation for, in one commentator's words, being 'a traditional "old" Labour, paternalistic style of authority …' (Dargan, 2002: 27), 'with strong, professionalised departments that bring dangers of a "non-corporate", or silo-based, culture of service delivery' (Davoudi and Healey, 1994: 13). Indeed, these charges have served to focus local political criticism: the 2004 Liberal Democrat administration placed community involvement high up the agenda of its manifesto and the party has more recently argued that Labour was taking Newcastle 'back to the days of decisions being taken in secret' and 'back to top-down, unaccountable, partisan politics' (Newcastle Liberal Democrats, 2012: 1). Together then, fairness commissions and the cooperative council ethos have been used to rebut these claims and set the agenda for a reformed organisational culture.

Newcastle's Fairness Commission and the promotion of liberal values

As Chapter 2 of this volume demonstrates, the Newcastle Fairness Commission drew on an expanded set of liberal principles as a means of approaching justice in the city. Its brief, which secured broad, cross-party support, was to set out fairness principles, assess evidence of the degree of fairness in the city and identify the critical policies that would need to be put in place to create and secure a fairer city (Newcastle Fairness Commission, 2012). The emphasis within both the brief and the Commission's final report was on distributing council services in such a way as to achieve a more equal distribution of opportunities and burdens to citizens across the city. This led to the production of four overarching principles, two of which – fair outcomes and fair opportunity – referred to the distribution of goods and bads within the city, while a further two – fair play and fair say – referenced citizens' rights to an even-handed and unbiased decision making process and to the chance of influence. The use of these generalised principles to conceptualise local justice issues in Newcastle had two immediate effects on the authority's external relationships. First, it enabled discourses of fairness to be made mobile and compatible with other local authorities seeking a joined-up critique of contrasting coalition discourses.[1] Second, it provided advice on questions of resource distribution to a timescale that responded to the rapid imposition of cuts by central government.

While a principles-led approach to pursuing fairness allowed Newcastle to look outwards towards its political and economic environment, its liberal foundation has been subject to a range of criticisms. Perhaps the most stark of these is that the generation of principles and ideals, while helpful for persuading citizens and policy makers to support common goals, is necessarily removed from the way in which urban space is actually experienced (Connolly and Steil, 2009) and is often ineffective at engaging with the contested dynamics involved in making particular decisions about the use of space. Susan Fainstein argues that:

> The fairly glaring weakness of [many of the dominant arguments on social justice] as practical tools is their lack of concern for the methods of achieving their ends, the absence of a formula for dealing with entrenched power, and their indifference to the costs and trade-offs that will be incurred by actually seeking to produce social justice. (Fainstein, 2009: 27)

Furthermore, the adoption of liberal principles in Newcastle might be seen as forming part of a wider culture of government in which the tendency, identified by Fainstein, for liberal theories to float above the realities of implementation, is exacerbated by an established separation of the realms of politics and administration, which frees up local politicians to concentrate on appealing to the external political and economic environment discussed above. One of the consequences of such separation is the direction of political attention to technical and spatial representations of injustice in the city and to principles for achieving desired future states, while the management of intervention proceeds on the axiom that justice can be made technical and rolled out via the administration.

One of the consequences of separating ideals from implementation, and politics from administration, is that any political stance taken towards fairness becomes predicated on a particular institutional context that defines how that stance should be carried forward. If this context is taken for granted then there is a danger that local government becomes unable to reflect on the relationship between the approach to government and its outcomes. A similar point is made by Young, who argues that the use of ideal principles to attend to issues of distributive justice across a city 'ignores and tends to obscure the institutional context within which those distributions take place, and which is at least partly the cause of patterns of distribution' (Young, 1990: 22). This, of course, has significant potential to hinder efforts to combat injustice.

The bias against critical reflection within liberal approaches to government serves to depoliticise public administration by defining this as separate to, and potentially obscured from, the realm where political agendas are set and strategies developed. Against this backdrop, practical illustration of actual experiences of injustices provides a necessary foil with the potential to add insights that would otherwise be obscured and to repoliticise this realm by emphasising the inequalities that pervade it. Conceptualising injustice and democratic practice in the terms and timeframes of those it affects makes it possible to challenge the atemporal nature of abstract templates and ideal principles. This not only allows patterns of governmental treatment to be identified but also raises questions about what it means to be 'fair' to communities that have suffered greater injustice in the past.

Introducing Cherry Tree View

Cherry Tree View (hereafter referred to as CTV) is the name given to a new block of self-contained units designed for households facing homelessness and in need of emergency accommodation. In 2009, under a Liberal Democrat administration, Newcastle City Council began the process of deciding where this block should be built and ultimately decided to locate it in Elswick, one of the most deprived parts of the city and one which already hosted a substantial proportion of the city's homeless provision. Planning decisions in the UK are typically subject to strict, centralised direction, however in some cases, such as CTV, national policy is silent. In the absence of statutory policy at the national or local levels it becomes necessary to answer policy questions through the making of an actual decision. While high level reports can sometimes fudge decisions or deal with issues in a vague way (Gaffikin and Sterrett, 2006), no such luxury is afforded to decision making at the level of individual projects, which cannot avoid the need to resolve competing perspectives and priorities.[2]

Context for the decision

The 1996 Housing Act places a duty on local authorities to provide accommodation to homeless people in priority need. This duty can be

Figure 10.1 South-facing aspect of Cherry Tree View with children's play area to the centre and adjacent housing to the right (out of shot)

Source: the author

fulfilled through private sector partners or by offering direct provision. None of those involved in the CTV dispute contested the principle of providing such accommodation; rather, it was the process and outcome of the Council's decision to relocate its existing provision that inflamed local residents. The CTV development entailed the decommissioning of three blocks of emergency accommodation located on an edge-of-city-centre site, directly adjacent to 'Science Central': one of the most significant development sites in the city. The case for renewal of the blocks was widely accepted; they had received little investment since their construction in 1972. However, the argument against reprovision on the same site was less clear cut. The CTV planning application noted that the applicant (Newcastle Council itself) considered that a new site would provide continuity of service and that its location would be 'more appropriate for accommodating families and vulnerable persons' (Director of Strategic Housing Planning and Transportation, 2010: paragraph 5). Objectors, by contrast, claimed they had been told informally that new homeless provision 'did not sit with the vision' for Science Central, imagined by its promoters as 'a flagship location for science and technology, a thriving environment for business and a beacon of sustainable living and leisure' (Science Central, 2014: not paginated). Thus, while it has never been accepted as such, the impetus for the conflict and the need for a new, and cheaper site fit neatly into a much repeated story of gentrification in which public sector disinvestment, and the emergence of a substantial rent gap, combine with a limited budget for replacement accommodation to generate pressure for displacement (Smith, 1979; Lees et al, 2010).[3]

The decision-making process

Those who objected to the site of the proposed new temporary accommodation argued that the outcome of the decision was wrong, but many were equally, if not more, affronted by the way in which the decision had been made. This ultimately led to a complaint to the Ombudsman on grounds of maladministration, which laid bare the formal process of decision making. The Ombudsman's report identified that discussions about the CTV location were taking place between senior officers and members of the Council in early 2009 and that, while the issue was not yet public, concerns were raised by the area's regeneration team. In June 2009, a report marked 'Confidential – not for publication' (Local Government Ombudsman, 2011: para 23) was brought to the Council's Executive on behalf of the Executive Director of Environment and Regeneration and its Director of Adult Services. The report considered fewer issues than would have been raised by a planning proposal, making no reference to the regeneration team's concerns or to the Council's strategic policies. However, its acceptance by the Executive authorised the preparation of proposals for the CTV site. From the point of view of objectors, and indeed the Ombudsman, the location of the development was decided in secret at this meeting since, in the absence of statutory policy dealing explicitly with the location of homeless hostels, the later question of whether to grant planning consent was guided by the merit of the proposal in front of the committee rather than the question of whether a more preferable location existed elsewhere.

There are obvious discrepancies between the process outlined above and a claimed political consensus on the importance of openness, accountability and responsiveness. Formal responsibility for the decision rested with the leadership of the then Liberal Democrat administration and there were certainly rumours among those living near to the chosen location that the Liberal Democrats were deflecting the development away from their political strongholds in the north of the city. However, even if such political drivers existed, decisions must still be 'justified': they must be framed within a particular discourse of justice, capable of gathering together and sympathetically conceptualising a range of considerations. Furthermore, this 'on the fly' mobilisation of alternative constructions of justice could not take place without the support of a wider group of actors beyond the core of senior politicians who sat on the Executive. Thus, during later public meetings, council officers made, what were at times, passionate arguments in favour of the choice of site. The rationalisation of the decision in this way can be understood as the permeation of a particular view of justice through both the political and public administrative infrastructure of the council, exhibited through the actual behaviour of decision making rather than the stated aims of policy documents. The existence of this divergent culture of justice was inseparable from the council's ability to process and make a decision in favour of the chosen site.

While the decision on CTV's location was taken in secret, and on stated grounds that did not take into account many of the Council's own policies and guidance, this does not preclude the possibility that it was also taken in the public interest, as the Executive envisaged it, or that it remains defensible as the 'best possible' option available to the council. Indeed, the construction of a public interest justification is evident from the arguments made in favour of the proposed site and these centred around the service-level benefits of the site and the limited negative effects it was deemed to have on the surrounding community and environment. Arguments for the chosen site typically referenced the high quality of the proposed development's design and the benefits it would bring for its users. While the Newcastle Fairness Commission had not yet been convened, it argues for a particular focus on providing assistance for the most disadvantaged. The argument made in favour of the facility could be read as consistent with this aim, since it prioritised the needs of the homeless, while arguing that the effects on others would be minimal. Officers argued that concerns around crime arising from the facility were ill-founded because the complex would be intensively managed with a comprehensive closed-circuit television (CCTV) system and designed to serve a wide range of homeless residents beyond those with drug and alcohol problems or on police bail. Proximity of the facility to the local college and to the city centre was also raised as an important factor, both in the report considered by the Executive and subsequently.

Indeed, the ability to provide high quality, local authority run emergency accommodation cannot be taken for granted. In a survey of 212 emergency accommodation projects outside London in 2001, May et al (2006) found that 91% were managed by voluntary or charitable organisations and just 8% by local authorities, while just under a fifth were only able to offer basic, night shelter accommodation, some of which was dirty or drug ridden. In contrast, the completed CTV development (pictured in Figure 10.1) features self-contained units with large windows, some of which extend to floor level, looking out over surrounding trees and foliage. To the south, the rooms have views over the Tyne Valley and there is a children's play area within the site, which is also within view of the rooms and overlooked by surrounding houses. A recent report on prevention of homelessness in the city identified CTV as a notable exception in an environment of severely limited funding for capital improvements and as one of six key strengths in Newcastle's approach (Harding et al, 2013b). Staff working at CTV also commented that the facility 'reduces the vulnerability of the people who are living there, who previously the environment didn't protect' and resulted in a 'completely different' response from clients (Harding et al, 2013a: 40). It was perhaps in anticipation of these benefits that, during the September 2010 meeting with the community, one officer went as far as accusing those residents who objected to the proposal of standing in the way of providing the best possible services to her clients.

This focus on service users' needs to legitimise the chosen location for the homeless accommodation provides a window into the institutional dynamics, which, in the case of CTV, made possible the emergence of a particular, practised culture of justice. The exclusion of planning and regeneration considerations from the report to the Executive can, in one sense, be seen merely as an instrumental tactic for securing or supporting political consent, but it can also be seen as reflective of the relative influence of the Directorate of Adult Services – who presided over a service that had been consistently well resourced and well regarded. The terms that framed the way in which the ethical nature of the CTV decision was comprehended were also reflective of a prioritisation of adult services. Thus, decision making was framed by priorities of acting quickly and on a limited budget. This in turn required that the council worked within conditions given to it at the time, resulting in a search of sites immediately available for development and ideally already in council ownership. In this sense, the CTV case entailed more than just conflict about the outcome of a decision but also conflict over the terms on which the public interest justification for that decision had been constructed, as well as the wider implications these terms might have for future decisions.

Objections to the particular form of utilitarian justice outlined above emphasised pervasive spatial imbalances in the location of homeless accommodation and, to varying extents, linked these to the council's willingness to work within the conditions immediately available to it, rather than to probe more deeply into the origins of those conditions.

The merits of a quick, cost constrained decision were contrasted with constructions of justice that emphasised the historic and systemic dimensions of past injustices. These arguments took on two forms: those that emphasised spatial inequalities and gestured towards some of the drivers behind these, and those that more explicitly concentrated on regeneration efforts and their associated, technical diagnoses of the systemic connections between Elswick and the city more widely.

Evidence of the distribution of homeless accommodation was pulled together by 'Ms B' – a local resident who lived opposite the CTV site and who would later go on to make a formal complaint to the Ombudsman. This information was later summarised by the Local Government Ombudsman, who noted that:

> Elswick and Westgate wards appear to have between them 31 units of accommodation housing a total of 626 people on a temporary or short term basis. The annual transient population will therefore be several times that number. The adjacent wards have, respectively, Benwell (none), Scotswood (none), Fenham (none) and Wingrove (three). A total of 21 temporary beds are shared amongst those four wards. (Local Government Ombudsman, 2011: para 14)

Of other wards in the city noted by the Ombudsman, the highest, an outlier, had seven with the next highest having five. This pattern indicates a concentration of homeless accommodation in wards around the city centre, with more deprived wards also having more homeless accommodation than other wards. The two most affluent areas of Jesmond and Gosforth (four wards) have just six homeless hostels with three of these being in South Jesmond ward, a mixed area that incorporates lower income and council accommodation to the south.

The purpose of collecting this information was to raise issues of distributive justice by connecting affluent locations to lower levels of homelessness provision and by similarly connecting homelessness provision with transient populations and police call-out incidents.[4] A wider connection between environmental burdens and deprivation is established by Davoudi and Brooks (2012) in their report on environmental justice in Newcastle, which accompanied the Newcastle Fairness Commission report. Both sets of evidence point to inequities in a form of provision that receives significant public financial support, thereby implying a degree of governmental responsibility for distributive injustice, which contrasts with the emphasis on market processes found in urban policy during the 2000–10 decade (Webb, 2010). Despite this, Ms B's representations chimed with objections made by regeneration organisations which, not necessarily agreeing on the causes of urban decline, sought to emphasise systemic issues ahead of short-term constraints.

Two central government-funded initiatives – Housing Market Renewal and the New Deal for Communities – had invested tens of millions of pounds in Elswick in an attempt to create a 'sustainable community' with settled residents, rather than transient households such as those who would be accommodated at CTV. These contradictions were laid out in an internal letter to a senior officer prior to the Executive's decision on which location to advance. This argued that:

> The neighbourhood is the most deprived in the City... It would be a very high risk decision to locate vulnerable people into an area experiencing the highest levels of stress in the City. In recent years we have been working with communities to develop diverse, mixed income neighbourhoods and embrace the principle of greater housing choice and private housing. This project will be difficult to reconcile with that strategy, especially given the existing level of hostel type accommodation in the area. There would appear to be very little benefit to the local community apart from the look of a modern residential development and 24/7 surveillance. Amenities in the area are poor and this development will do nothing to improve them or contribute to the economic vitality of the area. (Corporate Project Manager, 2009: 1)

Later objections sought to distinguish between this policy conflict and an outright opposition to the provision of homelessness services. Centre West – the successor organisation to Newcastle New Deal for Communities – thus argued that:

> This is not about 'nimby-ism' but about fairness to a community that is already paying a higher price in the deprivation stakes than the City as a whole. In the spirit of fairness we ask that the Wentworth Court application is not approved. (Centre West, 2011: paragraph 16.6)

Underlying both Ms B's representations and those of local regeneration organisations was a deeper awareness that Elswick has historically been characterised by processes that might, for operational reasons, lead to the continued concentration of transient households and homeless accommodation in the area. Where social and private housing is seen by potential residents as less desirable, there is a tendency for it to be filled by those with fewer options, and in some cases these environments have also been used, unofficially, as places that problematic tenants can be directed towards. Furthermore, a history of physical intervention in areas such as Elswick means that the local authority holds considerably more land assets than in more affluent parts of the city. A lack of market viability means these assets are more likely to be made available for public services whose clients are increasingly limited to the most vulnerable. In combination, these factors have the potential to favour the informal development of a 'social hospital' role for the area, in which both difficult to manage tenants and remedial public services are concentrated. The contribution of both Ms B's evidence and the representations made by local regeneration organisations was to contest this implicit logic, which was embedded in the terms on which the official justification of the CTV site rested. This was done by emphasising the disjunction between the service-orientated construction of utilitarian justice advanced by officers and the prevailing thrust of area-based policy at the time, which was seeking to strategically reposition Elswick within the city's housing market as a means of promoting social control and private sector investment. Thus, in the words of Ms B, "It's like the council's right hand doesn't know what the left hand is doing" (Weatherall, 2011: not paginated).

These objections were, however, not sufficient to persuade the council to refuse planning permission for CTV. Their chief impact was therefore to concentrate the complaint to the Ombudsman on the precise wording of the Council's adopted statutory policy for the Elswick area.

The role of policy in making justice accountable

The events outlined above tell a story about three competing constructions of justice in Newcastle, each supported by their own networks of political and administrative actors. The first construction was that of the party manifesto, promising visions of fairness and inclusivity. But this was found to be at odds with a second, emergent form of justification, which drove the implementation of CTV according to the values of a tight circle of policy makers. Ultimately, this circle was able to legitimise a definition of justice that could not be overturned or reframed by those outside the circle. A third, marginalised justice claim can thereby be observed in the representations of the Elswick community and some of the organisations tasked with governing it. The existence of these competing constructions should prompt us to ask critical questions about the democratic norms and institutions that steer a local polity towards supporting particular constructions over others. This in turn might help us to look at the Newcastle Fairness Commission in a similarly critical light – to enquire into the relationship between its approach to justice and the capacity for effective challenge of established cultures of practice.

The purpose of the Ombudsman's investigation was to assess whether maladministration had taken place. Maladministration was defined as the failure of a local authority to comply with the law or with its own policies. The test being imposed was therefore based on a similar separation of politics from administration to that which was discussed earlier in this chapter; it assumed the uptake of organisational principles confining the realm of administrative action to the implementation of clear, politically established goals. The report found that maladministration had not occurred, but emphasised that the reason for this was the Council's failure to adopt many of the draft policies it had been working on for the Elswick area. The Ombudsman explained that:

> The lack of a strategic policy for the area cannot be overstated. If a council has adopted a policy, the public has a right to expect that policy will influence every relevant decision the council makes. Through policy the public can hold the council to account. (Local Government Ombudsman, 2011: para 22)

Thus, the Ombudsman's argument was that she could not arrive at a verdict of maladministration because the council had effectively failed on two, related, fronts: the decision-making process was poor and the decision raised conflicts that required advance, democratic consideration and confirmation. The Council's failure to formally adopt an area-based policy for Elswick meant such confirmation had not taken place. The Council's main failing, in this sense, was its failure to properly direct and oversee its administrative functions in a transparent and accountable manner.

These conclusions demonstrate the capacity for a particular institutional dynamic to exist within local government: the distancing of hypothetical principles from operational practices, leading to a lack of oversight of individual decisions. There is less likelihood that this dynamic will affect some of the more affluent areas of Newcastle because supplementary planning policy and article 4 directions limit the number of houses in multiple occupation in parts of Jesmond and Gosforth.[5] This raises questions about why no statutory policy was in place to assist the careful management of the Elswick area and about whether this might change in future. Centre West's objection to the CTV planning application indicates that such a policy was offered to objectors as a means of controlling future developments (Centre West, 2011), while the Ombudsman's report records a formal commitment to consider 'the question of whether or not there is a need to put in place practical measures to restrict the density of similar properties in this area of the City' (Local Government Ombudsman, 2011: para49). When Labour took control of Newcastle City Council on 6 May 2011 it was implied that a policy had not been put in place for political reasons. Council Leader Nick Forbes stated:

> 'Four years ago I said when in opposition that something needed to be done to control the number of hostels in one area, but the proposal never got anywhere... Now that I'm leader of the council, I will make sure that once the finalised report comes out policies are put in place to make sure a catastrophic decision like this won't happen again.' (Weatherall, 2011: not paginated)

However, there is no evidence that this issue has since been considered. Nor is a policy included in Newcastle's joint core strategy, despite a request from the author of this chapter that one should be considered. With the political spotlight now elsewhere, Elswick remains a neighbourhood without a formally established vision for its future and the Ombudsman's concerns lie unheeded.

Issues of cultural legacy

At the very minimum, the CTV case illustrates the ongoing possibility of a systemic disconnect between local political leadership and the terms on which the administration of land use and investment issues is progressed. Broken promises to address this disconnect highlight the potential for systemic issues to be recast in politically partisan terms, internalising them within the political sphere and displacing critical scrutiny away from the relationship with the administration. However, while this establishes the potential for institutional practices to be reproduced by successive administrations it does not in itself provide any empirical evidence of this actually occurring.

It is at this point that the voices of those Elswick residents who objected to the CTV proposal take on renewed salience. Ms B was the most active of the resident objectors, responsible for the formal complaint to the Ombudsman and for ensuring that Council officers made good on their commitment to hold a community meeting in the wake of the Executive's decision. That meeting, however, was attended by around 40 other local residents, and it rapidly became clear that for many, the proposals amounted to a personal attack on them and their neighbours. Some took issue with the ethics of the officers before them and for their personal role in promoting CTV, and repeated parallels were drawn between the treatment of Elswick residents and the perceived treatment of more affluent areas of the city. This was far from being a debate about policy, evidence or rational argument. Rather, there was a clear perception that those in the room had been treated disrespectfully as a consequence of who they were and where they lived.

A look back at literature on planning and regeneration in Elswick sets the perceptions of residents at this meeting within the context of a historically fraught relationship between the Council and local residents. Much of this can be traced back to failed attempts to pursue block improvement during the early 1960s, which replaced some of 'the homes of the most prosperous families in the city' (Davies, 1972: 15) with dereliction and an increase in private renting, ultimately resulting in the mixture of smaller council housing and shared, privately rented properties, which characterises the area today. In a survey carried out at the time, Davies found that '... most of the people were distinctly bitter about what had happened to them and the area in which they lived' (Davies, 1972: 21).

This sense of injustice is also documented in later research. A study of regeneration in the early 1990s noted that tight timescales imposed by central government tended to stymie community engagement and promote 'back pocket' projects mainly originating from officers 'who, then, tended to go out and seek outside support' (Davoudi and Healey, 1994: 14). This created an 'uncomfortable coexistence' of partners, with one community representative stating, "we've got the private sector on our side against the council, and the council against the private sector" (Davoudi and Healey, 1994: 27). These dynamics also pervaded the later New Deal for Communities initiative, with one researcher recording that, 'Residents argue that they have been abandoned by a local government which treats them as though their lives and their needs are less important than the more affluent residents of the city' (Dargan, 2002: 22). In the words of one interviewee:

> 'You're talking about communities which have had years of neglect, years of feeling alienated and detached from decision-making, and not feeling that anything they've ever said has been taken on board, and nothing will ever change. That has been perpetuated for years and years.' (Dargan, 2002: 182)

Dargan found resident perceptions 'that the disadvantages they suffer – crime, ill-health, unemployment, a degraded local environment – are the direct result of poor quality service provision from the Council' (Dargan, 2002: 23). While Robinson argued that Elswick's history is characterised by the repeated, 'top-down imposition of "solutions"' (Robinson, 2005: 34). Others have attributed the distant nature of decision making in Elswick directly to the structure of the administration in Newcastle, with Davoudi and Healey (1994) arguing that departmental priorities got in the way of developing coherent, area-wide policies.

Conclusion

This chapter has drawn attention to some of the deficiencies within the liberal approach to fairness that has shaped contemporary debates in Newcastle, focusing in particular on the assumed capability of local democracy to roll out a programme of fairness based on theoretical principles and technical inquiry. The CTV decision illustrates, by contrast, the relatively effortless means by which local democratic institutions were able to construct and apply their own forms of justice with little regard to what the Ombudsman termed 'aspirational' corporate policies. The significance of such events lies to a great extent in the work that this arrangement does for wider practices of government. The separation of politics from administration facilitates a culture of 'looking out', to ways of positioning Newcastle politically and economically, through appeals to central government, to political movements or to opportunities for private investment, all of which depends on an ability to rapidly reorientate local political discourse. This institutional context provides the perfect conditions for absorbing abstract debates on fairness – or indeed inclusivity, participation or cooperation – and locking them within the political domain. By contrast, for ideas about justice to have traction with practice they must engage with the operational content of the administration. This is something that will require much more than the generation of principles and aspirations. It demands a direct engagement with the means by which these principles are negotiated at the level of daily decision making about the future of the city.

Despite these challenges, the author hopes that this chapter has shown how attention to the histories and attitudes of the social places within the city might invigorate public debate about the legacies of past injustices and about the political, economic and institutional processes through which injustice continues to be reproduced. Justice, in this conception, is an empirical question to be debated with reference to practical examples, not a technical programme that can be rolled out. It is only through debating these issues that wider discourses such as fairness and cooperation can be 'made real'. This call may be challenging for local politicians of both parties, but the risk of hiding behind administration is greater: failure to meet popular demands for inclusive and responsive services may see the generalised decline of liberal models of local government, and with them their emphasis on distributive justice. Locally, disillusionment with the city's centre-left consensus would create an electoral vacuum, which others on the far right may be all too willing to fill.

Notes

[1] The success of Wilkinson and Pickett's 2009 book *The Spirit Level* at reigniting support for a more materially equal society provided the impetus for a series of fairness commissions, established in the early years of the coalition government and reminiscent of efforts to use social justice to reinvigorate the party under John Smith's leadership (see Haddon, 2012).

[2] The author's early involvement with this case study arose through advocacy planning work with those objecting to the development, although details are also drawn from information compiled with the assistance of three postgraduate students in winter 2011 and spring 2012 as part of an investigation into the decision making process.

[3] One of the ironies in this case was the presence of substantial public sector subsidy of £6 million from the regional growth fund to support initial investment in Science Central and the fact that the project has struggled to attract investors even with this subsidy. Given Newcastle's economically weak position, pressure for displacement was to a large extent something that was manufactured by public policies seeking to advance what, in the wake of the great recession, has become a largely dysfunctional model of economic development.

[4] Separate evidence showed that police were called 40 times to the existing temporary accommodation in 2008/09 and 19 times in 2009/10 (Director of Strategic Housing, Planning and Transportation, 2010).

[5] These protections came about as a means of managing student housing but also apply to homeless accommodation.

References

Centre West (2011) *Centre West objection to Planning Application 2010/1435/01/DET – Newcastle City Council's proposal to build a homelessness facility at Wentworth Court*, Newcastle upon Tyne: Newcastle City Council.

Connolly, J. and Steil, J. (2009) 'Introduction: finding justice in the city', in P. Marcuse (ed) *Searching for the just city: Debates in urban theory and practice*, London: Routledge, pp 1-16.

Corporate Project Manager (2009) Email raising concerns about proposed temporary accommodation in Elswick.

Dargan, L. (2002) *A new approach to regeneration in Tyneside? The rhetoric and reality of the New Deal for Communities*, Newcastle upon Tyne: Newcastle University.

Davies, J.G. (1972) *The evangelistic bureaucrat: A study of a planning exercise in Newcastle upon Tyne*, London: Tavistock Publications.

Davoudi, S. and Brooks, E. (2012) *Environmental justice and the city: Final report*, [pdf] Newcastle upon Tyne: Newcastle University. Available at: http://www.ncl.ac.uk/socialrenewal/engagement/fairnesscommission/documents/environmental-justice-and-the-city-final.pdf

Davoudi, S. and Healey, P. (1994) *Perceptions of city challenge policy processes: The Newcastle case*, Newcastle upon Tyne: Newcastle University.

Director of Strategic Housing Planning and Transportation (2010) *Committee report reference 2010/1435/01/DET*, Newcastle upon Tyne.

Fainstein, S. (2009) 'Planning and the just city', in P. Marcuse (ed) *Searching for the just city: Debates in urban theory and practice*, London: Routledge, pp 19-39.

Gaffikin, F. and Sterrett, K. (2006) 'New visions for old cities: the role of visioning in planning', *Planning Theory & Practice*, 7(2): pp 159-78.

Haddon, C. (2012) *Making policy in opposition: The Commission on Social Justice, 1992-1994*, London: Institute for Government.

Harding, J., Irving, A., Fitzpatrick, S. and Pawson, H. (2013a) *Evaluation of Newcastle's 'co-operative' approach to the prevention and management of homelessness in light of changing government policy*, [online] Newcastle upon Tyne: Northumbria University. Available at: http://nrl.northumbria.ac.uk/15022/ [accessed January 2016].

Harding, J., Irving, A., Fitzpatrick, S. and Pawson, H. (2013b) *Evaluation of Newcastle's 'co-operative' approach to the prevention and management of homelessness in light of changing government policy (presentation to Youth Homeless North East)*, [pdf] Newcastle upon Tyne: Youth Homeless North East. Available at: http://www.newcastle.gov.uk/sites/drupalncc.newcastle.gov.uk/files/wwwfileroot/housing/evaluation_of_newcastles_co-operative_approach_final_report.pdf [accessed January 2016].

Lees, L., Slater, T.P.D. and Wyly, E.K. (2010) *The gentrification reader*, London: Routledge.

Local Government Ombudsman (2011) *Final decision letter – Investigation into complaint reference 10 012 300*. Not published.

May, J., Cloke, P. and Johnsen, S. (2006) 'Shelter at the margins: New Labour and the changing state of emergency accommodation for single homeless people in Britain', *Policy & Politics*, 34(4): 711-29.

Newcastle Fairness Commission (2012) *Report of the Newcastle Fairness Commission,* Newcastle upon Tyne: Newcastle Fairness Commission.

Newcastle Liberal Democrats (2012) *Liberal Democrat Manifesto for Newcastle 2012*, Newcastle upon Tyne: Newcastle Liberal Democrats.

Robinson, F. (2005) 'Regenerating the west end of Newcastle: what went wrong?', *Northern Economic Review*, 36: 15-42.

Science Central (2014) *Science Central*. [online] Available at: http://www.newcastlesciencecentral.com/ [Accessed January 2016].

Smith, N. (1979) 'Toward a theory of gentrification: a back to the city movement by capital, not people', *Journal of the American Planning Association*, 45(4): 538-48.

Weatherall, R. (2011) 'Newcastle City Council under fire over regeneration scheme', *The Journal*, [online] 13 August. Available at: http://www.journallive.co.uk/north-east-news/todays-news/2011/08/13/newcastle-city-council-under-fire-over-regeneration-scheme-61634-29226710/ [accessed January 2016].

Webb, D. (2010) 'Rethinking the role of markets in urban renewal: the housing market renewal initiative in England', *Housing, Theory and Society*, 27(4): 313-31.

Wilkinson, R.G. and Pickett, K. (2009) *The spirit level: Why more equal societies almost always do better*, London: Allen Lane.

Young, I.M. (1990) *Justice and the politics of difference*, Princeton: Princeton University Press.

SECTION FOUR

Social justice and life course

Derek Bell and Simin Davoudi

> Modern political theory asserted the equal moral worth of
> all persons, and social movements of the oppressed took
> this seriously as implying the inclusion of all persons in full
> citizenship status under the equal protection of the law.
> (Young, 1989: 250)

Liberal theories of justice, such as John Rawls' 'justice as fairness', seek
to achieve a fair distribution of resources and opportunities between
persons over their whole lives (Rawls, 1999). The 'whole lives' or
'lifetime' approach to thinking about justice may seem attractive
when we are imagining ideal principles of justice that are fair to all
persons. However, we should be aware that the kinds of *injustice* that
people experience may vary across the life course. At different stages
of the life course, we may have different needs and vulnerabilities,
require different resources and be seeking different opportunities. For
example, some of the needs of children tend to be quite different from
the needs of working age adults. Similarly, some of the vulnerabilities
of older people, in their 80s or 90s, may be quite different from the
vulnerabilities of younger people in their 20s or 30s. If we want to
understand injustice in the city and how it is (re-)produced, we need
to pay careful attention to how cities affect people throughout the life
course. We should not assume that justice requires 'laws and rules that
are blind to individual and group differences' (Young, 1989: 250). So
far, these issues have not received much attention by the main theorists
of justice and the city.

The three chapters that make up this section examine aspects of
injustice at three different points in the life course: among older
people; in schools; and in the workplace. In Chapter 11, Rose Gilroy
and Elizabeth Brooks examine older people's experience of social
injustice. Their chapter draws on interviews with older people living
in Newcastle. They use Iris Marion Young's account of oppression as a
framework for thinking about how older people experience injustice.
Gilroy and Brooks show the operation of exploitation, marginalisation,

violence, powerlessness and cultural imperialism in the lives of older people in Newcastle. This exercise of seeing older people's experiences through the lens of Young's theory of oppression highlights the distinctive ways in which older people experience injustice in their everyday life. Often these experiences of everyday injustice are hidden from view. Therefore, the first step toward justice for older people in the city is greater recognition and awareness of the many forms of injustice that they experience as part of everyday life. However, as Gilroy and Brooks argue, the next step is to turn awareness into strategic action that creates transformation. They outline the work that has been done by Newcastle City Council and its partners to make a reality of their commitment to become an age-friendly city. However, they note the difficulties of translating this commitment into action in a context where the City Council has competing priorities, not least the refashioning of Newcastle as a party city for younger people, and national government policies ensure continuing austerity for city governments. The many and diverse ways in which older people experience injustice in everyday life makes promoting justice for older people both extremely urgent and extremely challenging.

In Chapter 12, Karen Laing, Laura Mazzoli Smith and Liz Todd take us to the other end of the life course, when they examine the conceptions of justice that inform education policy and practice in England's city schools. They begin by emphasising the attractiveness of the concept of fairness, which seems to be in vogue across the political spectrum in discussions of education. They argue that the flagship schools policies of the Cameron government – 'closing the gap' in attainment between rich and poor, and increasing choice through academies and 'free' schools – reflect two contrasting theories of justice. 'Closing the gap' in attainment between rich and poor is underpinned by the liberal principle of fair equality of opportunity. In contrast, the choice agenda is underpinned by libertarian and neoliberal principles. Laing et al argue that this combination does not make for coherent schools policy. More importantly, they argue that focusing on these two issues leaves national schools policy blind to important aspects of fairness and justice. In particular, they emphasise the importance of 'relational justice', especially cultural justice and justice as recognition, which they argue is not given sufficient attention in national schools policy. They draw on their work with local schools in Newcastle to show that there is innovative practice that seeks to promote relational justice and, at least sometimes, does so by subverting the aims of national policies. In the practice of city schools, they find small examples of resistance to the dominant but unsatisfactory conceptions of justice that shape national schools policy. They conclude that these examples of local actions to promote relational justice suggest the need for a national policy focus on relational justice.

Chapter 13 examines fairness in the workplace. In this chapter, Jan Deckers brings the discussion of fairness and justice in the city to the place where most of the contributors to this volume spend their working life, Newcastle University. Deckers asks the question: what would be a fair pay policy for the University? His discussion has more general implications for any large employer located in one city but competing in a global marketplace for staff. He begins from the endorsement of the living wage in the report of the Living Wage Independent Advisory Panel to Newcastle City Council (2012). Deckers suggests that Newcastle University's pay policy is now consistent with the Panel's proposal. However, he argues that this is a very modest understanding of what justice requires from a large employer. He draws on liberal egalitarian principles of justice to argue for much more radical reform of the University's pay structure. On Deckers' account, unequal pay requires a rather different justification from the talent-based or market-based justifications that underpin the University's current pay structure. He acknowledges the common objection that failing to pay market salaries will lead to an exodus of staff. However, he notes that there are examples of successful companies that do have equal pay policies. Moreover, he suggests that justice requires that the University tries to develop a more egalitarian pay policy while monitoring its effects. If the hypothesised 'brain drain' occurs *and* it has a significant impact on the University's ability to continue to contribute to the common good of society through its research, teaching and provision of employment, unequal pay may be a necessary injustice.

The three chapters in this section explore (in)justice in the city during three different stages of the life course. Together they remind us that questions of justice and fairness are a pervasive feature of everyday life from our school days through working life and into older age. The institutions that (re)produce injustice – and that might challenge injustice – in the city are often closer to home than we might imagine even if their policies and practices appear determined by unquestionable logics. In their quite different ways, the contributors to this section remind us that the first step towards promoting justice is to question the *status quo* and ask difficult questions about whether the way we do things now is just to the people affected by our policies, practices and institutions. Once we question the justice or the inevitability of the *status quo*, we can develop and deploy new theories of justice, like those highlighted by the contributors to this section, to help us imagine and justify fairer alternative social arrangements.

References

Living Wage Independent Advisory Panel to Newcastle City Council (2012) *A Living Wage for Newcastle*. Available at: https://www.livingwage.co.uk/sites/default/files/images/A%20Living%20Wage%20for%20Newcastle%20REV1.pdf

Rawls, J. (2001) *Justice as fairness: A restatement*, Cambridge, MA: Harvard University Press.

Young, I.M. (1989) 'Polity and group difference: a critique of the ideal of universal citizenship', *Ethics* 99: 250-74.

ELEVEN

Fair shares for all: the challenge of demographic change

Rose Gilroy and Elizabeth Brooks

Introduction

This chapter focuses on older people's experience of social injustice, discussed here as oppression. We begin with a discussion of how 'old age' as a social category is being reconstructed before turning to consider the utility of oppression as a lens to explore the experiences of older people. Using the framework developed by Young (1990) this chapter considers the operation of exploitation, marginalisation, violence, powerlessness and cultural imperialism, drawing on national and local sources of evidence but more significantly on the narratives of older people living mainly in Newcastle. The discussion concludes by considering the work of Newcastle City Council and its partners in striving to make a reality of their age-friendly city commitment. To what extent do these partnership programmes create transformation or the possibility of transformative action?

Rethinking old age

While all socially constructed categories are in flux, the concept of 'old age', our understanding of what it is to be an older person, is now being contested and redefined (Hockey et al, 2013). In part, this is due to the greater number and proportion of people over 50 in global populations and the reasonable expectation that more people can anticipate living into their eighth decade or beyond. This in turn leads to a new landscape of later life that emerges as a multigenerational, highly differentiated experience that is impossible to encapsulate in traditional images. This has caused some commentators (for example, Clapham, 2014) to question whether age as a social category has any validity, though it is clearly still in common usage to determine access to a range of services and environments, which in themselves may be constructed in response to particular definitions of older age.

In response to the broad span of later life that might be some 50 years, new subcategories of 'old age' have emerged, with the most prevalent being the idea of the baby boomer. Much has been written on this cohort – in particular what might be more correctly termed the 'first wave' baby boomers born in the period after the Second World War – that has captured the public imagination with its, supposed, defining characteristics of individual choice making, prosperity, ownership and greater opportunities in the post work phase of life for self-actualisation. It is these characteristics that are associated with the concept of the 'third age'. Against this background new agendas have emerged. The 'successful ageing' agenda attempts to reframe later life as a time of possibilities in which individuals might make a continued, but different, contribution to society (Rowe and Kahn, 1997). This is a welcome development; however, 'the debate serves as a convenient shelter for a wide range of policy discourses and initiatives' (Walker, 2004: 75). In its guise as 'productive ageing', the vision has often been narrowed to the demand for deferred retirement (Higgs and Jones, 2009). As 'active ageing', it has been recast as a discussion of health and positive lifestyle choices. As Higgs et al (2009: 690) comment, this discourse has come to 'overwhelm our understanding of later life', as health is seen as not only central to any construct of a successful old age but increasingly a 'required goal' for individuals. In the current time of public finance constraint, it is expedient for neoliberal governments to promote the importance of individual responsibility (Means and Evans, 2014) and to set this within a discourse of ageing as a dire economic problem – the 'age quake' that threatens to further destabilise languishing economies.

If the idea of later life as a period of inevitable and progressive decline is firmly rejected by the baby boomers then a new construction of the 'fourth age' – sometimes termed the 'oldest old' – has emerged to encapsulate the onset of frailty that might encompass disability, bereavement, loneliness, incontinence and cognitive decline. It is as if we have created a 'scary room' into which we have pushed all those aspects of later age that *may* affect us and firmly bolted the door on this: for if successful ageing is about health and vitality then a decline into disability and frailty can too easily be seen as a personal failure. The fourth age has become in many ways the 'new old age' signalled not by chronology but by physical and social transitions. It is, however, important to note that as the baby boomers have transformed thinking about early stage post work life, it is anticipated they may challenge these fourth age concepts as they age into their ninth and tenth decades and beyond.

If the concept of later life is in flux and its language still emerging, the context of ageing has also changed. As the world becomes increasingly urbanised, so ageing becomes an increasingly urban experience. This has led to the World Health Organization's (WHO) Age-friendly Cities programme that established a worldwide network of cities committed to making physical changes in the urban fabric and improving the daily life experience of older citizens, not with a mission to serve any 'special needs', but rather to pay attention to older people as a matter of social justice:

> It should be normal in an age-friendly city for the natural and built environment to anticipate users with different capacities instead of designing for the mythical 'average' (ie young) person. An age-friendly city emphasises enablement rather than disablement; it is friendly for all ages and not just 'elder-friendly' (WHO, 2007: 72).

The challenge is not just to 'add in' older people, but by their inclusion to transform the urban experience, challenging not only those policy and societal practices that shape the physical fabric but all that restrict the lives of older people.

Turning to the framework of oppression

In exploring the experience of injustice in the lives of older people, Iris Marion Young's (1990) framework of oppression rejects simple explanations that suggest that a redistribution of material goods is the *complete* solution to inequality, but rather confronts the myriad ways in which power is exercised in society. In the UK there has been positive action to improve the incomes of older people through pushing back retirement and improving pensions; however, these benefits are unevenly experienced. Beyond matters of income and wealth, in the context of the UK and its shrinking welfare state, oppression can be uncovered in the 'everyday practices of a well intentioned liberal society' (Young, 1990: 41) and in the way cuts are made in publicly provided or procured services that may signal whose lives are valued and whose are not. Oppression is seen as [rooted in] 'unconscious assumptions and reactions of well meaning people in ordinary interactions, media and cultural stereotypes, and structural features of bureaucratic hierarchies and market mechanisms – in short, the normal processes of everyday life' (Young, 1990:41). The analysis that follows uses Young's five faces of oppression: exploitation, marginalisation, violence, powerlessness and cultural imperialism as ways of understanding the narratives of older people. The fieldwork was commissioned by Joseph Rowntree Foundation in June 2009 with the intention of looking at quality of life from older people's perspectives (Gilroy, 2009). Within an eight-week timescale, the research drew in the newly retired to those in their 90s and the terminally ill; the affluent and those on low incomes; those in a range of home settings including specialist housing and care homes; and from a diversity of faith and mother tongues. Where feasible, focus groups were held that drew together people with a common bond, often locality based. A total of 54 people took part in seven focus groups, including two where interpreters were used. A further 13 interviews were undertaken to explore some issues in greater depth and to include those seldom heard, including Jewish elders and frail, housebound people. To preserve anonymity, all participants are referred to by assigned, rather than their actual, names.

Exploitation

From a Marxist perspective, worker exploitation occurs when the labour of one group is controlled by and benefits others. In the context of older people, their exploitation could be seen as taking the form of substantial unpaid care work to sustain parents, spouse, adult family, friends and children. Clearly the state benefits from this economy of love and the savings to the public purse are very great. As carers of adults, older people provide an informal economic contribution of £11.4 billion in addition to the £6.6 billion of child care that they provide that enables their adult children to work and pay taxes. All this is in addition to the £5.8 billion of volunteering that older people give in a multitude of welfare, cultural, education and social arenas (Carers UK, 2014).

Closer to home in Newcastle, half of all unpaid care is given by those aged 50(+) and one third of those providing 50 hours or more of unpaid care per week is over 65 years of age (NCC, 2013). The personal cost to these carers in health terms may be severe. It is also evident that, for those who are mature workers, there may be financial penalties to be borne that impact on their own choice-making abilities in retirement. 'The peak age for caring is 45–65, resulting from the highest likelihood of needing to care for an older parent, meaning that the most intense pressure often comes at the peak of carers' careers when the loss of employment can become irreversible' (Carers UK, 2014: 45).

None of the participants in the fieldwork were providing child care, none were carers for parents, though one recent retiree had moved back into the locality with a view to looking after his parents-in-law in the near future. Only two were carers for their spouse, though several were now alone after years of care giving. How individuals view their caring responsibilities is clearly highly individualised. One woman spoke of her sick husband as a burden who took all her time and energy, while Mr Francis revealed the emotional cost to himself as he saw his wife become frailer and less able to engage:

Interviewer: 'The last thing I wanted to ask you was if you could change one thing that might improve your quality of life what might that be?'

Mr Francis: 'I think it would be my wife not being blind and disabled because in so many ways this is a constraint, it's not just you don't do things, it's that you haven't got an active partner, so for my part not so much my own health. The contact between us has really been very important and the fact that this has broken down in the last years since her health and sight have gone and the limitation that is imposed. It's really going back to social contact, rich social contact is the thing – even me, and I would have said I am not a very social person, I got my social contact within ... there is a lot of shared values with my wife, a profound bond right the way through, a core of shared concerns really.'

Care giving to a spouse is bound up with a sense of reciprocity and responsibility; for some it is part of the marriage vows of being with that person 'through sickness and in health'. For some it is a duty borne under sufferance; for others it is simply about love. In the context of older people, to talk of their unwaged care work as exploitation is consonant with Young's analytical framework but on a personal level may feel deeply wrong. This is, of course, the wicked issue in that love makes us complicit in our own exploitation. How does a just society better incorporate families into care systems without taking advantage of them? How does society support what might be a powerful shared experience (Horwitz, 2014)? More broadly, what does it say about our current view of later life that unsupported heavy duty care by older people is so prevalent as to seem unremarkable?

Marginalisation: a multifaceted picture

Poverty of resources

Marginalisation in a capitalist society, where income is frequently the key to a greater range of options, can be interpreted as lacking the financial competence to make choices and to feel part of the mainstream. A political commitment to raise pensioner households out of poverty has resulted in the average older person's household now having an income of £24,804 – just short of the average (individual) salary at £26,500 (IFS, 2013). Much of this increase can be attributed to greater engagement in the labour market by those over 60 due to changes in the state retirement age for men, and, particularly, for women. The spread of better occupational pensions has benefited the income of those under 75 but for older cohorts these schemes were largely unavailable, creating marked income differences (DWP, 2014). In the fieldwork this was reflected in the narratives of recent retirees, who were among the best off as outright homeowners, car drivers and with enough disposable income to pursue a range of activities. In spite of increases in older people's average incomes, 14% of pensioner households still live in poverty, measured as having 60% or less of median income after housing costs. Living on a low income is not confined to people in later life of course but as Ginn asserts, 'pensioners differ from the working age population in having no opportunity to increase their income in future: those who are poor remain so' (2010: 51).

The positioning of households on the spectrum of those with enough income to make choices is complex and two narratives illustrate this. The first voice is that of the Knox household. Mr and Mrs Knox, 67 and 69 respectively, live in a house they bought through the 'Right to Buy' in the mid Northumberland market town of Alnwick. While *Country Life* magazine (2002) stated it was the best place to live in the UK, Mr and Mrs Knox's home is on an estate where crime and antisocial behaviour are commonplace. Mrs Knox was a domestic at a large country house but lost her job through rheumatoid arthritis, which has left her largely housebound. Mr Knox was a lorry driver who was invalided out of his job 20 years earlier as a result of a traffic accident. Since then, their main source of income has been Mr Knox's disability living allowances, which he periodically had to fight to retain through tribunals. They have not retired into poverty; rather, it has been a shaping characteristic of their lives:

Mr Knox:	'Health and a little bit more cash, so, because I would like to take [wife] to a show, something to get her out of the four walls. Well really, how do you put it, it's no good having your health if you've got nae money. Because there's things you want to do, and you can't afford to do 'em. And we've never had a holiday ... never had a holiday. I just hadn't got the cash. I have never been away with my wife. How long have we been married? Forty-seven years?'
Mrs Knox:	'Forty-three years.'

One generation ahead, Miss Duncan, a 91-year-old former headmistress who never married, retired on a teacher's pension after more than 30 years' service. She lives in her own home in the city neighbourhood where she has lived all her life. She has been progressively losing her sight for 20 years and more recently has experienced some hearing loss. With no family and increasing frailty she is dependent on care workers three times daily for personal care for which she pays the full charges:

Miss Duncan:	'I tell you what older people resent, those who have a lot to pay for their care – I pay £150 per week, which is a lot of money and it's only because I worked and have a pension from teaching and people who had the same opportunities didn't take them or who spent every penny they had, get the same care and pay nothing or practically nothing. I hear that all the time from older people.'

While their working lives and incomes in retirement were markedly different, in later life both the retired professional woman and the retired manual workers' household have limited choices, the first through being penalised for her higher income by means testing and the second by a lifetime of low income and no savings. These are not stories of malnutrition or fuel poverty but of the monotony of daily life unrelieved by little opportunity for change and choice.

Poverty of mobility

In England in 2013 people in the top 20% for household income made a quarter more trips than those in the lowest 20%, and travelled twice as far. The key factor in personal mobility is access to a car (DfT, 2014:10). Finances are not the only reason that people do not drive;

many factors linked with later life can limit access to personal transport. Recognition of the restrictions placed on older people by lower income, the increasing likelihood of driving cessation (Ziegler and Schwanen, 2011) and evidence that poor mobility limits both physical activity and social interaction, has been addressed by the introduction of free local bus travel (Green et al, 2014). In the fieldwork, concerns about getting out and about by public transport were among the first issues raised by those in affluent and disadvantaged neighbourhoods. The contribution to bus services by local authorities has been subject to cuts, as Age UK (2014a) notes, with 46% of local authorities cutting spending on their supported bus services in 2013/14 and 36% cutting or removing services. In a Newcastle neighbourhood characterised by multiple deprivation, the bus service that used to operate through their estate and into the city centre had been withdrawn, leaving people with services accessed from the adjacent arterial road:

Mrs Clark: 'Why should people here have to get taxis – people who've had hip operations? You see some people are in agony – why should they have to get a taxi to get their pension? Who cares about old people – not the ward councillors! I wrote a two page letter saying that LinkUp should concentrate on areas like ours that have no service. Nothing has happened and I heard nothing at all from them.' (Disadvantaged neighbourhood focus group)

Judged on frequency, the services that run down the side of the estate are good but for large numbers of older people, 400 metres away or further, the journey to the bus stop was impossible. Pre-paid taxis were required for some focus group respondents to travel to a venue 250 metres from their home. The impact on mobility of life limiting illness is more marked in disadvantaged areas (Public Health England, 2014; ONS, 2014), but does not form part of the calculation made by transport planners or bus operators. As older people have commented, the offer of community transport is inadequate and taxis were a largely unaffordable luxury.

Mobility seen as exercise, as engaging with opportunities for social exchange, for exercising choice in shopping for daily needs, for its role in reflecting back an identity of a person with independent movement was the most important *material* concern for older people shared across the income range. This reflects the views of a local older people's discussion group that commented on government measures of material deprivation: 'People with finances can still be materially deprived e.g. lack of bus services/provision for elderly people and dangerous roads/busy roads unable to cross safely' (Newcastle Initiative on Changing Age, 2013: 9). Understanding the lack of material resources and mobility limitations demands a more nuanced approach. Beyond these there were other poverties to be endured.

Poverty of relationships

The research found older people who were well networked and engaged in pleasurable activities and exchanges. These included younger participants and two of the three oldest old, whose lives were enviably enriched through their faith community that had established social activities and support mechanisms. Age alone was not a predictor of loneliness or isolation but those without immediate family close by were more vulnerable as were those with limiting disabilities or with little or no English. For those like Mrs Shah who had to contend with all three, life had become a struggle to alleviate boredom and lonely days. Her social life is dependent on a local voluntary sector group that struggles to find the necessary funding:

Mrs Shah: 'Loneliness is a big problem. Now my husband is dead and my children are gone I feel isolated. Poor health stops me feeling independent. I need more company and more social contact. Loneliness is a very depressing thing. We live for coming out – even if only for a few minutes. There is only so much TV you can watch, only so many books that you want to read. If we could meet more often we would be less isolated. We meet together every Tuesday and if a letter comes we have to remember to bring it with us so someone can tell us what it says. It is easy to forget. Most days there is nothing to kill the time.' (Asian women's focus group)

Being connected, feeling valued, having friends, not just care workers employed to assist with daily living, was the most important issue after physical health – though it should be noted in that regard that waves of research now demonstrate that loneliness is as serious a health risk as obesity and smoking, with both physical and cognitive impacts (Age UK, 2012). Maintaining social connectivity and building new personal convoys of support is not only a challenge for individuals but for society as a whole.

Violence

Violence toward particular ethnic groups, older people, gay men and women, sexual violence against women in general and the chilling cosiness of 'domestic violence' are some of the most potent ways in which people categorised as 'other' are objectified. Statistics demonstrate that older people are least likely to be victims of any crime, much less violent crime, nevertheless surveys including evidence from Newcastle (NCC, 2013) suggest that people over 65 are least likely to report feeling safe in their locality after dark, leading to careful planning of both mode and time of travel. From the fieldwork, Mr and Mrs Knox continually have to manage intimidation, criminal and antisocial behaviour from their neighbours, including children:

Mr Knox: 'I mean they'll come round, they'll spit on you, they get nails and scratch your car, and if you say anything like, "Look, I'm going to see your mother." "What do you think she's going to do, like?" They vary from what, 11, from about 11, 12, downward. They'll come down here on an old bike with flat tyres, that'll go out. That bike will be thrown out into grass down by the road and they'll go out and pinch somebody's new one. Owt they see, they pinch. There's a family called [F], broke into my birdhouse and pulled some of the heads off my birds.'

Violence takes a number of forms and behind closed doors older people may be subject to physical, psychological, sexual and financial abuse that, because it happens in private, is difficult to capture or quantify (Fitzgerald, 2004); but public exposure – as in the 2013 jailing of a care worker in Newcastle for abusing dementia patients – can serve to open up the issues (Kennedy, 2013). Recent shocking reports revealed widespread neglect of older people in NHS hospital wards that left vulnerable elders in wet beds suffering from malnutrition and dehydration (Abraham, 2011). The Equality and Human Rights Commission (2014) has highlighted evidence of neglect and cruelty in care homes while the Resolution Foundation (2014) has revealed the impact of minimum (or even lower) wages on the quality of home care services procured by local authorities, which underlines the low value that is placed on older people's wellbeing. This can be viewed as the lack of compassion at the heart of the state's offer to vulnerable adults, but it is also evidence of the impossible decisions that many local authorities have to make in fulfilling their duty of care in times of public austerity:

Mrs Jeffries: 'My next door neighbour (private sheltered housing apartment block) is having big mental problems and they are doing wonderful jobs for her and at first they just came in to look at her. And in half an hour they have to do so much it is ridiculous, they cannot get her out of bed, she's very deaf, wash her, shower her, and give her her breakfast in half an hour. I've timed myself, I mean I just do what I want so I thought I'll try and rush myself, get out of bed, have a shower, have my breakfast, I can't do it in half an hour. Her flat is filthy now [sighs] they've now actually managed to get someone in to clean and do her shopping. She shouldn't be there but that's another worry but a home help used to be someone quite different, became your friend and people do need someone to have a cup of coffee with, not this rushing all the time because they have to get there poor souls and move on to the next one.' (Affluent neighbourhood focus group)

Beyond these experiences there was a current of incivility, frequently from bus drivers who did not give frailer people time to get to their seats or resented passengers who took time to board the bus. Miss Duncan, as a professional woman, now dependent through being blind and hard of hearing, was highly conscious of casual disrespect and battled against what she perceived as a societal view that she was incompetent:

Miss Duncan: 'One of the worst things that happen to older people is being talked down to ... there's another thing if there is a dispute of any kind or any doubt about it, you are doubted straight away because you are old – your word is not taken because you are old and that hurts.'

And it is this 'othering' and invisibility that Young talks of as the paradoxical oppression of 'cultural imperialism', which is understood as 'to experience how the dominant meanings of society render the particular perspective of one's own group invisible at the same time as they stereotype one's group and mark it out as the Other' (1990: 58-59). In so far as the active third ager has come to dominate the discourse, it is clear that those who have come to frailty and disability suffer from being seen as failed ageing people; it is also clear that those in the third age struggle to be seen as *not* frail, as *not* needing care, as '*not other*'. These struggles mirror the tension between those physically disabled people battling against assumptions that they are intellectually impaired while those with learning disabilities fight to be recognised and valued.

Powerlessness

Those who were dependent on needs assessments by professionals and were provided with services seen as appropriate to these needs were the voices of powerlessness in this study. Having concluded an interview with an older man in a care home, one of the authors saw him wheeled away and 'parked' with his back to a group of older women in chairs, where he was left without the possibility of conversation with any other person. These casual and unconscious displays of power were presumably commonplace. Beyond the care home, the gaps in the offer of the state made to those with no or insufficient command of the English language left older Asian women feeling helpless:

Mrs Gerai: 'I think our health is worse because we often miss hospital appointments. We get a letter and cannot read it. An interpreter has to be arranged to meet us at the hospital, sometimes they come to the wrong hospital or we go the wrong hospital. If we are at the wrong hospital we find it difficult to get to the right one. Sometimes the interpreter does not come at all. The interpreter cannot take us there; they can only meet us there. I need – we all need – an escort service. Ambulances need to be booked. Nothing is on our side.' (Asian women's focus group)

Those who received home care were vulnerable in areas where they risked exploitation through a restricted understanding of their needs:

Miss Duncan: Not being able to see I get very het up about my financial affairs. I think there should be someone to help those older people who don't have a family. You have no privacy because I have to ask the carers

to read a letter for me and it might be very personal
or something financial and I don't want everyone to
know what I have.

And yet Miss Duncan is one of the fortunate in receiving any service.
Statistics from Age UK (2014b) reveal the painful shortfall experienced
by many frail and vulnerable older people who are unable to access
either formal or family provided support. Some 870,000 people aged
65–89 who do not qualify for local authority support, cannot pay for
private care and have no family support, have to struggle as best they
can. This number includes four in five who need help taking their
medication (200,000 out of 240,000); over two thirds who find it hard
to eat on their own (160,000 out of 250,000); a half who struggle
to wash/get in the bath (500,000 out of 1,010,000); over two fifths
who find it difficult to get dressed (590,000 out of 1,300,000); more
than 1 in 3 who find it difficult to go to the toilet (120,000 out of
350,000); and 1 in 3 who find it hard to get out of bed on their own
(190,000 out of 570,000). The consequences for those lacking support
were indicated by a small scale qualitative study with people deemed
ineligible for social care by their social services department, which
identified a range of outcomes including examples of 'self reliance' that
could be seen as dangerous and potentially injurious to self-esteem
(Tanner, 2001). Newcastle City is one of the local authorities that has
restricted its offer of domiciliary support to those older people whose
needs are categorised as 'critical' (DoH and DCLG, 2014). Even in
this tightly targeted offer, it does not consistently offer a service that
pays attention to need and dignity.

Confronting oppression

The mapping of older people's experiences onto the architecture of
oppression is merely a first, though not inconsiderable step. The next
important step is for older people to begin to make the connections
between the transformations in minority civil rights they have
witnessed taking place in their adult lives and their own struggles as
older people to live with dignity, be treated with parity and to have
their own voices respectfully heard. A number of the baby boomer
generation have already shown themselves immune to the internalised
sense of lesser entitlement of previous cohorts and able to speak out
against the cultural and institutional bias against people in higher age
groups in the wider culture. The challenge is to move this into strategic
agenda for action.

In Newcastle, older people came together in the late 1990s, first through the Better Government for Older People pilot scheme and then as the Elders Council of Newcastle, to provide a mechanism for enabling older people to have a stronger voice and to provide a platform for older people to make a contribution to city life. The concept of uncovering older voices of experience to highlight areas for work is a core value of the organisation, as is working in partnership with policy makers and providers in the public, private and third private sectors to develop solutions. That older people can be heard and have access to key actors is an important step to changing the way policy actors do business and conceptualise older people's needs. However, the impact was only ever to be piecemeal without greater political commitment, which happened in 2011 when Newcastle City Council became a signatory to the Dublin declaration signalling its intention to become an age-friendly city, where everyone can flourish regardless of their life stage. The vision of Newcastle Age-Friendly City is to transform the city in ways that take account of the changing age profile when planning for the future, so that ageing is embedded in all policies speaking to other key agendas; to take an asset based approach to the role of older people in the city and take the indignity and dependency out of the way some people experience old age. Action goes ahead on multiple fronts, enlarging the conversation so more actors are made aware of what the changing nature of age might mean for them. Social justice arguments need to be reframed as good business strategies so that increased life expectancy is seen as an economic good, not only because older people are consumers but because they may stimulate opportunities for innovation. In the housing arena, it is about challenging the industry to explore the full spectrum of older people whose aspirations include new forms of housing and possibly new ways of living. In the cityscape, the Royal Institute of British Architects (RIBA, 2013) have questioned whether our traditional high streets, our notions of learning and living spaces, meet the challenge of an ageing society. This is a tough challenge given that post-industrial Newcastle has refashioned itself as a party city, based on the high alcohol consumption of younger people, where other groups, both older and younger, may feel uncomfortably out of place. How can the city address the tensions that arise from the impact of alcohol tourism on both social life and urban fabric?

In the face of increasing public sector cuts and service models based on crisis responses, there is a recognition that upstream investment is needed in neighbourhoods so that people can be supported to age in place. Creative practice with a locally based arts group that works collaboratively on socially engaged performance has helped unlock stories of local resilience and community assets in two typical city neighbourhoods. A key skill is determining impactful ways of confronting professionals with older people's lived realities. Social media, film making, dramatised narratives are more powerful than reports in alerting key actors in the local authority and third sector to how they may best deploy funds. That older people can develop greater resilience through their own actions is encouraged through small funds that facilitate the development of activities to address social isolation. Resilience is also promoted through increasing digital engagement, which is becoming more important in enabling older people to live full and independent lives, ranging from access to information; developing and maintaining social networks; and, access to assistive technologies. Digital inclusion may be a key to early intervention and action is being taken by the local authority's commitment to increasing access to superfast broadband and through increasing IT confidence via a digital drop-in service provided jointly with Northumbria University students.

The question, of course is, does recognition – the increasing volume of older people's voices; their engagement in the local policy arena – lead to transformation? In these tough financial times, we need to believe that a shared spatial imaginary will stimulate change and that actions that challenge the oppression of our streets, transport systems, care services and housing will lead to new ways of doing business.

References

Abraham, A. (2011) *Care and compassion? Report of the NHS Ombudsman,* London: Parliamentary and Health Service Ombudsman.

Age UK (2012) *Loneliness: The state we're in: Report for the Campaign to End Loneliness,* Abingdon: Age UK.

Age UK (2014a) *Agenda for later life: Public Policy for Later Life,* London: Age UK.

Age UK (2014b) '870,000 older people do not receive crucial care help', *Latest News,* 14 August.

Carers UK (2014) *Caring & Family Finances Inquiry UK Report,* London: Carers UK.

Clapham, D. (2014) 'Accommodation and support options for older people in Britain and Sweden', *European Network of Housing Research conference,* Edinburgh, 2-4 July.

Department for Transport (2014) *National Travel Survey, England, 2013,* [pdf] Available at: https://www.gov.uk/government/uploads/system/uploads/attachment_data/file/342160/nts2013-01.pdf [accessed January 2016].

Department of Health and Department of Communities and Local Government (2014) *Adult social care in England: An overview,* London: National Audit Office.

Department of Work and Pensions (2014) *The Pensioners' incomes series,* London: DWP.

Equality and Human Rights Commission (2014) *Close to home: An inquiry into older people and human rights in home care,* London: EHRC.

Fitzgerald, G. (2004) *Hidden voices: Older people's experiences of abuse,* London: Help the Aged.

Gilroy, R. (2009) *Elder Count,* unpublished report for Joseph Rowntree Foundation, copy available from the author r.c.gilroy@ncl.ac.uk.

Ginn, J. (2010) 'Unkindest cuts: the impact on older people', *Radical Statistics,* 103: 50-57.

Green, J., Jones, A. and Roberts, H. (2014) 'More than A to B: the role of free bus travel for the mobility and wellbeing of older citizens in London', *Ageing and Society,* 34(3): 472-94.

Higgs, P. and Jones, I.R. (2009) *Medical sociology and old age: Towards a sociology of health in later life,* Abingdon: Routledge.

Higgs, P., Leontowitsch, M., Stevenson, F. and Jones, I.R. (2009) 'Not just old and sick – the "will to health" in later life', *Ageing and Society,* 29(5): 687-707.

Hockey, J. Phillips, J. and Walford, N. (2013) 'Planning for an ageing society: voices from the planning profession', *Planning Practice and Research,* 28(5): 527-43.

Horwitz, W. (2014) *Looking forward to later life,* London: Community Links.

Institute of Fiscal Studies. (2013) *Living standards, poverty and inequality in the UK,* London: IFS.

Kennedy, B. (2013) 'Newcastle care home bully jailed for abusing frail dementia sufferers', *Newcastle Chronicle,* [online]. Available at: http://www.chroniclelive.co.uk/news/north-east-news/newcastle-care-home-bully-jailed-6313861 [accessed January 2016].

Means, R. and Evans, S. (2014) 'Communities of place and communities of interest? An exploration of their changing role in later life', *Ageing and Society,* 32(8): 1300-18.

Newcastle City Council (2013) *Know your Newcastle.* [online] Available at: http://www.wellbeingforlife.org.uk/know-your-city [accessed January 2016].

Newcastle Initiative on Changing Age (2013) *The Pensioner Material Deprivation Indicator, Years Ahead Task Group report,* Newcastle: Newcastle University.

ONS (2014) *Health inequality widest in older middle-aged census analysis shows*. [online] Available at: http://www.ons.gov.uk [accessed January 2016].

Public Health England (2014) *Newcastle upon Tyne: Health profile 2014*, London: Public Health England.

Resolution Foundation (2014) *Low pay Britain*, London: Resolution Foundation.

RIBA (2013) *Silver linings: The active third age in the city*, London: RIBA.

Rowe, J.W. and Kahn, J.L. (1997) 'Successful aging', *Gerontologist*, 37: 433-40.

Tanner, D. (2001). 'Sustaining the self in later life: supporting older people in the community', *Ageing and Society*, 21: 255-78.

Walker, A. (2004) 'The ESRC growing older programme 1999-2004', *Ageing and Society*, 24(5): 657-74.

World Health Organization (2007) *Global age-friendly cities: A guide*, [pdf] Available at: http://www.who.int/ageing/publications/Global_age_friendly_cities_Guide_English.pdf [accessed January 2016].

Young, I.M. (1990) *Justice and the politics of difference*, Pittsburgh, PA: University of Pennsylvania Press.

Ziegler, F. and Schwanen, T. (2011) 'I like to go out to be energised by different people: an exploratory analysis of mobility and wellbeing in later life', *Ageing and Society*, 31(5): 758-81.

TWELVE

Educating urban youth:
fair or foul?

Karen Laing, Laura Mazzoli Smith and Liz Todd

Behind claims to bring about fair educational policy or, indeed, budget cuts that are as fair as possible lie a mass of contradictory meanings. These contradictions are rarely made explicit. However, we argue that it is crucial to do so if it is going to be possible to debate what a fair education system might mean, and to find whether fairness in education is indeed possible. This chapter looks at the ideas of fairness underlying particular current national and local educational policy and practice and tries to assess implications for a fair education system. The context of this chapter is English education policy with examples from the city of Newcastle upon Tyne. However, similar policies are found in many international contexts.

The approach we take is to look at current educational policy and practice and identify the key ideas of fairness that seem to be portrayed. We first look at the accessibility and attractiveness of the concept of fairness and explore why it seems to be in vogue. Next we consider the focus in flagship educational policy on fairness as equality of opportunity as expressed in the targeting of resources on those deemed disadvantaged. We then consider additional aspects of fairness, which are not central to policy, but which are important to broaden current conceptions beyond distributive justice notions around 'closing the gap' in attainment between rich and poor, and beyond a marketised framework for organising schools. We assert the need for a focus in policy on many aspects of relational justice and suggest our seven principles of educational fairness as a way to operationalise both distributional and relational justice.

Understanding fairness

The idea that something is deemed either fair or unfair is one that is, pretty much, accessible to the general public. Young children have a keen sense of when something is unfair, and are often ready to declare this to those around them. In general parlance, fair is understood as good. Politicians, to indicate policies that will bring about a better life, use fairness as a key concept.

It is not difficult to find evidence for the need to improve – or indeed ensure – fairness. The view that inequalities in society in a number of key areas are not good for anyone is becoming an idea of our time, with the success of the book *The Spirit Level* (Wilkinson and Pickett, 2012). The UK is apparently becoming one of the most unequal industrialised countries on a number of indicators; for instance, the gap between the income of the top 10% of the population and the bottom 10% has multiplied by 14 in the last 25 years, according to the OECD (2008). The same report claims that there is 'nothing inevitable about growing inequalities' (OECD, 2008: 41) (see also Dorling, 2014). However, 31% of Newcastle's children, as against 22% nationally are defined as living in poverty. Statistics of this type evoke calls for a fairer society. For instance, the 2010 report by the Equality and Human Rights Commission, *How Fair is Britain?*, talks about new social and economic inequalities in Britain and the five critical 'gateways of opportunity', which can make the difference between success and failure in life: health and wellbeing; education and inclusion; work and wealth; safety and security and autonomy and voice.

Fairness is at once intuitive and instinctive and does not need definition (Ryan, 2006; Perkins, 2013): 'Fairness ... ought to yield an outcome that every rational person would agree on' (Ryan, 2006: 599). However, without working definitions, it cannot be very useful to policy, activism, research or theory. Using 'fair' to describe a policy hides its multiple and contradictory meanings. The common sense quality to fairness has led to its usage across the political spectrum.

A good deal of literature mentioning fairness quickly elides into discussions of justice and equality. Although different concepts, distinctions between fairness and social justice are not easy to define. 'Justice' is not always 'fair'. The term 'fair' (or, more usually, 'not fair!') probably features more often in everyday parlance. Dictionary definitions of 'fair' variously use terms such as equal, reasonable, moral and right, and a reference to the way people are treated. We draw on a long tradition of research and action in education, particularly in the sociology of education, that variously comes under the guise of social justice, equity and equality (for example, Tomlinson, 1982; Troyna and Carrington, 1990; Ball, 2004; Reay, 2004; Crozier and Davies, 2007; Gewirtz and Cribb, 2009).

Some of the alternative ideas underlying theoretical notions of fairness are contradictory. A fairer education system could be characterised by – choice within a marketised education system, equal opportunity, equal provision, or redistribution – to name just a few key ideas. These contradictions may not be obvious when politicians say they are working for a fairer society. This suggests there may be no single *fair education*. If that is the case, how can we make sense of the call to fairness in education? Our approach to this question is to consider some of the key education policies nationally and their application within Newcastle schools to explore which ideas of fairness are current, which seem to be omitted and to consider how easily different ideas of fairness sit together.

We look first at efforts to tackle the attainment gap, which draws on ideas of equality of opportunity but also on meritocratic thinking. We next look at policies that focus on choice based on ideas of libertarianism and the extension of a marketised economy to education. We then consider some understandings of fairness that seem less in evidence in today's education system, different aspects of relational justice, and find examples in local education practice.

'Closing the gap': equality of opportunity and meritocratic ideas of fairness

A key focus of the 2010-15 coalition government was to tackle the 'attainment gap'. This is the difference in average attainment between children from relatively rich households and those that are relatively poor (Goodman and Gregg, 2010). We know that already by the age of three there are big differences in the cognitive outcomes of poor children compared to those from better-off backgrounds and that this gap widens by the age of five. By the time young people take their GCSE exams, the gap between rich and poor in obtaining five good GCSEs (grades A*–C, including English and mathematics) is very large indeed. Only 21% of the poorest fifth manage to gain five good GCSEs compared to 75% of the top quintile – a gap of 54 percentage points (Goodman and Gregg, 2010).

In Newcastle's schools there is no evidence of a general problem with under attainment. Taking data from 2014, Newcastle's attainment is broadly in line with the national average at Key Stage 2. In 2014, at Key Stage 4 the gap between Newcastle and the national average has narrowed consistently over time and Newcastle is provisionally above the national average. At Key Stage 2 in Newcastle the attainment gap between pupil premium eligible pupils and their peers is similar to the national average. However, at Key Stage 4 the gap has widened, and it is greater than the national average. In Newcastle, pupil premium eligible pupils who do not attain the expected level are more likely to live in the most deprived parts of the city. There are local authorities elsewhere in the country, with similar cohorts of children to Newcastle (in terms of disadvantage and prior attainment), where a greater proportion of pupil premium eligible pupils achieved the expected level at Key Stage 4 in 2013. Newcastle has made great strides but there is still a way to go.

The 2010–15 coalition government's pupil premium policy gave funding (approximately £900–£1,200 per pupil) for each economically disadvantaged young person (so classified according to eligibility for a free school meal or having been looked after in public care) directly to schools. Children and young people may be eligible for a free school meal if a parent or carer is in receipt of one of a number of different welfare benefits as a result of no or low income. The aim of pupil premium is to increase social mobility by means of schools using the funding to put in place additional teaching support (and other kinds of interventions) and therefore have an impact on poorer pupils' basic educational attainment (that is literacy and numeracy) and other national exam results. We considered the ideas of fairness on which such a policy is based. This seems to be Rawls' classic principle of fair equality of opportunity and his related notion of distributional justice (Rawls, 2009). Distributional justice is about material goods, rights and duties in society and is concerned with both the principles for such distribution and also with beliefs about what makes for fair distribution. The other understanding of fairness that seems implicit to the notion of 'closing the gap' seems to be the meritocratic principle. There is often an implicit assumption that fairness is synonymous with a meritocratic educational system (Bamfield and Horton, 2010; Brighouse, 2010). This acknowledges that there will be educational differences in outcome, but these are justified if *processes are fair*. '… the intuitive case for educational equality is fairness-based; more specifically, it depends on the idea that, in order to be legitimate, inequalities should result from fair procedures' (Brighouse, 2010: 27).

While it seems that distributional justice is one of the key ideas of fairness in play in educational policy at present, some of the nuances of this approach to justice need to be acknowledged and the numerous considerations at play in implementing a form of distributive justice. We can identify different kinds of meritocracy, a 'weaker' and a 'stronger' definition. For example, a 'weaker' liberal definition focuses on equality of opportunity and the precise conditions in society that are needed for this to come about, while a 'stronger' liberal definition focuses on equality of outcome, intervening through positive discrimination for instance, to try and secure similar outcomes for different groups of people in society. In education, in the policy of closing the gap, the outcomes being equalised here are educational attainment, and more specifically attainment in formal school based tests and exams.

The pupil premium is, we suggest, a good example of the stronger liberal definition. It enables schools to put in place additional resources. Schools are then assessed on their ability to use these resources to raise the attainment of lower income pupils. In other words, there is the goal of using resources to equalise outcomes. Additionally, equality of opportunity is often used as a way to achieve the stronger equality of outcome. For many Newcastle schools, opportunities are offered via a range of activities and experiences outside the curriculum. We know that there is still a way to go in terms of equality of opportunity with regards to out of school activities. For example, in research carried out in 2010, Newcastle Council's Children's Rights Team looked at where young people from different areas of Newcastle go to take part in out of school activities (personal communication, Nick Brereton, Newcastle Council). They found a relationship between place and deprivation. Young people from the least deprived areas of Newcastle went to places that spanned a far wider geographical area than those living in the most deprived areas. The latter, in general, went to places that could roughly be located on a line from home to the city centre. It may be that access to a rich range of activities and opportunities is open to all, but the finding of a wider geographical reach of young people from more affluent areas suggests that they might have access to a wider range of activities.

We know that the support given by parents for children to attend a range of activities in addition to school contributes to the advantage experienced by middle-class children in educational success (Ball, 2010). There seem, therefore, to be differences in access to activities, but also in the location of activities attended by children who live in areas of the city that are associated with different socioeconomic positions and levels of income and employment. These findings are confirmed by the responses of the young people themselves, from the different geographical locations in Newcastle, speaking of their attitudes to school trips provided by school (Gosforth and Brunton Park are relatively affluent areas in comparison with the others). These responses came from focus groups carried out in 2010, by Newcastle Council's Children's Rights Team (unpublished fieldwork):

'Poor families get picked on 'cos they can't go on trips. Like a girl in my class, she is dead poor and a dickie nut [has nits].' (Boy, 9, Cowgate)

'Only the really rich families in our school can go on trips abroad, they cost £400 to £600.' (Girl, 12, Gosforth)

'If they can't pay they can't go on the longer trips, it's shan [sic, unfair], you need to sort it out like.' (Girl, 8, Fenham)

'The last trip was £10.50, but trips should be cheaper, like £1 to go somewhere for an hour.' (Boy, 8, Cowgate)

'You do have to pay for trips but it's not a lot really. I went to the Lake District and stayed for three nights. We had hikes, got taken away from the youth hostel and had to find our way back.' (Boy, 11, Brunton Park)

There is growing agreement in Newcastle for the need to increase opportunities available to children from poorer households. A Newcastle primary school with a very diverse intake in terms of family income is compiling a list of experiences that the school will try to provide for all pupils, such as 'meet an author' and 'plant an allotment'. The regional charity Schools North East is similarly working towards a regional entitlement curriculum through which every child would be entitled to and receive a variety of experiences.

The charity Children North East (CNE) with the North East Child Poverty Commission have developed a toolkit to poverty proof the school day. It uses this audit tool to work with schools to explore how the school day unwittingly exposes economically disadvantaged children and young people to stigma. This toolkit is a process that involves teaching staff and children/young people as a consultation group 'researching' and investigating the practices and policies of a particular school. More than 30 schools have applied to be part of this process, and see this area as being of such importance that they are willing to pay the CNE fee. The development of the toolkit involved children as researchers who visited other schools to ask questions about poverty. There were many instances in which children were unwittingly stigmatised, such as being asked to complete homework using the internet (when there was no internet access at home), never taking lessons to learn a musical instrument (since there are charges for lessons), and a lunch system that publicly in some way (however small) identified a child's school meal as free.

In conclusion so far, it seems national, regional and local policy presented here (pupil premium, entitlement to certain experiences) are concerned with distributional justice. Increased educational interventions and out of school activities for poorer students suggests a focus on equality of opportunity. However, there is a major policy focus aimed towards 'closing the gap' in attainment between rich and poor, which suggests that current meritocratic policies are geared more towards the stronger equality of outcome, than towards the weaker equality of opportunity. Schools are expected to demonstrate improved outcomes in terms of educational attainment for poorer pupils.

Freedom, choice and the market place

The principle of fairness in education, if it includes areas such as equality of opportunity and outcome, which tend to be most commonly invoked, also requires the principle of freedom of expression and choice. Freedom and choice constitutes, we suggest, a challenge to the idea of distributive justice. Such a challenge suggests the need for a balancing act between, for example, fairness and freedom – what can be legislated and mandated in terms of expectations of some kind of equality for instance, while not infringing personal liberties? Or put another way, how democratic can society be in terms of fair participation without enacting what may be for some, undemocratic laws? A key concept is that of libertarianism, which asserts that any acquisitions made from uncoerced contracting are by definition fair. As Sandel (2007) points out, for a libertarian, the right always comes before the good. Ideas of choice, freedom and libertarianism are of course linked to neoliberalism, and marketised policy in education.

A central policy of the 2010–15 coalition government in England that seems to be based on ideas of freedom, choice and the market place was the academisation of local authority schools. Academies are publicly funded independent schools that are not managed by a local authority. They can set pay and conditions for their staff, change the length of their terms and do not have to follow the national curriculum (mandatory for other schools). These freedoms are purported to bring advantages to the education of children. Once established, academies are run by an academy trust, which is a charitable company limited by guarantee. We ask questions as to whether other aspects of fairness, other than freedom and choice, are compromised in the academisation policy. Equality of opportunity may be at risk if schools offer different curricula. On the other hand, it is possible that academies can use their freedoms to offer additional opportunities for disadvantaged young people and there is some suggestion of this in national policy.

There is suggestion that there are a number of practices that could be regarded as compromising fairness (Academies Commission, 2013). There is media suggestion that academies manipulate admissions from certain groups of young people to achieve higher average exam results. Fairness may be compromised in the lack of financial transparency of publicly funded academies and the finding that there is little scrutiny of sponsors (Academies Commission, 2013). Implications for schools of the policy to change to academy status will depend to some extent on the development by the schools of fair practices. However, the additional funding for such schools in comparison with existing schools may be thought to compromise fairness, as might the lack of consultation with local communities that precedes decisions to set up academies.

There are other aspects of freedom that influence educational outcomes. Research suggests that the actions middle-class parents choose to take to secure the successful education of their children mean that advantaged children have benefited more than have the disadvantaged from policies aimed at the disadvantaged (Reay, 2004; Ball, 2010). The advantages achieved by higher income groups seem to reproduce class structures and class inequalities and therefore level down the achievements of the less well-off. There are a number of examples:

- The major increase in participation in higher education that has taken place in recent years has disproportionately benefited the middle classes (Elias and Purcell, 2012). We know that the impact of class on education is highly underestimated (Reay, 2004). However, this is not to ignore the evidence that many individual young people from disadvantaged communities have benefited from measures to improve participation in higher education (Lamont et al, 2011).
- A number of policies to do with school choice, gifted and talented and parental involvement are suggested to have reproduced educational advantage rather than to have contributed to reducing disadvantage (Reay, 2004).

There are a number of societal expectations on middle-class parents to use their not insubstantial resources to, for example, choose their children's school, navigate the selection and examination processes within schools, direct their children to additional resources outside school and encourage participation in an increasing range of extracurricular activities. This use of the market enables parents to ensure they are able to make effective choices for their children. There is a danger that education ceases to be an 'intrinsically valuable, shared resource which the state owes its citizens' and becomes a 'consumer product or an investment' (Ball, 2010: 160). Such a view of education is supported by state sponsored encouragement for parents to consider themselves as responsible for children's learning on the one hand and the punitive inspection regime that encourages a distrust of today's schooling on the other. Societal images in which youth are negatively portrayed plays on class fears that the disasters of youth need to be prevented by parental intervention. Child protection fears similarly encourage parent surveillance of youth leisure time.

The levelling down of the opportunities of the better-off as a means to achieve equal opportunities is a commonly stated potential problem in policies to reduce inequalities (Sen, 2002; Jacobs, 2010). Brighouse focuses on the curtailment of freedom of actions by parents, as this is a central locus for the education of the child and the unfair advantages that some are deemed to have. He suggests that we conceive of minimal conditions for valuable familial relationships that work towards educational equality, which we must not violate. So, for instance, reading to a child at bedtime should be allowed on this model, whereas sending a child to a fee-paying school generally should not. Brighouse says:

> ... giving great weight to family values does allow considerable space for pursuing educational equality by, for example, prohibiting elite private schools, desegregating schools by race, or socio-economic class, or abolishing academic selection, none of which undermine the ability of families to be successful in realizing the values they, uniquely can serve. (Brighouse, 2010: 38)

Tooley (2010) counters critics of markets in education by saying that over time, markets should produce improvements even if there are, at any given time, better or worse providers. He also states that rather than a lack of adequate information for choice being a problem, markets are better able to accommodate the more limited, tacit information available to people and even if not all consumers have access to the same information, as long as some do, this will be enough to produce the necessary level of competition between schools to drive up provision. However, Brighouse says that enthusiasts for school choice overestimate the quality of information that parents have and underestimate the transaction costs that consumers have. He also argues that schools cannot be compared to genuine markets as each consumer only has about five or six schools to choose from.

Parents are increasingly seen as consumers of education and investors in the cultural capital that their children represent. What this leads to in schools is the institutionalising of expectations based on class. In other words, there is a real danger in schools that:

> ... differences that are to do with income or class are taken to be essential and fixed characteristics and indicators of the capabilities of children ... that these differences are built into differentiations and opportunities and expectations in schools, becoming self-fulfilling ... in terms of performance. (Ball, 2010: 162)

In other words, the advantage of children outside school is equated with advanced ability inside school. One of the dangers of this is that differences between children in terms of resources and social and cultural capital from primary school onwards become translated into indicators of ability, and 'give rise to distinct academic identities' (Ball, 2010: 162). Children and their performances are 'essentialised rather than seen as socially, culturally, and economically "made up"' (Ball, 2010: 162).

To conclude thus far, we have suggested that freedom and choice, linked to neoliberal marketisation of schooling, underlies the current policy of school academisation. While libertarianism is a challenge to the idea of distributive justice, the policy of academisation might, in different ways, contribute to both ideas of fairness. However, the marketisation of schooling via academisation risks other kinds of injustice. In addition, the use of the market by advantaged parents compromises those policies aimed at disadvantaged parents. If advantage outside school is equated with advanced educational outcomes, then it is a short step to expect the converse, to see disadvantaged children as expected to have lower outcomes. This threatens the very basis of distributional justice.

Discussion: the omission from policy of relational justice

The approach we have taken to consider what a fair education policy might look like has so far been to look at current educational policy and practice and identify the key ideas of fairness that seem to be implicated. Our analysis so far of current educational policy in England has found two main groups of ideas that seem to be in play: those based on distributional justice and meritocracy (especially pupil premium); and those based on libertarianism, freedom, choice and neoliberalism (especially school academisation). We have suggested that distributional policies that aim to disproportionally benefit those who are disadvantaged (for example, providing school choice, higher education participation, gifted and talented programmes) can be compromised by the choice and freedom exercised by advantaged parents.

A full critique of distributional ideas of social justice and neoliberal ideas of freedom and choice is beyond the scope of this chapter. However, our analysis of current educational policy and practice has not only identified the key ideas of fairness that seem to be implicated, but has also looked at omissions. We considered what is missing from national policy in terms of important ideas or aspects of fairness. There is little sense in education policy of the vision of society, or even of education, to which pupil premium and academisation are intended to contribute. There is a suggestion that liberal and distributive ideals lack a vision of the good society (Wolff, 2010). Such a vision is also omitted from libertarian ideas of fairness. The focus should not, we suggest, be on the amount (here, of education) that can be privately enjoyed, but on aspects of human companionship and culture that can be shared, and which develop human potential. What seems to be omitted from both of the main groups of ideas of fairness that characterise current national educational policy is a range of ideas that come under the rubric of relational justice (Gewirtz, 1998). Relational justice is a recognition of the centrality of the nature of the relationships that structure society. This includes: 'issues of power and how we treat each other, both in terms of micro face-to-face interactions and in the sense of macro social and economic relations, which are mediated by institutions such as the state and market' (Gewirtz, 1998: 471).

In this section we discuss a range of ideas of relational justice and find examples of it in educational practice. Young's (2011) multidimensional conception of justice attempts to fuse together distributional and relational conceptions of justice. Young incorporates aspects of distributional justice through the recognition of marginalisation, powerlessness and violence as modes of oppression, as these constitute barriers to equality of opportunity. Young argues that a universal theory of social justice, by its nature abstract, presupposes no particular social life, whereas, 'In order to be a useful measure of actual justice and injustice, it must contain some substantive premises about social life

…' (Young, 2011: 4). There are many possible dimensions for a just social life, including: moral character (from Aristotle (1941) and more recently MacIntyre (1984)); the community ensuring the development of individual 'capabilities' (Sen, 2002; Nussbaum, 2011); and 'justice as mutuality' and 'justice as recognition' (Gewirtz, 1998).

Communitarian principles challenge libertarianism and utilitarianism for putting the right before the good (MacIntyre, 1984). However, communitarianism argues that a fundamentally unjust society cannot be upheld on the grounds of individual rights but on the moral character. Such communitarian principles are arguably of direct relevance to the communal institutions, which make up the bulk of our education system, with schools habituating young people in good moral habits and in how to use their reason and judgment well (Meyer et al, 2013). While there are few policies, local or national, that aim to develop good moral habits, an interesting discussion could ensue on the relationship between moral character and, for example, the call for schools to ensure that 'British values' are upheld or the need to teach sex and relationship education. Unlike the libertarian and utilitarian foci on rights, Aristotle developed an approach focused on the acquisition of habits of moral character that allow people to flourish and develop their abilities, leading to and enjoying a good life and being able to act justly. For Aristotle, immorality came from weakness in character, with people succumbing to sloth, opportunism and hedonism (Aristotle, 1941).

Drawing on Sen's (2002) idea from economics of capabilities, a community should ensure that its members develop the requisite 'capabilities' to partake in civic and political life (Nussbaum, 2011). This focus on taking part in civic and political life is not the same as making sure that individuals have access to educational opportunities, since the latter are usually focused more on raising individual educational attainment. Capabilities are the 'real and actual freedoms (opportunities) people have to do and be what they value being and doing' (Walker, 2010: 392). They are the actions one values doing, the approaches to living one's values: one's valued 'doings' and 'beings' (Walker, 2010: 392). In our evaluation of pupil premium (Carpenter et al, 2013), we found examples in which the head teacher used this funding for events and provisions beyond giving individual pupils more teaching in the key curriculum areas, for example, to fund time from a creative agent, an artist, to develop work with parents. These were not isolated examples. Such actions seem to suggest ideas of fairness based on a consideration of the needs of the community as a whole and not on some notion of individual needs. There is, therefore, much untapped potential for the concept of 'capabilities' to transform discussions of how to address the impact of educational disadvantage.

Two main relational conceptions brought to our attention by Gewirtz are 'justice as mutuality' and 'justice as recognition'. Justice as mutuality is encapsulated by Etzioni's (1995) theory of communitarianism, where citizens are bound together through a system of rights, duties and obligations, which balance out. There is, therefore, neither excessive autonomy, which erodes society, nor excessive collectivism, which erodes individual autonomy. For Etzioni, there is a moral deficit where there is an imbalance between rights and responsibilities. There is however no challenge to the dominant capitalist mode of relations of production and relations are explicitly forged between the dominant and the dominated. Such a framework has been influential in New Labour policy.

Justice as recognition rejects a universalism, which implies that everyone can be treated alike, in favour of an ethics of difference, or otherness, with a commitment to see commonality amidst different people and not to fall back on a politics of surveillance, control and discipline (Ball, 2013). Fraser (1997) proposes the related notion of 'cultural justice', in terms of the absence of cultural domination, non-recognition and disrespect. While educational policy draws on the principles of meritocracy, it rarely refers to class (Reay, 2012), and refers instead to income levels. Bamfield and Horton (2010) refer to a fully meritocratic system of education as being ambition-sensitive and endowment-insensitive. This is the common-sense intuitive conception, having a wide resonance because 'it accords with many people's innate sense of fairness, based around a belief in personal responsibility' (Bamfield and Horton, 2010: 15), justifying differences in educational outcome as long as they do not track class. However, the reality is that educational outcomes do track class very closely. Therefore, truly fair procedures in education demand work on background inequalities, which are often masked by the focus on fair procedures. A discussion of educational equity therefore necessarily entails a discussion of class and education, since 'the class gap in learning begins early in life' (Bamfield and Horton, 2010: 3).

Fraser's (1997) 'associational justice' is the enablement of different groups to participate fully in decisions that affect the conditions in which they live (Power and Gewirtz, 2001). For more than a decade, children have been asked their views on aspects of schools and public services. There are some impressive projects in which children play an active role in decision making. These demonstrate the agency of children and young people and their capacity to take responsibility in a way that does not always have to be structured for them by adults. One of these examples is the work of the Newcastle Children's Rights Team. In terms of equal citizenship, Newcastle has worked with children and young people from across Newcastle to develop a Children's Rights Charter (Newcastle Children's Trust, 2011). The team also developed its Youth Council in Newcastle in full collaboration with a diverse group of young people. Of course, seeking children's views is not always an indication or fair participation: when for example this is a 'smoke screen' to cuts in funding or, more usually, when this represents lip service to real participation.

More authentic forms of relational justice in the form of associational justice can be found today that are not lip service to participation. For example, in order to ensure young people have a real say in what happens in their school, and in their area and feel included and valued, one school in the North East has developed a range of opportunities for students to be consulted, have a voice, and to influence decision making throughout the school, in the local area, and at local authority level. This culture of participation is paramount and young people are encouraged and supported to make a difference in their community. There is a dedicated team to support the participation of young people in the area (called the participation group) and to promote youth voice. The school has a student council and the school cluster has a joint student council with each school sending two representatives. This is linked in to the local authority youth council and youth cabinet and an elected young mayor. The joint student council gets £400 each year to work on themes of their choice (Making Playgrounds Better and Sustainable Schools were past themes). They are supported in bidding for more money and thinking of mechanisms to involve the rest of the school. It meets once a term and has around 20–30 children at each meeting. In addition, the school runs a food and drink fellowship where children identify decision makers in the community and the local authority and can question and challenge them on issues that are of concern to young people. These decision makers are asked to commit to actions, and are held to account by the young people.

Relational justice encompasses a range of concepts to do with how we treat each other (at a micro and macro level) in the pursuit of a (however defined) good society. The various concepts include, for example, justice as mutuality (combining rights, duties and obligations); justice as recognition (an ethic of difference and otherness in how we treat each other); and associational justice (enabling participation in decision making). Although we did not identify these concepts as central to current flagship educational policy, we did identify examples from practice. In recent years there have been many interesting examples of young people's participation in decision making in decisions that affect services that they access, and we have presented a couple of examples.

Conclusion

Current flagship policies (namely, pupil premium, to close the attainment gap, and academisation, to give schools greater freedom) are underpinned by competing theories of fairness or justice (namely, egalitarian distributive justice and libertarianism). Omitted from national policy are the complex notions of relational justice. This includes a vision of the society, of communality, that schooling helps to create, and encompasses ideas of moral character, capabilities, ethics of difference, class, and participation in decision making. Important ideas of justice include cultural justice, justice as recognition and justice as mutuality. We find examples of local actions related to many of these that suggest the need for a national policy focus on relational justice. While we find no blueprint for a fair national education system, the seven principles of fair education that we developed in our work for the Newcastle Fairness Commission perhaps go as far as we are able to in the current analysis toward being a reasonably accessible way of communicating both distributional and relational justice:

- fair process as being treated the same;
- fair process in the way that 'different' provision is allocated or experienced;
- fairness as minimising divergence in educational attainments across social groups;
- fairness as achieving the same standard;
- fairness as meeting the needs of diverse individuals;
- fair participation in decision making and in the exercise of civic responsibility and the reciprocity between the individual and other people in society;
- fair participation in learning.

References
Academies Commission (2013) *Unleashing greatness: Getting the best from an academised system. Academies Commission January 2013*, London: Royal Society of Arts.
Aristotle, R.M. (1941) *The basic works of Aristotle*, New York: Random House.

Ball, S. (ed) (2004) *The RoutledgeFalmer Reader in sociology of education*, London: Routledge.

Ball, S.J. (2010) 'New class inequalities in education: why education policy may be looking in the wrong place! Education policy, civil society and social class', *International Journal of Sociology and Social Policy,* 30(3): 155-66.

Bamfield, L. and Horton, T. (2010) *What's fair? Applying fairness test to education*, London: Fabian Society, Webb Memorial Trust.

Brighouse, H. (2010) 'Educational equality and school reform', in G. Haydon (ed) *Educational equality and school reform*, London: Continuum, pp 15-70.

Carpenter, H., Papps, I., Bragg, J., Dyson, A., Harris, D., Kerr, K., Todd, L. and Laing, K. (2013) *Evaluation of pupil premium*. London: Department for Education.

Crozier, G. and Davies, J. (2007) 'Hard to reach parents or hard to reach schools? A discussion of home–school relations, with particular reference to Bangladeshi and Pakistani parents', *British Educational Research Journal,* 33(3): 295-313.

Dorling, D. (2014) *Inequality and the 1%*, London: Verso Books.

Elias, P. and Purcell, K. (2012) 'Higher education and social background', in *Understanding Society: Findings 2012,* [online] ESRC & ISERC. Available at: http://research.understandingsociety.org.uk/findings/findings-2012 [Accessed January 2016].

Equality and Human Rights Commission (2010) *How fair is Britain?* [pdf] London: EHRC. Available at: http://www.equalityhumanrights.com/sites/default/files/documents/triennial_review/how_fair_is_britain_-_complete_report.pdf [accessed January 2016].

Etzioni, A. (1995) *The responsive community: A communitarian perspective*, Presidential Address, American Sociological Association.

Fraser, N. (1997) *Justice interruptus: Critical reflections on the "postsocialist" condition*, London: Routledge.

Gewirtz, S. (1998) 'Conceptualizing social justice in education: mapping the territory', *Journal of Education Policy*, 13(4): 469-84.

Gewirtz, S. and Cribb, A. (2009) *Understanding education*, Cambridge: Polity Press.

Goodman, A. and Gregg, P. (2010) *Poorer children's educational attainment: How important are attitudes and behaviour?*, York: Joseph Rowntree Foundation.

Jacobs, L.A. (2010) 'Equality, adequacy, and stakes fairness: Retrieving the equal opportunities in education approach', *Theory and Research in Education*, 8(3): 249–68.

Lamont, E., Flack, J. and Wilkin, A. (2011) *An evaluation of the Research for Excellence Programme: Cohort one*, Slough: NFER & Sutton Trust.

MacIntyre, A. (1984) *After virtue*, Notre Dame: University of Notre Dame Press.

Meyer, H.-D., John, E.P.S., Chankseliani, M., and Uribe, L. (2013) *Fairness in access to Higher Education in a global perspective reconciling excellence, efficiency, and justice*. Rotterdam: Sense Publishers.

Newcastle Children's Trust (2011) *Newcastle children and young people's plan 2011*-2014, [pdf] Newcastle: Newcastle Children's Trust. Available at: http://www.newcastle.gov.uk/sites/drupalncc. newcastle.gov.uk/files/wwwfileroot/education-and-learning/grants/ cypp_11_14.pdf [accessed January 2016].

Nussbaum, M.C. (2011) *Creating capabilities*, Cambridge, MA: Harvard University Press.

OECD (2008) *Ten steps to equity in education. January 2008 policy brief*, [pdf] Paris: OECD. Available at: http://www.oecd.org/ dataoecd/21/45/39989494.pdf [accessed January 2016].

Perkins, A. (2013) 'Fairness commissions: is it possible for politics to play fair?', 3 September 2013, *The Guardian*. [online] Available at: http://www.theguardian.com/society/2013/sep/03/fairness-commissions-possible-politics-play-fair [accessed January 2016].

Power, S. and Gewirtz, S. (2001) 'Reading education action zones', *Journal of Education Policy*, 16(1): 39-51.

Rawls, J. (2009) *A theory of justice*, Cambridge, MA: Harvard University Press.

Reay, D. (2004) 'Educational and cultural capital: the implications of changing trends in education policies', *Cultural Trends*, 13(50): 73-86.

Reay, D. (2012) 'What would a socially just education system look like?: saving the minnows from the pike', *Journal of Education Policy*, 27(5): 587-99.

Ryan, A. (2006) 'Fairness and philosophy', *Social Research*, 73(2): 597-606.

Sandel, M.J. (ed) (2007) *Justice: A reader*, New York, NY: Oxford University Press.

Sen, A. (2002) 'Why health equity?', *Health Economics*, 11(8): 659-66.

Tomlinson, S. (1982) *A Sociology of special education*, London: Routledge and Kegan Paul.

Tooley, J. (2010) 'Moving from educational equality to improving the education of the least advantaged', in G. Haydon (ed) *Moving from educational equality to improving the education of the least advantaged*, London: Continuum, pp 96-129.

Troyna, B. and Carrington, B. (1990) *Education, racism and reform*, London: Routledge.

Walker, M. (2010) 'A human development and capabilities "prospective analysis" of global higher education policy', *Journal of Education Policy*, 25(4): 485–501.

Wilkinson, R. and Pickett, K. (2012) *The spirit level: Why equality is better for everyone*, London: Penguin.

Wolff, J. (2010) 'Fairness, respect and the egalitarian ethos revisited', *Journal of Ethics* 14(3): 335-50.

Young, I. M. (2011) *Justice and the politics of difference*, Princeton, NJ: Princeton University Press.

THIRTEEN

Fairness in Newcastle: theory and practice

Jan Deckers

Introduction

In 2011, Newcastle City Council set up the Newcastle Fairness Commission (NFC), a group of 18 people who were invited to prepare a report with the aim to set out the principles that would help Newcastle to become a fairer city. The NFC, which was chaired by Professor Chris Brink, the Vice Chancellor of Newcastle University, published its report in 2012 (NCC and Newcastle University, 2012). This article engages with what this report has to say about how salaries ought to be allocated within organisations, which it recognises as an important dimension of fairness. More specifically, the author shall engage with the question whether or not the theoretical recommendations made in the report ought to guide the practical allocation of financial resources in Newcastle University, the organisation that the author works for, and the third biggest employer in the city of Newcastle. The author's focus on Newcastle University stems from the belief that, as an employee, he has a greater right and duty to contribute to financial reform in his own, rather than in other organisations. Whereas the author shall not seek to argue for this position, which is based on his belief in participatory democracy, his hope is that these views will also inspire financial reform elsewhere.

A critical evaluation of the work of the Newcastle Fairness Commission

The NFC recognises that Newcastle is a relatively poor city, which it takes to be shown, for example, by the fact that it has more than 70,000 people who live in the 10% most deprived areas in the country, a relatively large proportion of people with significant debts, a relatively large proportion of children living in poverty, and an estimated 30% of households who suffer from fuel poverty (NCC and Newcastle University, 2012: 11). The region also has a higher rate of unemployment compared to the national average. While life expectancy is generally lower than the national average, some parts of the city suffer some of the highest rates of morbidity and mortality in the whole of the United Kingdom. The difference in life expectancy between some who live in some areas of the city and some who live in others exceeds 14 years (NCC and Newcastle University, 2012: 11).

The question might be asked how these facts relate to fairness. The author has argued elsewhere that the question of what is fair can be conceived entirely in terms of the question of what is, very broadly conceived, fair health care, and the author argued for granting all human beings a right to health care (Deckers, 2011). Whilst these arguments shall not be elaborated on here, it is interesting to note that a similar right is affirmed by article 25 of the Universal Declaration of Human Rights, which states that 'everyone has the right to a standard of living adequate for the health and wellbeing of himself and of his family, including food, clothing, housing and medical care and necessary social services'. Whereas this claim is problematic as even very high living standards may not be sufficient to support good health, the author believes that the NFC is nevertheless correct to infer unfairness from observed differences in the morbidity and mortality of different populations. Recognising that many, if not most people cannot enjoy good health unless others provide food, water, sanitation, shelter, and other health services or – within the prevailing capitalist economy – the financial means to secure these, the question of what is fair is therefore intimately connected with, but not limited to, the question of what would be a fair distribution of financial resources.

The NFC recognises that the distribution of financial resources is not merely an absolute, but also a relative concern. Indeed, a large body of empirical research supports the view that a person's right to health care cannot only be threatened by an absolute, but also by a relative lack of resources (Marmot et al, 1991; Daniels, 1999; Wilkinson and Pickett, 2010). Knowing where one is in 'the pecking order', the economic rank one occupies within a society or organisation, appears to be associated with a greater probability of suffering poor health when one is relatively low down and with a smaller probability of suffering poor health when one is relatively high up in the ranking order. In addition, empirical evidence supports the view that, all else being equal, people who live in more unequal societies have a greater chance of experiencing poor health compared to people who live in more egalitarian societies (Wilkinson and Pickett, 2010).

In light of these concerns with absolute and relative poverty, the NFC advocates 'reductions in the pay ratio between the highest and the lowest paid within companies' (NCC and Newcastle University, 2012: 39). The question must be asked, however, why we should allow pay gaps to exist in the first place. One alternative view is that we should pay everyone equally for each hour that they work. This egalitarian perspective is adopted by Suma, a cooperative company based in Elland, in the north of England (Corbett, 2013). Unlike Suma, the NFC adopts a sufficientarian view that allows some pay inequalities provided that there is progress towards a situation in which those who are paid the least receive a living wage (Newcastle City Council and Newcastle University, 2012: 37). In this, it follows a recommendation by the Living Wage Advisory Panel, set up in 2011 by Newcastle City Council. The Panel produced a report in 2012 that defines a living wage as 'the level of income needed to provide an acceptable standard of living in Britain to ensure good health, adequate child development and social inclusion' (Living Wage Independent Advisory Panel to Newcastle City Council, 2012: 3). This interest in a living wage is placed within the wider context of 'the election manifesto of the party that became the ruling group in May 2011', which 'made an explicit commitment to implement a Living Wage' (Living Wage Independent Advisory Panel to Newcastle City Council, 2012: 4). However, a similar commitment is shared much more widely, and can be found also in the 1961 European Social Charter of the Council of Europe, which stipulates a 'right of workers to a remuneration such as will give them and their families a decent standard of living' (European Social Charter of the Council of Europe, undated, part 2, article 4).

In line with more recent developments that have taken place elsewhere in relation to this proposed right, the panel expressed the view that the national living wage rate promoted by the Living Wage Foundation, which stood at £7.20 per hour at the time of publication, 'should be adopted in Newcastle' (Living Wage Independent Advisory Panel to Newcastle City Council, 2012: 11). This has now risen to £7.85, exceeding the national minimum wage, which varies with age and which was first introduced in the United Kingdom in 1999.[1] Subsequent to the publication of the panel's report, the living wage was implemented by Newcastle City Council on 1 November 2012 (NCC and Newcastle University, 2012). Whereas many other organisations have taken similar initiatives, a 2013 report revealed that about 20% of UK workers were still paid hourly rates below the living wage (Whittaker and Hurrell, 2013).

There is no doubt that the implementation of a living wage as a minimum threshold that every employee should be earning per hour of paid work might help to secure the right to health care for those who were being paid less than that beforehand. However, someone who is inspired by the writings of John Rawls might argue that, other morally significant factors being equal, income and wealth should ideally be divided equally unless paying workers unequally would confer a greater index of 'primary goods' (that is, morally significant goods that every rational human being can be assumed to want) over the lifetime of the least advantaged (Rawls, 1999: 266). Whereas it has been argued that, in reality, this view might be 'compatible with a bewildering array of distributive outcomes ... ranging from total equality to stark inequality' (Arnold, 2012: 105), Gerald Cohen (1997) has argued that Rawls' ideal society is inconceivable without assuming that its citizens would be driven by an egalitarian ethos. As Suma's pay structure exemplifies such an ethos – without wishing to make the claim that Cohen would necessarily have endorsed such a structure – the author shall engage in what follows with the question of whether or not Newcastle University might have good reasons to deviate from the egalitarian position adopted by Suma, which shall henceforth be referred to as the egalitarian baseline.

How to justify wage differentials within Newcastle University

One reason that might be proffered to justify differentiated wages is that some people are more successful at converting their efforts into goods and services that other people need or desire, and that their success should be allowed to be reflected in their wages. The modern world seems to be built – in very large measure – on this assumption. Bill Gates became very rich because he was able to develop products that many people desire. Those who adopt the view that success deserves to be rewarded might say that Gates deserves his riches on the basis of his success.

The problem with this view is that success is a relative notion. A farmer may be skilful at producing a great crop of potatoes, but he might still not be successful if there is an abundance of potatoes on the market in that particular season so that there would be little demand for them. Similarly, Gates might not have been successful if other people had either saturated the market with similar software before he had developed his, or been more fortunate to have the means to market the software that they had developed. In light of the fact that success depends on factors that are beyond one's control, it seems arbitrary to reward success. Even if some of these factors could be controlled, for example, by providing similar marketing opportunities to all, it remains unclear why success ought to be rewarded. For example, it is unclear to the author why the success of those who are able to produce pornographic films that appeal to many people ought to be rewarded as not all things that people are willing to pay for are necessarily in the interests of a good society.

Similar problems surround the view that it is not success, but talent that ought to be rewarded. Some people may never be granted the opportunities to show or develop their talents so that they are not rewarded for them. Even if these opportunities could be equalised, some may be very talented in producing goods and services that do not contribute to the good life, while others may produce goods and services that are not in demand but that would nevertheless be very good for humanity. Think, for example, of a very talented scholar at a university who produces a brilliant new theory, but whose theory is rejected and therefore never published because it clashes with the fashion of the day. The author concludes that success and talent depend largely on genetic, environmental, or social factors that are beyond one's control, and that they therefore do not provide good bases to reward people.

Perhaps effort – which the author defines in relation to either the disposition to work hard or the willingness to take on relatively high risks – provides a good reason why some people merit a higher income than others. Those who support this line of reasoning might argue that some people either work harder than others or take on greater risks, and that it would not be fair to refrain from rewarding them for their greater efforts, at least where the means are available to do so. Both X and Y may have an interest in receiving a high income, but only X may give this interest such importance that he would be prepared either to work hard for it or to take significant risks. Y, on the other hand, may value other things, and may not be prepared to make that much effort. It could therefore be argued that Y would not be wronged by being provided with a smaller income as he does not take an interest in working very hard or taking significant risks. Intuitively, this view seems attractive as it suggests that people can autonomously choose to earn more than others if they wish to do so. However, apart from the fact that rewarding effort per se does not guarantee that all have equal opportunities to make similar efforts, this scheme is not free from other problems.

A first problem is that effort per se does not seem to be sufficient to warrant pay differentials. It is plausible to hold that some efforts that are made to produce or provide some things are more worthwhile than others, even if the efforts that are made may be equal. If X works very hard at producing goods or providing services that do not contribute much to the common good, or perhaps even undermine it, it does not seem to be right to reward him for his efforts. This creates the problem of distinguishing between things that contribute to the common good and things that do not do so, which may be difficult in a pluralistic society. However, it is not because this is a difficult task that it should not be carried out. Many may agree, for example, that those who work hard to produce pornographic films do not contribute to the common good, contrary to university scholars who put a lot of effort into educating people or nurses who risk being infected while caring for Ebola victims.

Whereas establishing agreement on what sorts of things should count as positive efforts towards the common good in a pluralistic society might not be an insurmountable barrier, this does not solve all problems. A second problem is that there may be natural and cultural differences in people's capacities to work hard or to take on significant risks for the common good. Some may not be able to do so because of genetic factors that are beyond their control. Others may have been subjected to social factors that have predisposed them to be less prepared to work hard or to take on significant risks for the common good. Unless it could be decided to what extent someone's relative laziness or risk aversion was not the product of natural or social factors, it would seem to be unfair to discriminate against those who are either lazier or more risk averse through no fault of their own.

A third problem is that any proposal to reward effort for contributions to the common good by financial means runs the risk of providing an incentive for people to contribute for the wrong reason and may diminish people's motivation to contribute for the right reason. To use an example provided by Michael Sandel (2012: 9), if reading is something that is valued as a common (as well as a private) good, some might want to incentivise children's efforts to read books by rewarding them financially. The children may thus learn to appreciate reading not for its own sake, but merely for the fact that it provides a means towards receiving financial benefits. Even if children may improve their reading abilities by such a scheme, it might be argued that they would have been improved for the wrong reason, and that their overall development would have been stinted by the extrinsic incentive. Although some children may learn to appreciate reading for its own sake, this does not imply that the means by which they learnt to do so were appropriate. Some may have learnt that it is good to do particular things simply because they make money, rather than because they ought to be valued for their own sake.

In light of these problems, some might argue that we should sever all links between salary and success, talent, or effort, and that one's salary should be determined merely by one's needs. Those with greater needs would receive more money, regardless of their success, talents, or efforts at contributing to the common good. Provided that what counts as a need is subjected to social scrutiny rather than personal whim, this view seems attractive. The view that someone with a greater metabolic rate should be allowed to consume more food compared to someone with a lower metabolic rate, for example, seems intuitively defensible. However, the author is not convinced that we ought to relinquish altogether the idea that rewarding controllable effort for the common good should be permissible. To return to the example provided earlier, it would seem wrong to refrain from incentivising reading if it would undermine the common good more than doing so. Many activities, including reading, are not merely valuable for their own sake. If someone valued the ability to read a foreign language because they would be in a better position to do business with people who speak that language, it would seem to be prudent for a financial manager – who is conceived of here as a person with legitimate control over an organisation's finances – to incentivise the person in question financially for their commitment to learn that language if they expect that the incentive will produce greater contributions to the private good of the firm. Provided that the firm's private good also serves the common good, it would seem hard to oppose this unless it could be argued that the common good could be served better otherwise. Similarly, if some staff are expected to work during hours that might undermine their health more, for example, night time work or weekend work that might interfere negatively with people's interests in, respectively, rest and social opportunities, it would be reasonable to pay them more to compensate for the extra health risks that they take on by working during those hours so that they might be able to reduce their working hours. If this is accepted, some workers should be allowed to receive more income per hour worked compared to others on the basis of their greater controllable efforts for the common good, regardless of whether or not they have greater needs.

It is clear that rewarding controllable effort makes sense where it promotes the common good more than not doing so, unlike rewarding success, as the former does not depend on the arbitrary nature of the latter. However, in practice, it will often be the case that success is a necessary condition to justify rewarding controllable effort. An organisation that makes only just enough profit to be able to stave off absolute poverty for its employees, for example, would do well to disregard payment on the basis of controllable effort as using such a principle might condemn some employees to absolute poverty. It must, therefore, be pointed out that the author has only argued that rewarding workers for their controllable efforts for the common good can be justified, not that such efforts necessarily must be rewarded.

If we apply this line of thinking to Newcastle University, the author concludes that justice does not demand that it would be wrong for some to receive a nett hourly salary that exceeds the amount that other workers receive per hour worked. However, while the University's Council – which has the primary responsibility to control the University's finances – would do well to honour those who go to great lengths to pursue the private good of the University (and the government would do well to avoid taxing them if it does not clash with the common good), any wage differentials that are either maintained or implemented to honour hard workers should also reflect the valid points that Rawls makes where he points out that the amount of effort one makes is influenced by factors beyond one's control, including 'family and social circumstances' (Rawls, 1971: 74), as well as 'natural abilities and skills' (Rawls, 1971: 312; Rawls, 1999: 273-4). As it may be hard to determine to what extent someone's decision to make greater than average efforts is caused by voluntary choice or by involuntary factors, any concrete schemes to differentiate wages on the basis of controllable effort must be careful to avoid crossing the thin line between rewarding people fairly and discriminating unfairly.

Accordingly, the University should adopt a rigorous system to incorporate the 'controllable effort' factor, for example, a revised annual 'performance development review', so that those who either are expected to make or have made more controllable efforts compared to others are rewarded appropriately. This is not an argument for allowing people to be rewarded for the work that they do beyond the number of hours for which they are contracted. If some people are routinely working more hours than the number for which they are contracted, then this is their voluntary choice. To the extent that the voluntariness of any such choice is compromised by informal expectations, a case should be made for an increase in the number of contracted hours, rather than for a pay rise to compensate for the hours worked beyond one's contract.

Controllable effort, however, should not be the only factor that should be taken into consideration by the University's Council. There are a number of reasons why further deviations from the egalitarian baseline are appropriate.

First, the egalitarian baseline does not taken into account that workers contribute unequally to the common good through the unpaid work that they carry out to benefit those to whom they owe a duty of care. Many societies across the world fail to pay people for much of their productive activity, for example, for many tasks carried out within their families. The UK government is no exception. Many people who are not actively seeking (many hours of) paid work because of their caring duties are not being provided with any direct financial assistance to fulfil those duties, for example, people who look after elderly relatives who may have significant health care needs (Pickard, 2015). As women carry out more unpaid work than men, the injustice associated with unpaid work has been an important feminist issue (Himmelweit, 1995). It may account at least in part for why few women can be found among more senior staff at universities in the UK and elsewhere (Morley, 2014).

The critic might point out that these issues are for the government to resolve, and should not concern an organisation such as Newcastle University. This, however, is too simplistic. Consider a father who provides equal amounts of financial support to his children, where only one of the children has morally significant duties to someone who needs that child's financial support for their survival. Imagine that this resulted in significant hardship for the child in question. It would seem to be wrong for the father to provide his children with equal amounts of money, and it would seem to be right that he provides more support for the child with the needy dependant. By analogy, it might be said that every organisation owes a special duty of care towards its workers by virtue of the work ties that connect colleagues. As workers with morally significant unpaid duties may find it harder to enjoy a certain level of health care compared to others because of these duties, Newcastle University's Council ought to be particularly concerned about the wellbeing of these workers if it adopts the view that it has an equal duty of care towards all its workers.

This does not undermine the fact that workers must advocate political change so that those who are currently not being paid (sufficiently) for their contributions to the common good are rewarded by the UK government, as well as advocate for financial reform in other jurisdictions, which might, for example, be in the form of securing a basic income for all people – as proposed, for example, by the Basic Income Earth Network (Basic Income Earth Network, undated).

However, as long as insufficient political change has taken place at the level of the national government, Newcastle University's Council must ensure that all its workers are able to enjoy a certain standard of health care, rather than cater disproportionately for those who have relatively few unpaid duties. Accordingly, the University must differentiate wages to give due consideration to the different morally significant duties that its staff have in relation to unpaid work.

Second, the University must also recognise that some staff members may have had to spend a lot of money in order to receive the qualifications that make them suited for their jobs. To the extent that these qualifications were paid for by the workers themselves, who may need to pay back loans that they have taken out while they studied, the University ought to pay more for staff who have a legitimate case for help, so that their rights to health care are not jeopardised. As tuition fees in English and Welsh higher education were raised substantially a few years ago, it is likely that this will become a more serious consideration in the future for those students who had to fund a significant percentage of their education from loans and who would be disadvantaged unfairly compared to early school leavers if morally significant debts were not taken into consideration.

Third, the University must also consider that some staff must expend more resources to obtain an adequate level of health care compared to others. Some staff, for example, may have much more significant health problems compared to others that they cannot be held responsible for. Whereas the government and private insurance schemes should ideally protect those with greater health care needs, it seems reasonable to expect the University to help out where help by third parties is deemed to be inadequate. The University also has campuses overseas, namely in Malaysia and Singapore, where the cost of living differs from the cost of living in the UK. If some staff require less money to be provided with a basic standard of health care compared to others, this difference should be reflected in their wages, at least where a good case can be made that doing so outweighs the harm that such an adjustment might cause in maintaining economic inequalities between different countries.

Finally, if Newcastle University's current payment regime is unfair, the principle of restitutive justice demands that those who have benefited unfairly must compensate those who have been disadvantaged unfairly. Accordingly, some people may earn significantly less than the egalitarian baseline in the future. However, it is important to ensure that the extent to which some people's salaries are reduced to redress any historic injustices does not increase threats to workers' rights to health care overall.

So far the author has argued that decisions about people's salaries are best made by starting from an egalitarian baseline and that any changes from this baseline must be justified by reference to relative differences in controllable effort, duties in relation to unpaid work, morally significant debts, health care needs, and historic unfairness. A further qualification, however, will be required, as the scheme outlined so far fails to provide a satisfactory response to the 'brain drain' objection.

The brain drain objection

If the adoption of this pay system were to trigger a 'brain drain', whereby those who receive relatively high wages now leave the University in order to take on more lucrative jobs elsewhere, the University's quality would suffer. This is likely to result in a reduction in income, which would reduce every employee's salary. This levelling down objection must be taken seriously. If we assume the validity of the premise on which this objection relies, the University should also allow pay differentiation on the basis of success by rewarding those employees who are the most successful in bringing in income. This should be done not on the basis of the view that success ought to be rewarded, but on the basis of the view that not rewarding successful employees might jeopardise the rights to health care of all employees. The counterargument to this is that the state provides a safety net that secures rights to adequate health care for all, for example, by looking after those who might lose their jobs because of the brain drain. This would render this objection invalid unless it was deemed that the state does not do enough to secure the right to health care for all. If we assume that the state does not do enough in this respect, the prima facie unjustifiable local (intra-organisational) inequality associated with rewarding those who are successful should be tolerated to avert either absolute poverty or total inequality (where the adoption of a local egalitarian policy would disadvantage members of one organisation relative to members of other organisations), subject to one condition: a convincing case should be made that the latter presents the greater evil. Put differently and more concisely, inequalities that cannot be justified locally may be justifiable to stave off greater threats to workers' rights to health care.

However, the premise on which the argument relies must be questioned also: what evidence do we have to suspect that such a brain drain would happen? If evidence could be presented to support the view that a shift to a locally implemented more egalitarian division of financial resources might cause a brain drain, there would be grounds for concern. However, evidence could be presented to support the contrary view, namely that adopting a more egalitarian pay structure may motivate workers to stay rather than to leave. As mentioned earlier, an organisation that pays workers the same amount per hour worked is Suma, a food wholesaler founded in Leeds in 1977. Suma had 153 workers in 2012 and experienced an increase in turnover from £14.3 million in 2002 to £27.8 million in 2011, as well as an increase in its total wage bill from £1.7 million in 2002 to £4.3 million in 2011 (Corbett, 2013: 165-6). Having researched the organisation, Corbett writes that, 'the equal wage structure includes gross wages of £26,000 per annum for a five-day week, a profit related Christmas bonus, free cooked lunches, enhanced sick pay (three months on full pay), staff shopping at trade price, the option to take leave of up to six months, and a health plan' (Corbett, 2013; 175). His research also reveals that the equal pay structure that this organisation adopts is a significant 'source of pride' (Corbett, 2013: 175). These data might help to explain why more than a third of staff who worked for Suma in 1990 were still working for Suma in 2012 (Corbett, 2013: 165-70).

Whereas the example of Suma is no more than an anecdote because of its highly unusual pay structure, it reveals that it is by no means a certainty whether either the feared brain drain or the feared reduction in income would happen if the University were to develop a more egalitarian pay structure. If Suma's pay structure is cherished by many of its employees, some people might likewise be attracted to work and to continue working for the University precisely because of its superior pay policy. However, even if we accept that the feared brain drain would happen, and that this would trigger a reduction in the University's income and in the wages paid to its workers, the question must be asked whether the University should be concerned about such a reduction in light of the fact that it could currently pay every worker much more than the £7.85 hourly living wage rate that has been set by the Living Wage Foundation for workers outside London (Living Wage Foundation, undated). In 2014, the University spent 52% of its income on paying staff, to provide for the total of 5,081 full time equivalent staff that it possessed on 31 July 2014 (Newcastle University, 2014). Its wage bill amounted to £228.2 million in the academic year 2013-14 so that the average gross salary of each full time employee was just over £44,912. This figure substantially exceeds the average gross annual salary of full time employees in the UK in the year leading up to 5 April 2013, the latest year for which data are available at the time of writing, which was £26,884 (ONS, 2013). Some staff are expected to work 37 hours per week, and others 40 hours per week, but the proportion of staff within each category fluctuates. If we adopt a conservative estimate by assuming that everyone works 1,744 hours per year – the number of hours that people who are on the highest salary points are expected to work – the average gross hourly salary would amount to £25.75. In addition, the University also offers employees the option to be rewarded with a contribution to a defined pension scheme at a percentage of their salary, which might be conceived in terms of deferred pay. This shows that the hourly wage that a Newcastle University employee would be paid, if the income that is spent on salaries were divided equally, substantially exceeds the 2014 national living wage hourly rate of £7.85. The author's suggestion, therefore, is that the University should alter its pay policy by a gradual transition towards a more egalitarian pay structure. However, the consequences of doing so should be monitored carefully to avoid the possibility that too great a concern with local inequality might marginalise other threats to the right to adequate health care that every human being ought to possess, such as the threats of global inequality and absolute poverty. These threats might increase if the advent of a more egalitarian local ethos were to trigger a decline in the quality of the University's teaching and research.

Two small steps in the direction of a more egalitarian pay structure were taken when, in August 2013, some workers received a pay increase as the lowest point on the common pay spine became obsolete and when, in November 2013, some of the lowest paid staff were paid up to £300 extra. The latter, however, was no more than a one-off ex gratia payment (Newcastle University, 2014: 32). Consequently, every worker is guaranteed to earn at least £8.83 as the lowest point on the common pay scale produced a salary of £14,257 where someone on that point of the scale is expected to work 1,613 hours per year. This is a step in the right direction as, on 16 August 2012, the University had 404 staff whose hourly pay was less than the living wage (What Do They Know, undated). However, at the same time, the hourly pay difference ratio between the highest paid member of staff and the lowest paid was 17.8 to one (Times Higher Education, undated). Recent research has also revealed that the Vice Chancellor of Newcastle University earns 5.9 times more than the average member of staff is paid, and that there are 112 workers who are paid more than £100,000 per year (University and College Union, 2015: 36). It should be noted that this (5.9) is below the average of 6.4 for all higher education institutions that are included in the study and is the second lowest in the 23 comparable Russell Group Universities.

In the author's view, it is unlikely that threats to people's rights to health care would increase if the University took further steps in the direction of an egalitarian pay structure. It is clear, however, that revising pay structures will not be the only thing that is required to develop a more egalitarian ethos. A further measure, for example, would be to drop academic titles as it is unclear why those who have obtained particular degrees or professional positions should expect to be addressed differently compared to everyone else merely because they have those degrees or positions (Morand and Merriman, 2012: 138). There is a significant danger that using those titles serves to maintain and reinforce traditional divisions between superior and subordinate people. In the interest of equality, the name of 'advisor' may also be preferred to that of 'supervisor'.

Conclusion

As the right to health care can, in many situations, only be respected through the availability of adequate resources and as many resources can only be procured by means of money in the prevailing economy, any initiative to promote fairness must tend carefully to the grossly unequal distribution of resources across people and societies. This has been perceived by the NFC, which recognises that the health of many people in Newcastle is jeopardised by an absolute and relative lack of resources, which is why it recommended that organisations should implement a living wage as the minimum wage that all workers should enjoy, as well as reduce pay ratios. These recommendations were compared with the alternative distribution scheme adopted by Suma, which uses an unqualified 'equal pay for equal time' principle to distribute wages. Whereas this principle might appeal to those who follow Cohen in adopting the view that an egalitarian ethos should guide the implementation of Rawlsian justice, the author questioned the desirability of using this principle in relation to the issue of how Newcastle University ought to divide its wage bill. The author argued that decisions about people's salaries are best made by starting from an egalitarian baseline and that any changes from this baseline must be justified by reference to relative differences in controllable effort, duties in relation to unpaid work, morally significant debts, health care needs, and historic unfairness. Newcastle University's Council must justify deviations from the proposed salary scheme by arguing that the prima facie wrongness of pay inequality outside these parameters is outweighed by the greater good that might be served, and the same applies to other organisations.

Note

[1] Since April 2016, the national minimum wage has been superceded by the 'National Living Wage' (with rates lower than those set by the Living Wage Foundation).

References

Arnold, S. (2012) 'The difference principle at work', *The Journal of Political Philosophy*, 20(1): 94-118.

Basic Income Earth Network (undated) [online] Available at: http://www.basicincome.org/bien/ [Accessed January 2016].

Cohen, G. (1997) 'Where the action is: on the site of distributive justice', *Philosophy & Public Affairs*, 26(1): 3-30.

Corbett, S. (2013) *The social quality of participatory democracy: Social empowerment in the workplace and local community. A thesis submitted for the degree of Doctor of Philosophy (PhD)*, University of Sheffield: Department of Sociological Studies.

Deckers, J. (2011) 'Negative "GHIs," the right to health protection, and future generations', *Journal of Bioethical Inquiry*, 8(2): 165-76.

European Social Charter of the Council of Europe (undated) [online] Available at: http://conventions.coe.int/Treaty/en/Treaties/Html/035.htm [accessed January 2016].

Himmelweit, S. (1995) 'The discovery of "unpaid work": the social consequences of the expansion of "work"', *Feminist Economics*, 1(2): 1-19.

Living Wage Foundation (undated) [online] Available at: http://www.livingwage.org.uk/calculation [Accessed January 2016].

Living Wage Independent Advisory Panel to Newcastle City Council (2012) *A living wage for Newcastle*, [pdf] Available at: http://www.newcastle.gov.uk/sites/drupalncc.newcastle.gov.uk/files/wwwfileroot/your-council/communications_and_marketing/a_living_wage_for_newcastle_-_april_2012.pdf [accessed January 2016].

Marmot, M., Stansfeld, S., Patel, C. et al (1991) 'Health inequalities among British civil servants: the Whitehall II study', *The Lancet*, 337(8754): 1387-93.

Morley, L. (2014) 'Lost leaders: women in the global academy', *Higher Education Research & Development*, 33(1): 114-128.

Newcastle City Council and Newcastle University (2012) *Fair share, fair play, fair go, fair say. Report of the Newcastle Fairness Commission*, [pdf] Available at: https://www.newcastle.gov.uk/sites/drupalncc.newcastle.gov.uk/files/wwwfileroot/your-council/equality_and_diversity/fairness_report_web.pdf [Accessed January 2016].

Newcastle University (2014) *Financial statements*, [online] Available at: http://www.ncl.ac.uk/foi/publication-scheme/spending/financialstatements.htm [accessed January 2016].

Office for National Statistics (2013) *Statistical bulletin: Annual survey of hours and earnings, 2013. Provisional results*, [online] Available at: http://www.ons.gov.uk/ons/rel/ashe/annual-survey-of-hours-and-earnings/2013-provisional-results/info-ashe-2013.html [accessed January 2016].

Pickard, L. (2015). 'A growing care gap? The supply of unpaid care for older people by their adult children in England to 2032', *Ageing and Society*, 35(1): 96-123.

Rawls, J. (1971) *A theory of justice*, Cambridge, MA: The Belknap Press of Harvard University Press.

Rawls, J. (1999) *A theory of justice* (revised edition), Cambridge, MA: Harvard University Press.

Sandel, M. (2012) *What money can't buy*, London: Allen Lane.

Times Higher Education (undated) [online] Available at: http://www.timeshighereducation.co.uk/download?ac=8048 [accessed January 2016].

University and College Union (2015) *Transparency at the top? Senior pay and perks in UK universities*, [pdf] Available at: http://www.ucu.org.uk/media/pdf/0/0/ucu_transparencyatthetop_mar15.pdf [accessed January 2016].

What Do They Know (undated) *Living wage*, [online] Available at; https://www.whatdotheyknow.com/request/living_wage_8 [accessed January 2016].

Whittaker, M. and Hurrell, A. (2013) *Low pay Britain 2013*, [online] London: The Resolution Foundation. Available at: http://www.resolutionfoundation.org/publications/low-pay-britain-2013/ [accessed January 2016].

Wilkinson, R. and Pickett, K. (2010) *The spirit level. Why equality is better for everyone*. London: Penguin Books.

FOURTEEN

A fairer city: towards a pluralistic, relational and multi-scalar perspective

Derek Bell and Simin Davoudi

Disparities breed resentment and mistrust. The perception that some are gaining access to advantages and opportunities denied to others is an unhealthy and dangerous situation. For communities to thrive people must feel they are being treated fairly and have equal chances to enjoy a good quality of life ... We can choose another way, and strive to make inclusion, equity and fairness cornerstones for the construction of a better city (NCC, 2012: 5).

Introduction: a just city?

The above are the words of Nick Forbes, Leader of Newcastle City Council, when he launched the Newcastle Fairness Commission in July 2011. His statement indicates both an acknowledgment of the growing inequalities in the city and a call for ways of reducing the unfairness of the city. The launch made Newcastle upon Tyne one of a small number of UK cities that have officially recognised the importance of thinking about how to promote fairness and social justice by setting up a Fairness Commission. A key trigger was the substantial cuts to the City Council's budget under the austerity policies of the Coalition government. This has since been considered by Newcastle City Council, and a number of other northern and mainly Labour-led councils, as unfair *to* the city. The 2010 Comprehensive Spending Review cut the local governments' budget by an average of 4.4%. However, some of the most deprived local authorities received cuts of 8.9% compared to cuts of only 1% or less in the most affluent ones (Davoudi and Madanipour, 2015: 94). An example of the latter is Guildford in Surrey where the 2010–13 cuts were about £16 per resident, while in Newcastle (an example of the former) it was £162 (Harris, 2014: 9). In 2013–14 Newcastle

City Council cut £37 million from its spending and is cutting another £38 million in 2015–16 (at the time of writing), with more cuts to follow in the following years (Harris, 2014: 9).

The Fairness Commission was established in the context of this diminishing public expenditure with the aim of:

- Setting out a strong set of principles of how the concept of fairness could be given practical effect in Newcastle, in a way that would secure broad endorsement from across the city.
- Critically assessing evidence of the degree of fairness, cohesion and equality within Newcastle; informing and making use of the proposed Newcastle Future Needs Assessment.
- Identifying the critical policies and 'Civic Contract' that would need to be put in place to create and secure a fairer city, and to challenge us all to implement them. (NCC, 2012: 5)

In July 2012, the Commission presented an extended set of (liberal) fairness principles to guide the City Council's policies. It provided some illustrative examples of how those principles might inform decisions on particular issues. The aim was 'to provide […] a toolkit for fair decision-making' (NCC, 2012: 45) for a city government that wants to promote fairness *in* the city. Despite this, the Council's spending decisions have faced considerable opposition from local people, community groups and voluntary organisations. This is reflected in the following statement by one of the residents, "The facility was absolutely brilliant – the community used to come but the council decided that it wasn't viable and that it was going to close ... they had other options, they didn't listen to us" (quoted in Denton, 2014). For the critics, the Council's decisions are exacerbating the existing injustices *in* the city by further disadvantaging those who are already disadvantaged. Indeed, the cuts to some services, such as social care and community libraries, may be increasing the injustice *of* the city as they reconfigure the city's physical and socioeconomic 'infrastructure' and make the production and reproduction of injustice more 'hard-wired' into the city. The heated debates about budget decisions in Newcastle – and other cities in the UK and elsewhere – highlight the many challenges of moving towards a fairer city or even avoiding contemporary cities becoming more unjust.

In this concluding chapter we reflect on three key questions: how should we theorise justice and fairness *in* and *of* the city? What methods should we use to inform our judgment about claims of injustices? What are the strategies of resistance to injustices *in* and *of* the city?

Our discussion will draw on the arguments and evidence provided by the contributors to this volume. It is, therefore, informed by thinking about cities in general and Newcastle in particular. In keeping with our emphasis on 'ordinary' cities, we believe that the issues that we discuss are likely to be relevant for all cities while acknowledging that 'city' is a plural phenomenon and each city has its own particular challenges and opportunities that reflect its particular history and circumstances. We also consider 'city' as more than its physical attributes and as socially produced.

The structure of the chapter mirrors the above three questions. So, after this introduction, section two will focus on the different conceptions of justice *in* and *of* the city that are found in contributions to this volume. These draw on diverse theoretical traditions with some extending liberal theories of justice and others developing alternatives to liberalism. We argue that this diversity reflects both the complexity and the contested character of the interrelationship between justice and the city. To this debate we add two further considerations, which we call justice *for* the city and justice *by* the city. We suggest that the alternative perspectives on (in)justice and the city can help us develop a more sophisticated understanding of the many and various ways in which cities can be unjust.

In section three, we discuss different ways of studying justice in and of the city, highlighting some of the advantages of qualitative methods. In section four, we reflect on two further issues that our contributors have raised: the difficulty that city governments have in translating rhetorical commitments to fairness into actual reduction of injustices in and of the city; and the resistance to unjust processes and practices that we find in the everyday life of people in the city. We argue that the discussion of these issues in this volume points to the importance of the connection between justice and democracy. If we do not invigorate democracy in our cities, we are unlikely to move towards fairer cities. We conclude the chapter by summarising some of the key points for future research and political action.

Theorising the *just city*

In Chapter 1, we provided a brief outline of alternative approaches to thinking about justice in political philosophy, beginning with debates within liberalism and then outlining critical alternatives to them. We also set out some of the main strands of thinking about justice and the city. In particular, we focused on Susan Fainstein's liberal multiculturalist account of justice *in* the city and the more radical accounts of the injustice *of* the city set out by David Harvey and Henri Lefebvre, who draw on Marxist ideas and theories of spatial justice. In subsequent chapters, we have seen many of these approaches and theories drawn upon to think about injustice and unfairness in practice.

In this section, we suggest that a useful way forward for advancing the debates about theorising (in)justice *and* the city is to focus on three critical issues. First, we need to adopt a *pluralistic* understanding of justice which, as the contributions to this volume show, acknowledges the inadequacy of an exclusive focus on distribution and recognises the need for deeper understanding of the relationships among different kinds of (in)justice. We suggest that this is an area where the coming together of both normative political theory and social sciences can lead to promising results.

Second, we need to adopt a *relational* understanding of the 'city' as a social, spatial, environmental and material construct, which functions as both the site where injustices happen and the agent that produces them. We have discussed this at length in Chapter 1 of this volume.

Third, we aim to advance the debate further and suggest that the discussions of justice *in* and *of* the city should be extended to address two further questions: what can a city justly claim from those 'outside' the city; and what can a city do to act justly to those 'outside' the city? This requires adopting a *multi-scalar* approach, which enables us to explore how justice at one spatial scale (however defined) exacerbates or ameliorates injustice at another scale – from the neighbourhood through the city and the nation-state to the planet? How are (in)justices produced and reproduced in the drawing and redrawing of the territorial, administrative, jurisdictional boundaries? We, therefore, argue that a full account of justice *and* the city must consider justice *for* the city and justice *by* the city as well as justice *in* and *of* the city. We suggest that this leads to a pluralistic, relational and multi-scalar approach to thinking about justice and the city. In the following account we summarise how these three theoretical issues have informed and been reflected in the contributions to this volume.

One common feature of the discussions in this volume has been (implicit or explicit) dissatisfaction with an exclusive focus on the just distribution of resources, which is often associated with political liberals such as John Rawls or Ronald Dworkin. Our contributors have either sought to *modify* political liberalism or *reject* it. Those who sought to *modify* political liberalism have done so in two main ways. First, some have focused on particular goods (and bads), such as greenspace (Davoudi and Brooks, Chapter 2), food (Midgley and Coulson, Chapter 5) and transport (Palacin et al, Chapter 4)), which are often not explicitly considered by political liberals, who tend to be interested in the conventional currency of 'resources', understood in terms of income and wealth. This kind of modification directs attention to questions about the fair distribution of goods that political liberalism ignores (such as greenspace and transport) or simply takes for granted (such as food). Second, some contributors have modified political liberalism by suggesting that there is more to justice than the fair distribution of goods and bads. In many cases, they have drawn on elements of other theories of justice such as, democratic proceduralism, multiculturalism, environmental justice and spatial justice. For example, most of the contributors have emphasised the importance of procedural justice or democracy as an important element of any theory of justice in the city. While they do not share the democratic proceduralist's belief that the outcome of a democratic process is necessarily just, they do believe that democracy is an essential feature of a just city.

Several contributors, including Davoudi and Brooks (Chapter 2), Gilroy and Brooks (Chapter 11), Laing et al (Chapter 12) and Woolner (Chapter 3), draw on the work of Iris Marion Young and Nancy Fraser on justice as recognition. Davoudi and Brooks regard recognition as an additional element in a liberal-democratic-multiculturalist theory of justice. For others, justice as recognition and the importance it attaches to relations among persons is an important corrective to liberalism's focus on the atomised individuals and the opportunities they have and the resources they own. We have already seen that Davoudi and Brooks draw on environmental justice while ideas of spatial justice are used by Palacin et al among others.

The contributors who sought to reject political liberalism have drawn primarily on Marxism and spatial justice. For example, Webb (Chapter 10) argues that the idealism of political liberalism fails to take account of the economic and political history of the city and the power relations produced by that history. Thus, public commitments to distributive justice by city governments – even when based on a liberal-democratic-multiculturalist ideal of justice – often have limited effect when faced with historical economic and political injustices. Several chapters draw on the more radical ideas of spatial justice in Lefebvre's work on the right to the city, including Speak and Kumar (Chapter 6), Pugalis et al (Chapter 7) and Strachan and Lopez-Capel (Chapter 8). For Speak and Kumar, the primary focus is on how the construction of the city – spatially-politically-economically-culturally – produces and reproduces injustice. In contrast, Pugalis et al and Strachan and Lopez-Capel examine how the city is constructed differently by marginalised groups or groups that do not enjoy the right to the city or the rights to centrality and difference. For all of them, Lefebvre's work offers a better way of thinking about the *in*justice *of* the city because it not only highlights pervasive injustices that liberalism misses, but also provides accounts of how injustice is (re)produced and how it is always resisted and contested in the everyday lives of those treated unjustly.

Our contributors reject an exclusive focus on the just distribution of resources for different reasons and offer different alternatives. However, together their discussions point towards four fruitful avenues for future research. Below we present these in relation to justice in, of, for, and by the city.

Justice in the city

There seems to be an agreement among the contributors that *ideal* justice *in* the city requires more than a just distribution of resources. It requires a more pluralistic framing of justice, which recognises and takes into account issues such as recognition and democratic procedures. To illustrate this point, let's imagine a hypothetical city in which resources were distributed justly but there was not justice *in* the city. In such a city, some people might have better access to greenspace, while others suffer more from air pollution. Or, some people might have easy access to political power while others are excluded from participation in the governance of the city. Or, some might suffer discrimination on grounds of race, culture or gender while others benefit from being part of a dominating group. Or, some might control the means of production while others have little or no choice about what work to do, who to work for, or where to work. Or, some might be able to exercise their right to the city while others have limited access (physically, culturally and socially) to most parts of the city and have no agency for (re)making the city and themselves in the process.

The disagreement among our contributors about which of these features would make a city more or less unjust might simply reflect broader disagreements among traditions of thought. Indeed, it seems likely that justice in the city will always remain a contested ideal and an unfinished business. However, it would be premature to assume that no progress could be made through critical engagement between traditions and approaches and attempts to reduce injustices. So far, political theorists have paid little attention to the idea of justice in the city (understood as an administrative/territorial unit) or the literature on justice and the city. However, ideas developed for thinking about justice in the nation-state – and globally – have been employed by others to think about justice in the city. We might plausibly expect that political theorists could usefully contribute to discussions about how to develop those ideas in a new context. The real benefits come from an understanding of the city not as a passive context in which injustice happens but as an active agent that exacerbates and even generates injustices.

Thus, the first avenue for future research relates to questions such as: what are the *ideal* principles of justice *in* the city? Should these include principles for the distribution of specific goods and bads (such as food, greenspace and poor air quality)? What is the best defence of a liberal-democratic-multiculturalist account of justice in the city? How are Lefebvre's key rights related to – or what do they add to – ideas that are central to liberal, democratic and multiculturalist conceptions of justice?

Justice of *the city*

We agree with those contributors who are concerned about the idealism of political liberalism and the failure of political liberals to address two critical questions: How is injustice (re)produced in the city? How can we reduce actually existing injustices and move towards our ideal of justice in the city? These are questions that other traditions – notably, Marxists and spatial justice theorists but also some multiculturalists and democratic theorists – have taken more seriously. They are, of course, also questions that can be – and have been – addressed by a range of social sciences. We suggest that it might be useful to reconceptualise these questions in terms of our idea of the justice *of* the city.

This leads to a second avenue for future research in relation to questions such as: how does the physical-spatial-social-political-economic-cultural infrastructure *of* the city (re)produce injustice among the people living *in* the city? How might the infrastructure *of* the city be changed to reduce injustice among the people living *in* the city? How might we bring about – or contribute towards – the necessary changes to the infrastructure *of* the city given the constraints imposed by the existing injustice of the infrastructure *of* the city? We believe that this way of thinking about the causes of injustice in the city might have two advantages. First, it might help us avoid simplistic approaches to tackling injustice, such as making public commitments to fairness. Second, it might help us recognise the systemic character of the city and, derivatively, of the injustice of the city. If we are going to tackle injustice in the city, we need to understand the city as a complex system with non-linear emergent possibilities capable of (re)producing (in)justices.

We have suggested two avenues for future research on theorising justice *in* and *of* the city. The first would explore alternative ideals of justice in the city and requires insights from political theorists' work on justice at other scales. The second would explore the city as a physical-spatial-social-political-economic-cultural complex system that (re)produces (in)justice. This requires insights from social scientists.

Justice *for the city*

A third avenue for research arises from the importance of justice *for* the city and relates to questions such as: what can a city justly claim from those outside the city? As we saw earlier, the local governments in many cities in the north of England, including Newcastle, have argued that the Coalition Government's austerity policies have unfairly reduced their budgets. They seek justice *for* their cities. In this case, they claim that the national government should treat them justly by providing them with a fair share of national resources. Claims of justice *for* the city might also be made against other cities, regions, states, international institutions and corporations. In many cases, these claims might not be about a fair share of resources but rather about other forms of just treatment. For example, justice *for* a city might require neighbouring cities, regions or states to limit their use of resources (such as water) and reduce pollution from their industries. Or, it might require that multinational corporations reinvest more of their profits in the cities that produce them rather than extracting surplus value from one city and exporting it to their shareholders in another. We believe that a full account of justice *and* the city must include an account of justice *for* the city: what can a city legitimately claim as a matter of justice from those who live and work 'outside' their city boundaries and whose actions (or omissions) affect the lives of people living 'inside' the city boundaries? How can we account for the multiple and complex population, environmental, economic and cultural flows between the 'inside' and 'outside'? How are actual and imagined scales/boundaries (territorial, administrative, social and cultural) (re)drawn and who benefits and who loses from them?

Justice *by the city*

A fourth avenue for research relates to what we call justice *by* the city and raises questions such as: what must a city do to act justly to those outside the city? A city is not only affected by what others do; it also affects others by its actions. For example, many of the policies developed by cities, including economic, housing and transport policies, will have effects on people living outside who commute into the city for work or leisure from neighbouring regions. Cities can also have significant effects well beyond their territorial borders. For example, a city's carbon emissions contribute to global climate change while its economic development policies are often designed to produce inward flows of labour and capital from other parts of the world. It is reasonable to ask of a city: is it doing justice to others? Is justice being done *by* the city? Thus, a full account of justice *and* the city must include an account of justice *by* the city. What must a city do (or not do) as a matter of justice for (or to) those outside the city whose lives are affected by the actions of the city and its people?

To summarise, we have suggested that a full account of justice *and* the city must consider justice *for* the city and justice *by* the city as well as justice *in* and *of* the city. A city should consider not only justice within its borders (justice *in* and *of* the city) but also justice in its relations beyond its borders (justice *for* and *by* the city). We use the term 'borders' not as a fixed or given delineation of the city, but as a fluid, socially constructed and politically contested concept. In addition to the need for better theorisation of each of these four aspects of justice *and* the city, more work needs to be done on how they might be integrated into a theory of *the just city*. There are many research questions that have not yet been explored in a systematic way, such as: should what a city can justly claim from others depend on whether there is justice *in* the city? If a city is not treated justly by others, could there still be justice *in* the city? Can a city treat others unjustly to promote justice *of* and *in* the city? We might also ask: how does a theory of *the just city* relate to accounts of justice at other scales? Thinking about justice *and* the city suggests a rather different way of thinking about justice more generally. We have seen that contemporary political philosophy tends to think about justice only at two scales – the nation-state and the world. Thinking about justice *and* the city should remind us that in our everyday lives we think about justice or fairness at a much more diverse range of scales and in a more diverse range of places and relationships – including the family, the friendship group, the school, the workplace, the market, the neighbourhood, the community and the city. Justice and fairness in each of these – and many other spaces, places and relationships – may not require the same thing. For example, the principles for a *just city* are not likely to be the same as the principles for a *fair school*. However, we know that what happens in a city affects what happens in the schools in that city (and vice versa). The connections between (in)justice in different spaces, places and relationships should be part of a pluralistic, relational and multi-scalar theory of justice that takes us beyond the disembodied, de-contextualised atomism that is often associated with static and mono-scalar liberal theories of justice.

In this section, we have suggested that theorising *the just city* is a complex and ambitious inter-disciplinary research programme, which may be part of a radically different way of thinking about justice and fairness across multiple scales, places and relationships.

Methods for studying (in)justice *in* and *of* the city

The contributors to this volume mainly use qualitative methods to study injustice *in* and *of* the city. For example, Gilroy and Brooks' chapter (Chapter 11) is based on interviews with older people living in Newcastle. They analyse their interview data using Young's account of the five faces of oppression to identify examples of injustice. Webb's chapter (Chapter 10) draws on observation and documentary analysis to reconstruct a case study of injustice in the west end of Newcastle. Midgley and Coulson (Chapter 5) provide an account of the development of the idea of food justice and the food justice movement in the UK and illustrate its potential with two Newcastle-based case studies based on interview data. Woolner (Chapter 3) presents a selection of case study vignettes, based on observation and interviews in schools, which illustrate how schools in areas suffering from environmental and social injustice can develop innovative ways of improving the lives of their students and communities. Laing et al (Chapter 12) use a combination of documentary analysis and case study vignettes based on observation and interview data to explore how competing conceptions of justice are manifest in English education policy and the everyday practices of teachers. Similar qualitative methods, drawing on observation, interviews and documentary analysis, are used in many of the other chapters to examine injustice, ways of challenging or overcoming injustice, and the conceptions of justice that underpin the policies and practices of the institutions and actors being discussed.

In one sense, the dominance of qualitative methods simply reflects our choice of contributors and their methodological preferences. However, it also reflects most of our contributors' beliefs that justice *in* and *of* the city is about more than the just distribution of income or wealth. It is relatively easy to use quantitative data to study inequality of income and wealth but it is more difficult to use them to study procedural injustice (or inequalities of political power) and much more difficult to use them to study misrecognition or inequalities of status or respect. The difficulties of studying non-distributive injustice *in* the city are twofold. First, we just have less data on non-distributive injustice because it is often more difficult and expensive to collect. Second, some forms of non-distributive injustice, especially injustice in recognition, are not best understood as quantifiable inequalities between the experiences of different people. Instead, they are better understood as qualitative injustices in the relationships between people or between people and institutions, such as being disrespected or being ignored. We could, of course, count the number of people who self-identify as having been treated unjustly or even attempt to use other observational methods to count the number of people that we – as observers – believe have been treated unjustly. We could – if we had the data – even create maps quantifying the different proportions of people in different territorial spaces who have been treated unjustly (and correlate them with other demographic features of those territories, including other injustices or inequalities).

However, quantifying the number of people treated unjustly is not the same as being able to identify injustice by comparing the quantities of a good (or bad) that different people own or experience and considering whether the differences in quantity are inconsistent with principles for the fair distribution of that good or bad. We should avoid thinking that if we cannot use quantitative data to identify inequalities and injustices, they do not exist. However, we should aim to collect more data – qualitative and quantitative – that helps us to understand both the injustice *in* and the injustice *of* cities. The trend towards thinking of cities as complex systems and using 'big data' to better understand how they work and, in particular how to make them more sustainable, means that we will come to know more and more about some aspects of the lives of a city's inhabitants and its 'infrastructure'. It is, however, less clear that the quantitative data that are collected and analysed through, increasingly, 'urban observatories' will tell us what we need to understand about many of the injustices *in* or *of* our cities. Therefore, we believe that there would be real value in an interdisciplinary programme of research specifically informed by thinking about justice *in* and *of* the city that sought to create different forms of knowledge.

It is also important to note that most studies of justice (both quantitative and qualitative) adopt what we may call a top-down approach; that is, claims of (in)justice are studied by the experts (the researcher). We believe that this dominant approach should be complemented with more inclusive and interpretive methods, which involve people who are the subject of the study. It is only through detailed and rich narratives of people's perceptions and experiences of injustice that we can begin to understand what it means to be treated unfairly. It also helps provide a situated understanding of (in)justice, which takes full account of the context and the power relations. Finally, if we can improve our understanding of the injustices *in* and *of* cities, we may stand a better chance of identifying more effective ways of promoting just cities. We do not, however, suggest that the reason for injustice is the lack of awareness or information about it, but rather argue that research and dialogue can help change the discourse that is dominated by the liberal view of justice and 'enlarge the boundaries of action' (Fainstein, 2009: 35).

Resisting injustice

In this section, we reflect on the implications of two further themes that have emerged from the contributions to this volume. The first theme, noted by several contributors, is that rhetorical commitments from city governments to creating fairer cities coexist with the continuing injustice *in* and *of* our cities. Public commitments to justice and fairness often do not translate into reduced injustice. The second theme is that people through their everyday lives are challenging what they perceive as unjust and by doing so are remaking the city and themselves. We can resist injustice without changing local (or national) government policy. Moreover, changing local government policy might do little to reduce injustice because government policies may be ineffective or even counter-productive in the complex systems that are cities. We believe that these two themes point towards a more radical conception of the politics of the city, associated with the work of Dikeç and Lefebvre. This conception has two key features. First, resisting injustice is – and must be – something that we are always engaged with in our daily lives. Second, resisting injustice in the city is inextricably linked to the activation of agency in the many, democratisation of the city and its reconfiguration, so that the power to make and remake the city is not concentrated in the few. In other words, reducing injustice requires the explicit and self-conscious politicisation and democratisation of the everyday life of the citizens.

The first theme – that rhetorical commitments from city governments to creating fairer cities coexist with the continuing injustice *in* and *of* our cities – is most clearly articulated in Webb's case study (Chapter 10) of the controversial siting of a homeless hostel in one of the historically most disadvantaged areas of Newcastle. He argues that Newcastle City Council's commitment to a liberal-multiculturalist conception of justice, exemplified by its endorsement of the Newcastle Fairness Commission report, had little or no effect on its decisions in this case. The decision-making process was undemocratic because it was neither transparent nor inclusive. Moreover, the decision is not best explained by Newcastle City Council's commitment to liberal principles of fairness or distributive justice. Instead, it is best explained by a historical institutionalist analysis, which recognises the importance of path-dependencies, political considerations and the power of economic interests in the decision-making process. The difficulty of translating public commitments into justice-promoting practice is also highlighted by other contributors. We see this, for example, in Gilroy and Brooks' discussion (Chapter 11) of the difficulties of realising Newcastle's public commitment to be an age-friendly city, and Palacin et al's account (Chapter 4) of the difficulties of realising commitments to fairer and more sustainable transport systems.

The second theme – that people through their everyday lives are challenging what they perceive as unjust and by doing so are remaking the city and themselves – is a recurring theme in several chapters, including those by Woolner (Chapter 3), Laing et al (Chapter 12) and Strachan and Lopez-Capel (Chapter 8). Woolner shows how schools in disadvantaged areas can resist social and environmental injustice through the creative use of their – often limited – space to grow their own food. On her account, these communal gardens remake the schoolyard and can play a key role in reconfiguring the relationship between the wider school community (including teachers, children, parents and others living near the school), the environment and the process of learning. In the process of growing together, the school community remakes itself – albeit in a small way – and resists the injustice *of* a city where the physical infrastructure, especially the road system, exposes some children to more polluted air and more noise than their better-off neighbours across the city. Laing et al (Chapter 12) discuss how schools can resist dominant conceptions of justice, which shape education policy narratives and are blind to important injustices, through creative use of resources in ways that subvert the original intention of policy makers. Strachan and Lopez-Capel (Chapter 8) also find examples of everyday resistance in the meaning that disadvantaged young people attach to the city's marginal places where they live and play. These examples of small, everyday acts – of remaking the city and remaking themselves and their communities – suggest that we should not understand the injustice *of* the city as fixed or static. The city is a social construct, with the voices of those experiencing injustice *in* the city being marginalised rather than silenced.

Together, these two themes in the contributions to this volume point to an understanding of the politics of the city that is very different from the liberal conception of politics. On the liberal account, we can separate the 'political' from the 'personal' so that politics is seen to be about what the state does, rather than what we do. In contrast, a recurring theme in this volume is that everyday life is political because injustice *in* the city is (re)created through the unjust physical-economic-social-cultural organisation *of* the city's – and its inhabitants' – everyday life. We concur with this perspective and agree that in the acts of everyday life we are recreating or resisting injustice, albeit without always being conscious of our actions and their implications. The pursuit of justice requires reflexivity (self-conscious reflection) on how our actions affect the (re)construction *of* the complex system that is the everyday life of the unjust city.

At the societal level, the pursuit of justice *in* the city requires the democratisation of the city. Scholars whose work is grounded in Lefebvre's 'right to the city' have called for emancipatory politics for mobilising the marginalised. For example, Dikeç suggests that:

> Right to the city implies not only a formulation of certain rights and the cultivation of the political among city inhabitants, but also a reconsideration of the spatial dynamics that make the city. It, therefore, should not be conceived merely as a practice of claiming and asserting rights, but should also be conceptualized in a way so that it puts on the agenda the *dynamics* (for example, property markets) and *principles* (for example, urban policy, land-use policy, planning laws) of the ways in which social relations are spatialized in the city (Dikeç, 2009: 83).

This requires putting the emphasis on the mechanisms through which the city is materialised; mechanisms such as land and property rights and the alliances between policy and corporate actors that work in favour of global capital interests. It requires focusing on how certain legal, political, economic, cultural and spatial practices and processes lend themselves to the constant reproduction of unjust cities.

Some of the contributors to this volume have highlighted the need to move from critiques to the identification of pragmatic alternatives through engagement with local communities. What emerges from almost all the contributions is the need to give voice to the disadvantaged and enable their agency. We concur with these views because we cannot hope to reduce injustice without increasing democracy by empowering those who frequently and sometimes systematically experience injustice and remain marginal to the organisation of the city's everyday life. This may seem as if it just shifts the problem: why should we expect democratisation unless there is already empowerment of those who are politically marginalised? The short answer is that we should not *expect* democratisation but we should *hope* and *strive* for it. We should seek to promote self-conscious reflection, including our own, on the political injustice of the undemocratic city and we should resist the concentration of power in the hands of the few in cities.

In this section, we have argued that promoting justice *in* the city is not something that we should leave to local governments. Resistance to injustice is a common feature of everyday life at the margins. It is this resistance that must be empowered to reconfigure the organisation of the everyday life of the city – materially, legally, economically, socially and culturally. So, reducing injustice in cities is tightly connected to increasing democracy. And increasing democracy is tightly connected to reflexivity and resistance to the political injustice of the undemocratic city.

Conclusion

In this chapter, we have tried to identify some key themes in the contributions to this volume and explore their implications for research and action. We have argued that there is important work for political philosophers and social scientists to do. We need a meeting of minds between political philosophers and urban theorists to better understand the idea of a *just city*. We also need to draw on different traditions of inquiry that have different epistemology and methodology and employ a range of quantitative and qualitative data to help us *see* a fuller picture of injustice *in* the city and better understand how the complex everyday life *of* the city (re)produces injustice. However, research is not enough. Researchers can seek to promote the self-conscious reflection on the organisation of the city that might make change possible, but they cannot create that change. As Marcuse et al (2009) argue, the 'search for the just city' requires a coherent frame for actions and deliberation. However, it also requires that people, who through their everyday life already challenge what they perceive as unjust, can exercise their 'right to centrality', so that they are able to do more than remake the city in the margins. Justice *in* and *of* the city depends on the empowerment of people who suffer injustice.

References

Davoudi, S. and Madanipour, A. (2015) 'Localism and post-social governmentality', in S. Davoudi and A. Madanipour (eds) *Reconsidering localism,* London: Routledge, pp 77-103.

Denton, M. (2014) 'Newcastle City Council cuts: Who's to blame?', *BBC News North East & Cumbria,* [online] Available at: http://www.bbc.co.uk/news/uk-england-tyne-27437441 [accessed January 2016].

Dikeç, M. (2009) 'Justice and the spatial imagination', in P. Marcuse, J. Connolly, J. Novy, I. Olivo, C. Potter and J. Steil (eds) *Searching for the just city: Debates in urban theory and practice,* London: Routledge, pp 72-89.

Fainstein, S. (2009) 'Planning and the just city', in P. Marcuse, J. Connolly, J. Novy, I. Olivo, C. Potter and J. Steil (eds) *Searching for the just city: Debates in urban theory and practice,* London: Routledge, pp 19-40.

Harris, J. (2014) 'Is saving Newcastle a mission impossible?', *The Guardian,* [online] pp 1-22. Available at: http://www.theguardian.com/news/2014/nov/24/-sp-is-saving-newcastle-mission-impossible [accessed January 2016].

Marcuse, P., Connolly, J., Novy, J., Olivo, I., Potter, C. and Steil, J. (eds) (2009) *Searching for the just city: Debates in urban theory and practice,* London: Routledge.

NCC (Newcastle City Council) (2012) *Fair share, fair play, fair go, fair say, Report of the Newcastle Fairness Commission,* Newcastle upon Tyne: NCC.

Index

Note: page numbers in italic type refer to tables and figures.